THE SOONG SISTERS

Eling   Mayling   Chingling

THE
SOONG
SISTERS

BY EMILY HAHN

DOUBLEDAY, DORAN & COMPANY, INC.

GARDEN CITY   1941   NEW YORK

PRINTED AT THE *Country Life Press*, GARDEN CITY, N. Y., U. S. A.

Apology

A<small>N ATTEMPT</small> was made at the beginning of this book's writing to follow the Wade system of spelling for Chinese names, but when upon completion of the work the author submitted it to several savants in succession, requesting them to correct her Wade, the most dire results obtained. Each expert leaped at the chance; each expert disagreed violently with everything that had been decided by someone else, and at the end the spelling was in a worse muddle than ever. The writer has done her best but knows it is not good enough, and meekly bends her head before the inevitable storm.

Acknowledgment

T HIS BOOK should be dedicated to the Japanese, since without their aid and assistance it would never have been written—or would have been done better, which is as good an excuse as any for a dedication. Twice the notes and several chapters were lost when my room was bombed, and the working manuscript was carried into and out of dugouts so often that it became indecipherable. Early photographs of the Soong sisters and of the rest of the family are scarce because of the fact that the Kung ancestral home in Shansi, where many of these mementoes were stored, has been looted by Japanese soldiers. The Soong house in Shanghai, also because of the Japanese, cannot be used as a source of material.

Thanks are due Zau Sinmay for searching out and translating for me the Chinese sources I have used, and to Mr P. C. Kuo (Kuo Ping-chia) for correcting many of my mistakes in historical fact and for finding such necessaries as paper and typewriter ribbon in Chungking when these commodities were scarcer even than peace

ACKNOWLEDGMENT

and quiet. Thanks are due Miss Corin Bernfeld for her constant attention to this work in progress: between air raids, huddled over a charcoal burner, she read it assiduously, criticized it severely, and kept me at work. Thanks are due Mrs Tilman Durdin and Mrs Jack Young, who typed the script and sent it back to me across country by sampan, pony, sedan chair or coolie. Thanks are due the Press Hostel for lending me what books they still had. Thanks are due my very good friends, the Reverend and Mrs J. G. Endicott, who let me use their house and children for relaxation, their attic for work, and their long experience in China for purposes of argument and inspiration.

I wish to thank Dr Richard L. Pearse of Durham for the valuable material he collected for me in America. I thank "Billie Lee" of *T'ien Hsia* for all the help she gave me in Hongkong. I owe very much to Mr Randall Gould of the Shanghai *Evening Post,* from whose writings I have not only borrowed but taken outright, and from whose time I extracted large amounts whenever I wanted something looked up at long distance.

Thanks are due especially to Messrs Edward Gammell and A. Gidley Baird of the Asiatic Petroleum Company. When every available living place in Chungking had been bombed, they took in myself as well as a large number of other refugees, and in the "safety zone" of the South Bank the book was at last completed, in full view of the burning, shattered, unconquered city. The kindness of Messrs Gammell and Baird, who put themselves at great inconvenience for many months, almost caused me to remove whatever adverse comments I have made anent western imperialism in the Far East. Almost, but not quite.

E. H.

Hongkong, October 30, 1940.

THE AUTHOR and the publishers are indebted to the following for permission to include quotations from their work:

Harper & Brothers, for two quotations from *This Is Our China,* by Mme Chiang Kai-shek.

Henriette Herz, for a quotation from an article by Edgar Snow.

Fulton Oursler, for a quotation from his interview with Mme Chiang Kai-shek, reprinted from *Liberty Magazine.*

Penguin Books, Inc., for a quotation from *China Struggles for Unity,* by John Martin Douglas Pringle and Marthe Rajchman.

The *Nation,* for an extract from "Madame Sun Keeps Faith," by Randall Gould.

Current History and Forum for a quotation from "China Unconquerable," by Mme Sun Yat-sen, and for a quotation from an article by Mme Chiang Kai-shek.

Carol Hill, for an extract from *Personal History,* by Vincent Sheean, published by Doubleday, Doran & Company, Inc.

Mr Michael Bradshaw, for material contained in his article "Charlie Soong's Education" in the Raleigh (N.C.) *News and Observer.*

[*ix*]

Contents

CONTENTS

Illustrations

[*xiii*]

THE SOONG SISTERS early accepted the simplest American fashion of spelling their names—Eling, Chingling and Mayling. Strict sinologues, according to the complicated Wade system (which has borrowed rules from most of the dead and living languages of the world), spell the same names Ai-ling, Ch'ing-ling and Mei-ling. There are various ways of translating the syllables; it is an interesting subject and worth a little attention here.

Family or clan names in China, although they are simple characters, i.e., Chinese words, are a little specialized by virtue of the fact that they have been used as appellations for a long time. Thus, although a man may be Mr Chang, those who know him or read his name in the paper will not automatically think of him as Mr "Open" any more than we conceive a mental picture of a blacksmith working at his forge as soon as we hear the name of Smith. To us Mr Smith is simply Mr Smith, and he is nothing more. But the personal "Christian" name of a Chinese, usually made up of two Chinese words, is not quite so ordinary; each man has a name especially composed of some significant combination, selected at will by his people. Whether he retains the label chosen by his parents or uses another of his own choice—Chinese are much more in the habit of changing their names than we are—the syllables are picked out with an eye to the meaning of the words. A popular girl's name, for example, is Pei-yu, which means "Hanging Jade." Now we Occidentals are not accustomed to this fashion of nomenclature, and when we first hear such a name translated into our own language we are pleasurably impressed. Even when we become used to it, we still feel a little thrill at using the pretty phrase; such a name enhances the owner's attraction in our ears. Just so might a Chinese or a Japanese be pleased to know that "Theodora" means "Gift of God": once he knows this he will probably think "Gift of God" subconsciously whenever he pronounces the name "Theodora." The word will mean more to him, actually, than it does to us, for we have long since ceased to appreciate the syllables as anything more than a convenient name for a certain girl. On his own side he is so used to names like "Hanging Jade" and "Plum Blossom Under the Moon" that they have lost their significance for him even though they have been composed originally with an eye to esthetic effect.

The Soong sisters, therefore, should properly be known to us as Eling, Chingling and Mayling, rather than as "Loving Mood," "Happy Mood" and "Beautiful Mood," clumsy nomenclature beloved of the American magazines and newspapers, irritatingly and exaggeratedly "quaint."

It is not uncommon that Chinese parents should label their children in series, preserving a sort of family resemblance of names by using a common first or second syllable. The "ling" of Eling, Chingling and Mayling means "life" or "age" in the sense of lifetime or era, rather than "mood." But it is likely that this character was chosen more for the sake of euphony than for meaning; unless the Chinese paterfamilias is scholarly to the point of snobbery, he does not fret too much about such trifles. Almost any highsounding, abstractly virtuous character will do.

INTRODUCTION

Perhaps it was half believed that the character "ling" might impart long life to those who bore it as appellation: Mei-ling, "Beauty, the Long-living."

One friend of the Soongs goes so far as to say that this "ling" means no more than does the "ling" in "darling"; that it is, in short, merely a loving diminutive. The theory is tempting but too amusing and pat to be taken seriously; nevertheless, since it has been put forward by a Chinese, it is safe to suppose at least that the intrinsic *value* of the character, in translation, is not great.

"Eling," or "Ai-ling," means "Friendly Life" (or Era) or "Long-living Kindliness." "Chingling" means "Glorious Life." "Mei-ling" means "Beautiful Life." If we ignore the second syllable and translate the other words as nouns, which according to Chinese grammar we have every right to do, Madame Kung may be called "Kindliness," Madame Sun "Gloria," and Madame Chiang "Beauty." By this time, at any rate, they are celebrated names that mean just about as much as the "Elizabeth" of England's queen or the "Eleanor" of Mrs Roosevelt. The comparison is not very good, because the Soongs are Chinese ladies, who would insist that their personal names have no importance whatever. They are better known to their people as Mesdames Kung, Sun and Chiang.

Chinese fortunetellers claim a talent superior to that of their gypsy brothers-in-trade; and any one of them can tell a fortune at a distance, without even seeing his subject. If you have a friend whose fate interests you, and who cannot go to consult a seer for himself, you have only to tell the fortuneteller what day and what year he was born, and you will be able to learn everything about him and his future down to the last detail.

These prophets use their talents to amuse themselves when they have no customers; from time to time they peer into the destiny of the man of the hour, be he a contemporary general, a new-rich gangster or a president. The Soong family is popular among fortunetellers, although it is to be doubted that any Soong has ever been superstitious enough to consult one. The sisters especially have been discussed, observed and singled out for study.

Fortunetellers are character readers, too; some of them, like phrenologists, can describe a man's personality by studying the shape and contours of his face and head. There are books in Chinese that outguess Lombroso, prophesying criminal careers for people who possess a certain type of nose and divulging many a character trait from the height of a forehead. This knowledge is general and follows set rules; just as the life line of a hand means the same to any palm reader who is up in his work, so the shape of a face denotes the same characteristic to no matter what fortuneteller. They are all agreed, for example, that the three Soong sisters are alike in possessing the quality of *peng fu yuin:* in other words, they are pearls among women, "husband-helpers." Praise could go no higher. One does not, of course, need a fortuneteller's information on this subject; the smallest child in China is well aware that Mesdames Kung, Sun and Chiang are excellent wives and helpmeets. But the seers do not stop with this; they use the countless photographs of Madame Chiang that appear in the daily papers, the few available prints of Madame Sun, and the very rare pictures of Madame Kung; with these they indulge in a bit of unsolicited character reading now and then, publishing the results in the hope of a little modest advertising. I have yet to hear that any one of the ladies has paid attention to these offerings, but public interest in the seers' pronouncements is always immense.

Eling's face, according to these prophets of the market place, is of the "melon-seed" or "goose-egg" type, smoothly oval in shape. This oval face is much admired in China, where one of the tests for beauty is to make certain that a lady's lower jaw is invisible from the back: Madame Kung, they say, passes this test with flying colors. A melon-seed face is more than merely beautiful; it denotes great cleverness and an admirably practical habit of mind. Madame Kung dislikes being photographed, and as a result her face is not really well known to the masses. The description of her character as far as it goes is quite accurate.

[*xviii*]

INTRODUCTION

Chingling's face is round and small, with delicate, perfectly formed features. It is a countenance of nobility and dignity, the face of a princess. She gives an impression of physical fragility through which her sturdy spirit shines.

Mayling is sometimes considered the chief beauty among the sisters, but she does not photograph well, and her pictures do not do her justice. Her cheekbones are noticeably high; this feature first of all attracts the attention of the fortuneteller. "Power," he says, placing a sure finger upon the pictured face. One is left skeptically wondering if he would have been so sure of an unknown lady, an unfamiliar face. . . . To be sure, he did not read power into Madame Kung's countenance, although he must have known enough to expect he might find it there. No, the melonseed face remains unread, delicately oval in shape, inscrutable.

The Revolution of 1911 brought about many emancipations, chiefly that of Chinese women. We who read history, when we consider the Chinese Revolution, think first of the unbinding of the feet, but there were other unbindings more significant, if not so dramatic. In Chinese domestic life, women had always held a certain power, but even there they became immeasurably freer after 1911, and all the public world was virgin territory to them; they advanced eagerly, yet fearfully, with slow steps.

The Chinese woman has never been as downtrodden as was her Japanese sister across the sea. There has never been any of that kneeling in China, that rapt devotion in the Temple of Service that makes gods of the most ordinary and unlovely Japanese men. Nevertheless concubinage and slavery were heavy shackles; nor were they thrown off all at once. The freeing of women in China has progressed very slowly; concubinage, for example, was outlawed only a few years ago, and still exists, and the old-fashioned peasant women of certain provinces in the backwoods still bind their baby daughters' feet. All the definite changes took place only in the big cities, where young women embraced the new fashion

[*xix*]

with feverish enthusiasm. Some of them had played a personal part in attaining their liberty; a few girls had even carried bombs and thrown them, and fought in revolutionary battles, side by side with their men companions. But in the country these reforms went gently, by degrees.

It is fairly obvious to anybody familiar with the Chinese temperament that the women of the upper and middle classes, those with enough means to have retained their natural animal spirits, had never been nonentities in society, even during pre-Revolution days. Enormous power was wielded in family circles by the old lady, the dowager mother-in-law; and henpecked husbands are as old a joke in China as anywhere else in the world. Those beauties who were aware of their feminine power, whose wishes were carried out anyway, without personal effort, were among the loudest decriers of the new freedom. It has always been thus. Only the really new type of girl, the ever-present Modern, demanded her right to education and an opportunity for public service. The Revolution, in short, took place just in time for Charles Soong's daughters.

No, the Chinese have never been shocked by the Soong sisters' assumption of power and responsibility. True, the American directness with which Soong Mayling sometimes goes about her appointed tasks may have startled the public at the beginning of her career, but it is an old story now, and the chief fact, the Soong Dynasty itself, was never a new story at all. There is, of course, a proverb to match the occasion. The Chinese are never at a loss for a proverb. This one has become popular as the popularity of the Soongs increases:

"Value not males, but the birth of females."

Back in the Tang Dynasty, when Yang Kwei-fei conquered the Emperor's heart with her plump beauty, he granted lucrative appointments to all her male relatives. Nowadays, the saying is repeated in good faith or in bitterness with never-diminishing relish wherever gossips get together, wherever people debate on politics (nobody in China ever fears the accusation of being bromidic): "Value not males, but the birth of females." Not all disappointed parents, you see, exposed their girl babies to the elements in China, even in the bad old days. There was always the chance that the little girl might grow up a Yang Kwei-fei or a Soong.

It would be quite useless to explain to a traditionally educated Chinese that Kwei-fei was of an entirely different type of woman from the Soongs. The way of a woman with a government is always the same, he would say wisely; anyway, who cares? Smart girls, the Soongs—good girls. Well might their father be proud of them as he looks on from heaven, the world of ancestors.

Yet our stubborn listener is wrong, from beginning to end. Yang Kwei-fei, if she still keeps an eye on this troubled planet, must look in amazement at the actions of China's rulers. Who are these strange women whose lives are all outside the palace gates? What manner of empress is this who travels from province to province, making speeches to the dangerous mob? Why will she not allow herself to be hailed as empress? One can only guess at Kwei-fei's utter bewilderment when she contemplates Madame Sun. Only Madame Kung would be at all comprehensible to the pretty Kwei-fei; her type is immortal and has endured from the beginning of China's history. China and only China produces the Elings of the world; mother and statesman together.

As for Charles Soong, his heaven is not the sort of afterworld from which ancestors look benignly or critically upon the actions of their descendants. Charles Soong dwells serenely in a Methodist heaven, and visits the world no longer in mortal shape. The odors of the banquet, the appetizing vapors of cooked meats and wine are not for him; his chair is empty on New Year's Eve. Indeed, no chair awaits him: his ghost is nowhere expected. The Soong New Year is a Christian holiday.

E. H.

THE SOONG SISTERS

CHAPTER I

Charlie Soong Gets an American Education

EVEN BEFORE there began to be that resentment against the Western missionaries in China, which was to culminate in the Boxer uprising, and which was almost to stamp out Asiatic Christianity for the sixth time, certain scholars and courtiers in Peking began to evince an interest in European culture. The Dowager Empress herself, the Manchu Tzu Hsi, disliked the barbarians of the outer world, but she was willing to examine their claims to civilization. It is typical of the Chinese mind that these elegants should have been tolerant enough to admit the possibility of any civilization at all outside of the Middle Kingdom. Sincerely believing all non-Chinese to be little better than savages, they still realized that people who had for centuries been sending messengers to China might be able to teach them a few things worth knowing. Marco Polo had been a valuable adviser to Kublai Khan, after all. Now there came news of universities in the capitals of Europe and in America, and the academic curiosity of the savants was aroused.

[1]

The Empress went so far as to offer a prize to such enterprising people as dared to go abroad and spend some years imbibing the wisdom, such as it was, of the West. She decreed that anybody who learned in a satisfactory manner such lessons as the foreign universities had to offer would be granted the honorable title of "Yang Han Ling": literally, that he should be considered worthy to dwell in the "Forest of Pencils." The man elected to the "Yang Han Ling" would be known as Best Foreign Scholar, and was expected to have at his finger tips *all* knowledge pertaining to mathematics, philosophy, politics, literature, and the gamut of science from astrology to oceanography. Quite evidently, Tzu Hsi and her subjects had an exalted idea of the ideal foreign scholar's saturation point; or perhaps she really did think it possible for a Chinese to achieve all there was of Western knowledge in a few years.

As usual, however, the Court made do with second-best, and many returned students who fell short, one supposes, of these requirements did nevertheless acquire right of entry to the Pencil Forest. This honor, with its suggestion of imperial approval bestowed upon Western-style education, was the cause of a new fashion; the Grand Tour of the Western World. Young scions of rich families set out to acquire degrees from Oxford or Cambridge or Harvard or Paris. It seems strange to us today that Chinese parents should take so lightheartedly to a program that bade fair to undermine their own civilization, but it did not seem to occur to the young men's people that three or four years in Europe or America could possibly send back the younger generation in a dissatisfied state, ambitious to remold their world.

To understand this trustful attitude, we must remember the genuine contempt which the Chinese felt for any country but their own. It was inconceivable to them that there should be any dangerous attraction in such an inferior culture as the West could offer. They were absolutely confident that any Chinese youth armed with a decent background and a good training in the Classics was completely protected against barbarous ideas; he could go abroad and browse in the fields of foreign education,

[2]

taking what he chose and rejecting the rest, and in the end return to China still the perfect scholar and gentleman. Of course if he should choose to bring back some new, amusing philosophy for the delectation of his peers, so much the better. The nightmare of modern science had as yet no terrors for the Chinese; they could not foresee the bitter struggle which they were shortly to undergo, or the battles they were to fight, vainly trying to keep unchanged their old ways of life. To their innocent minds all knowledge was good, and to be acquired for its own sake.

There followed exciting days for many young men, sent off as they were thousands of miles to make their university homes among strangers. Some adapted themselves quickly, others remained withdrawn from their foreign fellow students and were miserably lonely and homesick. But they all learned something. Seventy-five years ago saw the first joke in China of the "returned student" with his haughty airs, his foreign clothes and his scraps of English and French which he trots out when he wants to be impressive: today the joke is still good, and audiences titter when he appears on the stage, a stock figure of comedy in modern Chinese drama.

Yet he was more than a figure of fun; he was an object of envy to ambitious boys who had not shared his chance to see the world. The new fashion affected the hopes and desires of more and more of China's young people; a foreign education was to become after a time as much a part of an upper-class Chinese child's aspiration as is a college education to our own Middle West youngsters. In 1870 the Grand Tour was still a privilege of the most wealthy families' sons, but there was one honest young man in China who dreamed a dream to which he had no right.

He too sailed for America, but his future in the West as it had been mapped out for him was of a different sort. His was no idle pleasant outlook of elegant study and snobbish retirement; he was destined for a simple hard-working life. The first step for him was to help his uncle, like a good obedient young man, in one of the family shops in Boston.

[3]

Soong Yao-ju's family had sober, cut-and-dried plans for him, in which the newfangled foreign education played no part. Yao-ju himself had other ideas, but he kept his own counsel after the usual manner of nine-year-old boys.

It is not a matter of record which boat took Soong Yao-ju to America and thus in one trip changed the future of China forever. He told his children later that even at that age he was rebelling against the notion of becoming a shopkeeper and fitting into the conventional complicated pattern of a trading family in nine-teenth-century China. The Soongs came originally from Shansi, fleeing from a civil war to Hainan some years before Yao-ju's birth. In the generation before his they had joined the other pioneers of South China and sent out branches to America, founding businesses up and down the east coast of the United States. In China they say that the Cantonese have always been travelers and traders: Yao-ju's family adopted the customs and talents of their neighbors. We in America know only the outside of those shops in Chinatown which we pass when we go slumming, peering curiously into the dark windows as we make our way to a meal of chop suey and chicken chow mein. To us they are just little shops, independent businesses, we assume, which belong to stray Chinese who have somehow drifted into our cities.

Actually, few Chinese shops inside or outside of China do not belong to some vast family of traders. Each small establishment is an outlier of the system; each proprietor is some relation of the owning family. Most of the big fortunes of China have been founded on tiny, dingy one-room shops or big, elaborate restaurants and curio marts stationed here and there throughout the provinces, and the Chinese "stores" in America and Australia and France and England are founded on the same system.

Yao-ju was sent with an uncle to one of his family's outposts in Boston, where he was supposed to learn the business American fashion, which is also Chinese fashion, from the ground up. The

Charles (Charlie) Soong

uncle was on his mother's side and was the first tea-and-silk merchant to emigrate to America; he was owner of the shop and had no son. Therefore he followed the old custom and adopted Yao-ju as his heir and successor, to return with him to Boston and learn the intricacies of trade: the boy was to grow up in that city in his adopted father's house. Someday, decreed the family dictator, Yao-ju would be a shopkeeper on his own, but that day was a long way off. The nine-year-old boy would not be a man according to Chinese opinion for at least another six years.

Yao-ju served his apprenticeship for three of those years, living a Chinese life in a Chinese house in the heart of Boston. Then he made an acquaintance that was to change his entire career. Two boys from Shanghai began to drop into the shop to chat with their compatriot. Wan Bing-chung and New Shan-chow, cousins, had been sent to the United States as members of the Chinese Educational Mission, a gallant venture organized by Dr Yung Wing, a Cantonese graduate of Yale. The mission was to last only ten years, but one of Fate's patterns began to be woven when those two boys, future brothers-in-law of a Shanghai girl who was to marry Yao-ju, first strolled into the Boston shop.

The two young students talked to the wistful little boy behind the counter, telling him of their life at school and of the camp where they were sent each summer. Probably they boasted a little. They visited the shop frequently and kept criticizing young Soon—that is how he spelled his name in those days—for remaining behind the counter and being satisfied with night school, in America, where a first-class education was so easy to obtain. (They considered it first-class.) Yao-ju listened, and his mouth watered for a similar chance. Urged by his new friends, he approached his uncle with a request for permission to leave his work and go to school regularly.

It was no use. Naturally his uncle and what other members of the family were in America did not sympathize with such an outlandish ambition. Yao-ju had his future, a very good one; he was to act as all the other Soons had acted, working like an industrious little ant to build his clan higher and higher, and developing into a shrewd trader and a credit to the family. That was that.

The insidious influence of America, however, had penetrated into that Chinese house. When Yao-ju was thirteen or fourteen he acted like an American boy and did what an American boy would have done—he ran away. It was unfilial, but inevitable. He knew Boston Harbor by heart, and he simply stowed away aboard the cutter S.S. *Schuyler Colfax,* "a second-class sidewheeler," which as it happened was bound for the South. Not that Yao-ju knew or cared where it was bound for; he just wanted to get away.

Of course he was caught and brought before the captain, Charles Jones. Captain Jones was a kindly man and pious. He must have had some imagination besides. Instead of simply kicking young Yao-ju ashore at the next port, he began to wonder how and why it had come about that a Chinese boy had stowed away on his ship at Boston. Yao-ju, eager and bright and terribly in earnest, told him all about it—how he wanted to go to school and his uncle wouldn't let him. He was growing up: a little later it would be too late for him. He begged for permission to work his way, to stay out of Boston and the shop, to find a chance to fulfill the destiny he had chosen instead of that which was being forced upon him.

Yao-ju had always possessed a definite personality, and the captain, as mentioned, was both kindly and pious. He felt rather guilty about that uncle in Boston, but after all he was bound for the South, and in the meantime he could think it over. . . . Yao-ju got the job, as cabin boy.

On Sundays the captain talked to him about Christianity. Whenever the *Colfax* came into Boston Harbor, Yao-ju disappeared mysteriously and reappeared only when they were safely away from that dangerous city. Really there wasn't much the captain could do about returning him to his uncle. . . . But when the *Colfax* came into Wilmington, North Carolina, during a voyage, the skipper went ashore purposefully and looked up friends of his, Colonel Roger Moore and Mrs Chadwick, who was an ardent worker in the Southern Methodist Church. They discussed Yao-ju,

[6]

and Mrs Chadwick handed him over with his problem to the Reverend T. Page Ricaud, pastor of the Fifth Street Methodist Episcopal Church, South. Dr Ricaud was fascinated by the story of the little heathen and his spiritual search. As a result Soon Yao-ju was baptized as Charles Jones Soon. He asked for that name as a Chinese compliment to his first benefactor.

An occurrence like this must have attracted considerable attention in the quiet city of Wilmington, and when Dr Ricaud several months later brought young Soon to the attention of General Julian S. Carr, it was the natural outcome of what had already happened. General Carr of Durham was a Confederate soldier, a textile manufacturer, a rich man and a philanthropist. He decided to consider giving the boy the education he wanted. Therefore Charlie's next step toward the Chinese Revolution was made into the little town of Durham, N.C., to which the general summoned him on approval. He came, he was seen, he conquered. The general took him into his own large house, where for many days he was more or less on exhibit to the other children of the neighborhood, who had never before seen a Chinese.

The general selected for Charlie the Methodist Trinity College, then a small place in Randolph County. The first year the boy spent in preparatory school, but he learned very quickly and was soon doing college work. He lived at Professor W. T. Gannaway's home and studied with the president of the college, Dr Braxton Craven. Mrs Craven helped him in the first difficult steps when his English was still uncertain. Already it had occurred to these good people that Charlie Jones Soon must have been sent to them by Providence for a special purpose. Properly trained, could he not be a source of great good in his native land? Before Christmas of the first year the boy was at Trinity he was taken into the church, and Dr Craven preached on the text, "Go ye into all the world and preach the gospel to every creature."

One can imagine the high hopes held by his friends of Charlie's future godly works among the heathen of his native land. It was the time described by Pearl Buck in one of her best books, *Fight-*

ing Angel: all over America church folk were eagerly collecting funds to support their missionaries, stern young people with a "call" to go out and save the souls of benighted pigtailed Chinamen. Charlie's benefactors must have thought this cabin boy had been sent to them as a manifestation of the Divine Plan. American missionaries were very well in their way, but how much more effective a home-trained native pastor could be! It behooved all good Methodists to treat him kindly and to cherish and instruct him in the ways of the Lord.

Meantime the founder of the Soong family was living as General Carr's own son, calling the veteran "Father Carr" and worrying about his financial dependence upon the older man. During school vacations he insisted upon earning what he could by selling books and cord hammocks, which he had learned to make aboard the *Colfax,* from house to house. It was all very much like a Horatio Alger book: Charlie was indeed a typical Alger hero, bright and good and independent and willing and poor and lucky. Civilization does seem to follow the lines laid down for it by its current literature. General Carr, the Alger millionaire, reaped his proper reward twenty years later when he went out to China. "They treated me like a king there," he used to say musingly—"like a king. . . ." In the meantime Charlie, after two years at Trinity, was transferred to Vanderbilt University in Nashville, Tennessee, in order that he might come into contact with returned missionaries.

He was not happy about leaving the Cravens. He gave one of his hammocks to Mrs Craven and made a careful and courteous speech of thanks, then broke down and "threw his arms about her neck and kissed her good-by."

In the School of Religion at Vanderbilt, from 1882 to 1885, Charlie seems to have made friends with everyone except the acting dean, Dr George B. Winton, who wrote rather sourly:

Soong, or Soon as we called him . . . was a harum-scarum little fellow, full of life and fun, but not a very good student. He gave no

Charles Jones Soong

evidence of having any special interest in religion, even less in preaching. As a matter of fact, when he went back to China he soon became interested in some business enterprise. In the course of time he married a woman who must have been definitely his superior.

No doubt the important item in Dr Winton's report is that which follows the phrase "As a matter of fact." These afterthoughts are usually significant. Charlie's departure from the service of the Church puzzled and grieved many of his old friends, and at the time he was not at liberty to explain his action. Let us see what a contemporary, the Reverend Mr Tuttle, remembers of him:

For two or more years I enjoyed the pleasure of personal acquaintance with Brother Soong, having met him at Vanderbilt University in 1883. In 1885, during my first year at Fifth Avenue, he spent several weeks at my home, and the people of that church felt that he was their son in the gospel and missionary to his native land. He preached for Fifth Avenue Church two or more times during his stay with me, speaking good English, and to the spiritual edification of all who heard him.

Another classmate, James C. Fink, says:

The writer was a student there at the time and had the pleasure of having the acquaintance and friendship of Charlie Soon (he dropped the "g"). He was of a most genial and friendly nature, and I remember that on introducing him to some of the boys, he smilingly remarked, "I'd radder be soon den too late."

His roommate at Vanderbilt (J. B. Wright, later pastor at Cairo, Georgia) says that he was short but strongly built, of a jovial disposition, and very popular with all the students.

He continued to spend his summers with "Father Carr" at Durham and was a favorite of one of the town's leading businessmen, James H. Southgate: he became devoted to Mr Southgate's sister Miss Annie. He sent her a photograph from Vanderbilt and corresponded with her, after he returned to China, until she died in 1886.

He had written in one letter to her, "I love you more than anyone in America." When the news reached him of her death he wrote to Southgate:

It is a matter of great sorrow to learn of the death of Miss Annie, though on the contrary do rejoice to know that she is happier in heaven than could possibly be on earth. And no doubt all these work for good to them that love God. May God comfort you all and sustain you with His tender love and grace and finally when our work is done in this life we may all meet her on that happy shore where there is no parting.

Miss Annie was one of my best friends. Her Christian example is worthy of attention. When I left America I had no idea of such event would have occurred so soon and that we are not permitted to meet again on this side of Jordan. O this is sad to think of the sweetest flower God has plucked off and took away from us; but that very identical flower is blooming in the garden of God in heaven. Happy art thou who sleeps in the Lord. And thrice happy art thou who being translated from earthly sorrow to heavenly joy. May God keep us from sin and weakness and finally translate us to His home where we will meet all our friends and loved ones and to live with Christ forever.

It is a fragment of Charles Soong himself, direct from his heart, that is exposed in this letter. Enmeshed in the conventionalities of two cultures, tied up with quotations, down in the middle of the tangle we see the puzzled and homesick boy.

Even in America he must have had a good deal of the charm that was to set a new fashion in teaching when he went to Shanghai. It is pleasant to speculate on the meetings that were held in Wilmington and Durham, the tea parties and committees and sewing circles that must have gathered to discuss the fate of the Chinese boy. One sees him firmly installed in the favor of the little town, going from door to door to sell his cord hammocks, greeted in each house by church members who had already, of course, met him or at least taken a peep at the general's strange protégé. No doubt he was often invited indoors for a cup of coffee and a piece of pie before he sold his hammock. Oh, the peaceful gardens of Durham and the neat cord hammock that swung in each, all for the good of the heathen Chinee!

In later years, telling his children about those school days in North Carolina, he was fond of remembering a certain Hallowe'en night soon after he was first entered at Trinity. He came into his room in the dark that evening to encounter a grinning pumpkin head sitting in the corner, a candle flame flickering behind the holes of eyes and mouthful of jagged teeth. Now a Hallowe'en pumpkin head is no novelty to an American boy, but Charlie had never seen one before. At first he had no idea what it could be, and then he had far too many ideas. He stopped dead in his tracks and stared, while his hidden classmates stifled their giggles. It is possible that Charlie Soon thought swiftly of ghosts before he reminded himself that now he was a Christian boy who didn't believe in such things. . . .

"He didn't hesitate more than a second," said his daughter Eling, telling her father's story more than fifty years later. "He walked straight up to that pumpkin and punched it in the nose. Of course it smashed. After that the boys never made fun of him any more."

A photograph of Charlie in North Carolina shows a sturdy boy in the American clothes of his time, his hair parted almost in the middle and slicked down on each side. The legs are crossed, the hands disposed in a carefully careless position. He is staring straight ahead, an earnest frown on his young brow. His nose turns up, and his mouth and chin are determined. He looks a healthy, hopeful young man, the sort who comes into his convictions early.

The picture, with its fancy-scrolled chair and background of drapery, is a perfect period piece. It is difficult to believe, while looking at it, in Charlie's background: the twisted streets, the incense-laden temples, the low green fields of the Orient. This young man's very watch chain, draped jauntily across his waistcoat, speaks of American classrooms and student church meetings.

It is bewildering to turn from the daguerreotype and read the legend over it:

INFLUENCE FELT IN MODERN CHINA

CHAPTER II
Shanghai in 1890

At the risk of being dull, we must pause for a moment to look at the country and the city to which Charlie Jones Soong returned with his message and his young hopes. Those of you who know China will not have to read this chapter.

A truthful map of the Middle Kingdom about 1890 would be woefully spotted and particolored, every portion of territory under the influence of some greedy foreign power that was biding its time and waiting its chance to grab more land outright. The Imperial Court at Peking depended for its existence on these powers of the Western world: China's rulers were lulled by international conspiracy into playing a harmless game of independence, and they remained stubbornly blind to the charity on which they leaned. Each day the Court continued to function was one day more granted by the powers, whose diplomats saw their trade increasing satisfactorily enough under these strange conditions. Everybody realized that it would someday be necessary to close down the theater at Peking and take over the last shreds of power, but for the moment there was no need to hurry. Tentative division had already been made. China was in the bag.

Nominally the ruler was the Emperor Kuang Hsu, second to last of the Ch'ing Dynasty, but the redoubtable dowager Tzu Hsi had taken from his shoulders the chief burdens and responsibility of his station. That amazing woman was tenacious but intelligent, within the boundaries of her universe. She was, however, completely ignorant of the world outside the kingdom, and the contempt which all high-minded Manchus felt for the Western barbarians was her fatal blind spot. It is doubtful if she ever appreciated the true significance of what was happening to China, even at the end of her career; most likely with every concession she made to the powers she told herself that she was outwitting the enemy and paying out land that would of its own accord come back to its rightful owners in good time. Fate and the gods were on her side, because they had always been.

Tzu Hsi lived to see her domain shrink considerably. The vast collection of races and territories then known as China was being nibbled away swiftly and surely by the foreign marauders. Burma had been annexed by Great Britain; Macao ceded to Portugal; Russia had taken the greatest part of Ili up north; Annam was now a French protectorate. Tzu Hsi wielded Kuang Hsu's scepter, but it was rotten at the heart, ready to break as soon as she should attempt to brandish it.

The official machinery too was becoming westernized. Although about the Court the Forbidden City was still splendidly Oriental, and the palaces were full of lacquer and jade treasures, the world outside was changing. The money for this splendor came in great part from the maritime customs, working efficiently on a British system, under British control. The treaty ports at Tientsin, Hankow, Chinkiang, Kiukiang, Newchwang and Canton contained foreign "concessions" leased in perpetuity to foreigners, and Shanghai had been given up almost completely to the Westerners. These hospitable cities were in immense contrast to the congested

Canton "factories" of earlier days, wherein foreigners had lived as prisoners for the privilege of trading with the haughty Chinese.

Everywhere on the fringe of the hinterland except in the Court itself the new civilization was penetrating, raucous and speedy and redolent of machine oil, like the first railway built in China, between Shanghai and Woosung. *It* was promptly bought and destroyed by the Chinese, who carried the rails to Formosa and abandoned them there on the beach. But one cannot go on forever buying up the Future and destroying it. . . .

Step by step with the new science, the spiritual culture of the West was creeping in. Roman Catholic priests from France and Protestant preachers from England and America brought with them doctors who knew how to administer powerful drugs along with their religious teachings. These pioneers found the way fairly open to anybody who did not fear the privations of existence in the Chinese countryside. The year 1890 saw the inception of riots against missions in the Yangtze Valley, but there was no great uprising, no general resentment to hint of the Boxers who were to sweep the country ten years later. The missions flourished, on the whole. In this land of religious tolerance, where Buddhists and the followers of Lao Tze mingled and worshiped together peacefully, sharing the philosophy of Confucius, Christianity spread swiftly.

The Christian missionaries to China were probably never completely relaxed and off their guard, nor was their life remarkably easy, but the Middle Kingdom as a dwelling place compared favorably with perilous Africa and India. By 1890 there were thousands of Christian communicants in China, and many native preachers.

Compared to the interior, Shanghai was even then a luxurious metropolis. Its reputation had already created a new verb in the English dictionary, but it was now far more than a harbor wherein sailors made merry or bewailed having been kidnaped. Since 1843 it had been a treaty port. After the signing of the Treaty of Nanking, the British, who had for the most righteous if nebulous reasons stormed the walls of the old fishing village, came back from further triumphs to open a port there, foreseeing the time when this little cluster of houses on the mud flats would be an important center of trade between the Chinese interior and the European marts. They hoped to create a totally foreign city of their own, admitting Chinese only to do necessary work as servants and shopkeepers. Nobody supposed that within the century Shanghai would become the haven of harried refugees, fleeing from the perils of civil war to seek the protection of foreign governments. By the time Charles Soong returned in 1886, Shanghai was one of the world's cities. Its appearance calls for some description.

It is not always true that an old fashion is more picturesque than a new. The tourists who leap eagerly from their ships down on the Bund or in Yangtzepoo seldom fail to exclaim bitterly at their first glimpse of China, which apparently consists of crowded tram lines and high brick walls. Except for the rickshas, curio shops and Chinese people, there is nothing about downtown Shanghai that the traveling families and Cook's tourists could not see in New York or London. Disillusioned, they wander about the streets and stare scornfully at hotels and department stores, telling one another that the white man's advent has spoiled everything. There is simply nothing to photograph. In the old days, they muse sadly, Shanghai must have been a paradise of yellow-tiled temples and glittering red houses; dwarf trees and goldfish ponds and carved stone lions have no doubt all been sacrificed in the interests of commerce.

Before 1937 these pilgrims in search of romance were somewhat appeased by a visit to the "native city"; in Nantao was a bazaar of the most delightful shops, full of ivory and jade carvings, pictures and scrolls, embroidery, lacquer. In the center of the twisted street system a real old temple could be entered by anybody; there were painted gods there and burning incense, and always one or two old women kowtowing and praying aloud. This, said the tourists happily, was more like it. This was a fragment of the real old Shanghai. This was *China*. The long trip across the Pacific or around the Suez Canal had not after all been in vain, even if they did not have the time or the money to go on to Peking. Thomas

Burke and Ernest Bramah would always mean more, now that one had a genuine memory of Old China—before the white man came.

Today, though Nantao and the Chinese city of Shanghai are smoking ruins, no valuable landmark of China's history, none of her real beauty has vanished from this place. It is just as well for the dreams of the travelers that they cannot see a real old Chinese city of the past century. Peking is open today, but Peking was the capital of the empire, and even there the famous beauty spots were hidden from the public. The Forbidden City guarded its treasures behind wall after wall. In Soochow, in Hangchow, in Yangchow, in Nanking, in all the beloved cities of China the common people have always lived in dismal-looking low-lying houses, and those rich men and the recluses who had gardens kept them jealously hidden from everybody save the hallowed family and a few friends of the clan. Old Shanghai had no open bazaar in the Chinese city for many years; the market place where the country people came in for holidays was a workaday place, nothing like Nantao's glittering streets. The few jade merchants and picture dealers hid their wares within dark houses. The pawnshops of China, where the greatest treasures on the market are still to be found, were then, as they are now, dingy houses as carefully locked and guarded as bank strong-rooms.

Ancient Chinese city streets were narrow and dirty; for fresh air and fountains and the trees celebrated in the old poems one must have permission to pass through the small, lowering doors set in the high gray walls on either side of the street. It was small wonder that even China's rich men and their children were eager to move to the wide streets of Shanghai, where even in the middle of the city the air was not fetid and the public highways were clear of filth. They moved in by the hundred, abandoning their villas in the country and their little huts near the ditches. The rich men began playing with the toys of the foreigners; the poor men looked for city work.

By 1890 Shanghai was on the eve of a great industrialization that was to place cotton mills on the fringe of the slums and attract thousands more of the country people. Until the advent of the mills Shanghai's aspect had been that of a small town, or rather of a conglomeration of towns, for already the nationals were herding themselves into cliques. The French Concession and the Settlement made a natural division between two grounds, although the French had not as yet built up to their first limits, and stayed down near the middle of town, which was marked by Soochow Creek. People still lived for the most part near the British consulate.

Their houses were built in solid blocks, with deep verandas all along the fronts. The new buildings were uncompromisingly foreign in style, as though the invading Westerners were already homesick and wished to obliterate any reminder of the Orient. In their nostalgia they sacrificed every chance of comfort that Chinese houses would have afforded; they froze in the winter and baked in the summer, sheltered by ugly red brick. Otherwise their lives underwent an inevitable change; tempo slowed down, and little by little the insidious effect of cheap labor had its way. A man grew so used to being lazy out in China that he dreaded going home, and Shanghai filled up with coolies, servants and Chinese clerks.

For foreigners the Astor House was the center of social activity, although churches and meeting houses also held secondary places of importance. At the Astor House bar tradespeople gathered every morning for an eleven-o'clock drink. It was at the Astor House that the important foreign balls were always held, in the banquet hall, but the Chinese at that time did not join in these revels. They had their own restaurants and clubs when the menfolk wished to seek amusement; they seldom entertained in their homes. These were surrounded by walls, as if their owners still lived in bandit-haunted country. One sees these walls today enclosing large tracts of land that has become of fabulous value, along Bubbling Well Road and the busy streets of Frenchtown. Great iron gates guard the outer courtyards, and while the limousines of the owners wait for admission, a half-dozen servants must scurry about inside, unlocking and drawing back the bolts. We catch glimpses, when this happens, of bamboo pavilions and elaborate mazes of artificial

[18]

craggy rocks between a series of small sagging-roofed houses. Then the gate clangs shut, cutting off that secret world, and the traffic of a modern city rushes past on oil-stained concrete.

Pidgin English was a real language then, and one had to be able to use it fluently. It was just beginning to be fashionable among the higher-class Chinese to teach proper English to their children. On the whole it was only the Christian Chinese and the "compradores" who were at all friendly with the foreigners. The only social contact between the races was an occasional chilly banquet given by a Chinese man in honor of a foreigner, or vice versa. In either case the banquet was a "stag" affair; nobody dreamed of inviting respectable women to help entertain the guests. Chinese women of the higher class were simply invisible. They went out only to temple on state occasions, or on long visits to their relations' houses.

Their husbands and sons, on the contrary, took the air in state every day, riding in their carriages in full panoply, with elaborately dressed grooms escorting them on ponies, one in front, one on each side, and several coming along in the rear. It was a regular little parade, very gay and bright with fluttering silks and jingling bells. Bells were everywhere, on the harness and the carriage. Through the sober streets they trotted, while the foreigners in their dull clothes stood and gaped from the pavements and called them all, with a happy disregard for exactitude, "mandarins."

CHAPTER III

Charlie Soong's Family

CHARLIE returned to China—or, rather, he went to Shanghai—in 1886. It was the one place on that side of the world that he could have borne to live in during the first difficult period of readjustment, and he always felt more at home in the bustling, sprawling Western city than he did in the interior. He wrote to his American friends that he was preaching at Woosung, the village at the mouth of the Whangpoo, and at Soochow, and Kiensan. At Woosung, which was his first center of activity, he also taught at the denominational school, and in one of his classes was a student who was to become China's ambassador and leading educationalist, Dr Hu Shih. Dr Hu remembers that when the new teacher first "stalked on the platform," his square body and homely face made all the students giggle. They were accustomed to the traditional professor of China, grave and delicate and slender, with conventionalized mannerisms. Hu Shih expected that Soong would leave the room for shame; instead he began to speak, and the boys immediately fell silent and respected him. He was a good teacher.

In those days all the Chinese missions of the Southern Methodist Church were under the jurisdiction of Dr Young J. Allen, who, judging from all reports, did not find the burden too heavy for his taste. He was a bit of a dictator in his way, which was a stern one, and Charlie speaks in one letter of three men who had themselves appointed to posts in Japan because "none of these missionaries could stand the 'one man power' at Shanghai." Charlie upon his return was naturally anxious to visit his parents in the South, and Dr Allen wouldn't let him. In a letter to Mr Southgate he writes,

No. I haven't been to see my parents as yet. Dr Allen said I may go during the coming Chinese New Year and not before then. I am very much displeased with this sort of authority; but I must bear it patiently. If I were to take a rash action the people at home (my Durham friends especially) might think that I am an unloyal Methodist and a lawbreaker; so I have kept as silent as a mouse. But when the fullness of time has come, I will shake off all the assuming authority of the present superintendent in spite of all his protestation, assuming authority and his detestation of native ministry. The great "Chogul" [?] was the man who wanted to dismiss all the native ministers from preaching a year ago. And he is the man who ignores my privileges and equality which I am entitled to. I don't like to work under him—I will apply for transmission to Japan.

He did not succeed in his application and had to remain under Dr Allen. Even so he stayed with the Church as preacher for a few years more, learning a bitter lesson after the happy school days in North Carolina. Note that Charlie Soong reversed the usual process: he met with unpleasantness from foreigners only after he returned to China, and he looked upon America as home. That is one reason some of his children today are so very much Americanized. Like any fond father, Charlie wanted them all to be educated at "home," and they were.

[21]

Oh yes, the children. Charlie had returned at the age of twenty-three, and in a year or so he married Miss Nyi, named Kwei Tseng. From the biography that is sent out, according to tradition, by his heirs upon the death of an important person in China, we learn of Mrs Soong,

She was the second daughter of our maternal grandfather, Yuin San; his native town was originally Yuyiao [near Ningpo, in Chekiang Province]. He was a scholar and well learned in law. He was a political adviser, which work took him to Chuan Sha; there he settled down and thereafter lived with his family.

Our maternal grandmother was of the Hsu family, which is very well known in the west part of Shanghai. [The district of "Sikawei" was named after the family; literally, "Hsu's corner."] There has been a Hsu in official life in an unbroken line since the illustrious Wen Ting-kung [Hsu Kwang-ki] down to Fu Yuin, our maternal great-grandfather, who was of the sixteenth generation of Wen Ting-kung's descendants. He was a commander of the army that protected the districts, and fought at Shanghai, Paoshan, Nan Wei and Chuan Sha, where he was killed in battle. In admiration of his courage and his accomplishments the authorities built a temple dedicated to his honor at his birthplace, and up until today the inhabitants have never stopped paying tribute to him.

Ever since the end of the Ming Dynasty, after Wen Ting-kung was converted to Christianity and began to respect the new education, the family has maintained this tradition, treating their children in a manner absolutely free of sex prejudice. Our maternal grandmother and our mother were baptized Protestants when they were children, and faithfully obeyed the Ten Commandments. Our mother was very clever and was her parents' favorite. When she was only three or four years old she began her studies under a private tutor: she entered school at the age of eight; at fourteen, she was promoted to the Pei Wan Girls' High School at the West Gate and was graduated at seventeen. She was particularly good in mathematics, and she loved the piano. At eighteen she was married to our father, Yao-ju. They gave birth to us six children: Eling, Chingling, Tseven, Mayling, Tseliang, Tsean.

At that time our father was a resident of Shanghai, a minister of the Southern Methodist Church, but he had entered the industrial world. He was also helping Dr Sun Yat-sen to carry out the Revolution, and he worked day and night at this. Our mother looked after the domestic affairs and managed to make both ends meet, and whatever money she saved from food and clothing she too donated to the revolutionary cause. She also helped the poor and was a patron of schools and churches.

Although our parents were not very well off, yet she helped us all to live in happiness and comfort, and this she kept up through the most difficult times. . . .

Hsu Kwang-ki, Mrs Soong's ancestor, now called by his post-humous title "Wen Ting-kung, Learned and Resolute Duke," was one of the first Christians in China, an ancestor of Mrs Charles Soong, and so forefather to the Christian Soong sisters.

Perhaps Mrs Soong's chief ambition in life was to make her children as self-reliant as possible, by teaching and example. Her method was Spartan. It is the custom among our writers to sentimentalize over the joys of childhood's freedom, but life for a Chinese child of the past generation was far from being a careless appreciation of this world's pleasures. His training really began when he could remember and recognize a picture, sometimes at three, sometimes at four years old; then he was started in on his "characters," the ideographs that form the Chinese words. There are thousands of characters in the Chinese language, and it is an immeasurably bigger task to learn them than to remember our alphabet and its combinations.

There was also the code of manners. A Chinese child must be versed in this rigid ceremony as soon as possible; it is still the backbone of his social life. Calligraphy must be practiced assiduously. Then there is a strict and thorough training in the Classics, the study of which is the essence of Chinese education, with discussion and composition and rewriting of the text. A certain exercise known as *"tui-tui"* consists of question and answer; the schoolmaster suggests any word, "Black" for instance, and the student must rejoin immediately with an opposite to that word: "White."

[23]

That is a simple "tui-tui" for beginners, but many of them are long quotations in which each word, the form *and* the meaning must be opposed. An example:

> One explosion firecrackers sends off old [year]:
> Many thousand house-scrolls take on new.

The little Soongs, however, were to be spared the less important refinements of the classic education. Shanghai had several foreign-style schools to which Charlie gravitated as naturally as a dove flies home. His Americanism was not diluted during these years; it was the guiding force of his life. Although he had set to earnestly to study Chinese as soon as he returned to Shanghai, his manners and customs did not really undergo much of a change. He was a practical man, and when at last he gave up his career as a missionary and parted without tears from Dr Allen, he found plenty of proselytizing still to do. He had been shocked, as most Americans are shocked, by China's laborers, the way they were forced to work like beasts of burden and the manner in which they had to live; Charlie Soong was not a man to be shocked at conditions and yet refrain from attempting to reform them. His nature and his training sent him straight into the work of industrializing Shanghai. He was the first agent for foreign machinery in the city, and he himself learned to install the equipment for flour and cotton mills. In this way he became connected with a large flour mill belonging to a Sun family (not to be confused with Sun Yat-sen), still leaders among the industrial Chinese of Shanghai. Charlie installed the machinery and worked in the mill and held some of the shares. The Soong family still holds these shares.

It was at this time that his friendship with Sun Yat-sen began to affect his career. Bereft of the first hope of his life, to help China to redemption by means of the gospel, he must have welcomed the political ideas of the future revolutionist. There is no record, for obvious reasons, of the steps by which the friends came to their ultimate plan, but from this time on Charlie Soong was sworn to the cause, and for the rest of his life he was Sun's stand-by, organizer, secretary, and cover for the secret activities of the Doctor, who was to be for many years more a fugitive.

The children looked upon Sun as an uncle, and to Charlie he represented that pure flame of principles without which the Americanized, mission-trained man would have found life rather empty and unsympathetic in China.

A little later he founded a publishing house. Those of his acquaintances who wondered at the change put it down at last to a hangover of his missionary aspirations, for Bibles were the chief output of his press, or perhaps a few of them thought that Soong foresaw a large demand for literature and was being clever. For years the real reason of the enterprise was kept secret, but students of the life of Dr Sun Yat-sen now know that Charlie Soong's printing press turned out revolutionary articles and pamphlets for the little doctor. No other printer dared take on the job; the Imperial Court was watchful and its methods bloodthirsty. Dr Sun therefore depended upon his friend and co-worker, who cheerfully risked his life and the welfare of his family for this new dream which had taken the place of the old. He published Bibles and tracts and pamphlets preaching peace on earth and revolution: he gave his Bibles away in the street and then went home to discuss new plans of overthrowing the government with Sun Wen.

Sun stayed in their house whenever he came to Shanghai. The children took him as much for granted as they did any member of the family. There were for them more important stresses and strains in the home that interested their young minds more than did China's political future. They were being brought up according to a certain plan, an original medley of Oriental and Western ideas, and there was a sharp division between their parents' individual interpretations of this plan. In short, their father was genial and hearty and easy to manage, but their mother was none of these.

In China it is the custom to consider the father in courtesy but the mother in fact as the mainspring of all family communal life, and to pay her elaborate respect accordingly. We hear a good deal about the Chinese mother, and most of it is true: her self-sacrifice, her strict adherence to principle, her executive ability in managing all the complexities of a large, compact family group. . . . One trait she often has, however, which is not so praiseworthy: her love of power. The peculiarly narrow and deep limits of her life develop this passion to a dangerous degree. The average old-fashioned Chinese *tai-tai* is all too often the ruin of her sons. She makes them too dependent upon herself; they turn out to be spoiled darlings, weaklings, cherished creatures who have been so carefully and lovingly swaddled that they are spiritually unable to stand alone.

Mrs Soong—Charlie now spelled his name with the "g"—was an early example of the new type of Chinese matron. Her education and home training had made her a Christian of the evangelist type, with a strong belief in the efficacy of prayer and the abiding value of "good works" on the small, personal scale, the sort of thing which was soon to develop into social service. If you ask any Shanghai resident today what he remembers of Mrs Soong, he will reply, "She was always going out to give things to poor people." She held strongly to the forms of her religion, whereas her husband had an easier conscience for detail. She was known as a saint; the outside world considered her the best woman in the world, *but* . . .

In her home she was a Spartan disciplinarian. She had the best authority in the world for her inflexible decrees; the Church itself was the basis for her energetic rule. The children must behave because of God. They could not dance or engage in other unseemly relaxations because God wouldn't like it. Her own affection she disciplined and suppressed; the children were more difficult to manage. Chingling, a dreamy and pretty child, was her favorite, probably because she was quiet and obedient. Eling, the eldest, was a tomboy and distressingly ebullient, and Mrs Soong's task of bringing her up was not made any the easier by Charlie's obvious preference for this little limb of Satan. Still she persevered, stifling her own feelings to the point of sending the children away to school at an earlier age than even the English do. Remember that this action was the more iconoclastic because she treated the girls just as she did the boys. Her daughters were the first to go abroad.

Their very early years, however, they spent at home, and that home was a concrete symbol of Charlie's existence. As one might expect, he had never conformed to the manners and ideas of his Shanghai business contemporaries. China simply made him impatient, and he had a way of tearing along on his own affairs, along his own lines, without waiting for China. One of his chief fetishes, for example, was punctuality, and he could never reconcile himself to the Chinese idea of time, which is vague to the point of oblivion. In a land where it is considered quite good form to be two hours early or three hours late, Soong had plenty of opportunity to criticize bitterly and frankly those compatriots of his who made no attempt to emulate his virtues—and he never neglected an opportunity of the kind. It is not surprising that he failed at first to achieve universal popularity among the merchants of Shanghai, but he stuck to his guns. Today he has almost won the battle, though it is too late for his comfort. To be late or early in modern Shanghai business circles is enough to brand a man as passé.

Otherwise also Charlie was uncomfortably American. He was very frank and outspoken at a time when all polite people practiced the art of evasion, and courtesy consisted of long-winded, elaborate and beautifully insincere compliments. Nobody expected sincerity —nobody, that is, except Charles Soong. He could not have shocked the gentlefolk of China more if he had gone naked to his work every morning. Indeed his truthfulness, his impatience of Chinese convention, *was* a sort of nakedness, and his contemporaries had to avert their eyes. Yet he won his way. They first feared, then watched, then imitated Charlie Soong.

The house in Hongkew was branded just another Soong eccentricity, because it was out in the wilderness. Friends of the Soongs gasped at their daring and secretly admired them for it. Today the house is surrounded for miles by close-packed city, and until the Japanese took Hongkew in 1937 the family was still collecting rent

[27]

on it. In those days it stood in green fields and was surrounded by date palms and other trees rare in Shanghai. A stream ran by the front. The architecture was of the half-Chinese, half-foreign type that most Shanghai residents chose, and thus set off their city from the other treaty ports, where Chinese residences are still for the most part of the old style. A front wall enclosed the first courtyard, designed to cut off the stream from the nursery, but the children soon learned to climb it and play in the fields. They clambered up and down the trees and disturbed the villagers of the neighborhood so much that the prudent Charlie gave the country people small sums of money to bribe them into leaving his babies alone. After that the small Soongs had the run of the countryside.

In front the house stretched in a straight line behind the courtyard and was divided into four big, high rooms—Charlie's study, the dining room, a Chinese parlor furnished with redwood tables and stiff little chairs, and a foreign-style parlor with piano and comfortable chairs and sofas. The rooms faced south, as all good Shanghai rooms do, to a wide veranda where the family often ate out-of-doors. Behind were smaller rooms with staircase and lavatory. Both were unusual, the staircase because it meant an upper story. The four upstairs rooms were bedrooms: parents', girls', boys' and guests'. Two small rooms and two bathrooms were behind these, the bathrooms fitted with pretty Soochow tubs, with yellow dragons coiling around the outside and green glaze inside. Cold water was laid on; hot water prepared downstairs and carried up. Until electricity came out Hongkew way, the heating was furnished by gas radiators, a refinement that many foreigners in Shanghai did without. The beds, instead of the hard, flat, wooden structures still used by most Chinese, were good, comfortable, mattressed American couches. The neighbors would come in just to peer at those beds, to feel them with critical jabbing fingers, and to agree with each other that they were most unhealthy and dangerous for the children.

The second house behind, separated by a smaller courtyard, contained in similar arrangement the servants' quarters, the kitchen and stores. Behind this again was a large vegetable garden where Charlie Soong loved to work, and thus enhance his reputation, if such a thing were possible, for eccentricity. An educated man, a scholar and teacher, working like a farmer? What next?

Charlie in all his life could not settle down to Chinese cuisine, and Mrs Soong became perforce an excellent foreign-style cook. A pantry behind the dining room contained a stove where she did her baking and roasting, though in the kitchen proper the family servants had their own way; she taught her daughters the mysteries of American cooking in that pantry. Chingling and Mayling are accomplished cooks today, and many of Madame Chiang's friends can vouch for her ginger cookies and Christmas cakes, but Eling, the wild one, never cared for those lessons. Her one accomplishment in the kitchen is roast chicken, and she can still roast a chicken as well as any American housewife. As to the Chinese food, the Soong cook was of course a man, and the girls did not think of entering his domain. Their mother taught them what a young girl should know of such things—noodles, small cakes and so forth.

Good girls in those days knew how to embroider pictures on silk, to make the oddly shaped little designs that were to be sewn into slippers, and to reproduce characters in silken thread so delicately that you would swear they were brushed in ink. Mrs Soong herself did not care for needlework; she read and studied too much to spare the time for it. Nevertheless she was eager that her daughters should become proficient in the art, and she hired a teacher of the conventional type—a decayed gentlewoman, a widow with enough education to write characters. The Chinese word for "needlework" sounds very much like the word "beggarwoman." (The Chinese language is the best in the world for punning, since almost every word in it sounds like something else.) Eling, already bored with the prospect of sitting still long enough to sew a fine seam, pounced on that pun and used it to avenge her tortured spirit by way of the widow. Naturally her little sisters followed her example.

It was a long time before the teacher discovered why her pupils giggled so much when they addressed her, but when she did she immediately went to Mrs Soong and complained. The mother's reaction was direct; she felt that Eling had outraged the proprieties of the Chinese *jeune fille* and had been un-Christian besides. She scolded her daughter sharply, and would have gone on to further punishment if her husband had not stepped in and taken Eling's part. He himself liked to see the children independent and outspoken, and he sympathized with the little girl's hatred of sewing, but he knew better than to say so. Instead he reminded his wife that it was after all unnecessary and wasteful to spoil the child's eyes with such delicate work when the best embroidery cost only a few dollars to buy. Eyes were better employed in reading— *Little Women,* for example. Mrs Soong may have been convinced; at any rate she let Eling, but only Eling, off embroidery from that day on, and Madame Kung herself bears witness, without regret, that she cannot even today sew three straight stitches.

Charlie loved to sing. He had a fine, resonant voice, and the little Soongs became accustomed to the music of the West rather than to Chinese melody. Eling showed a similar talent and often sang duets with him during the evenings of the summer vacation; she learned from him the songs that he had picked up in North Carolina and in Tennessee. She spent a good deal of time with her father; her position as eldest and her nature made them especially congenial. Charlie was fond of bicycling and was one of the first in Shanghai to acquire a wheel. On Eling's tenth birthday he gave her a bicycle; she was the first Chinese girl to own one. She often went out riding with Charlie; when they came to the end of Nanking Road at the Bund, she would circle round and round the huge Sikh traffic policeman who stood there, while her terrified father commanded her in vain to stop.

Long before this, however, Eling's formal education had begun, and she started a fashion in the Soong family, in all innocence, of beginning school at an extraordinary early age. Charlie by this time was becoming popular among the Shanghai burghers, and his interest in the West, his knowledge of America, were assets. Already, before the Revolution of 1911, these dwellers in Halfway House were looking across the sea. The small Christian community accepted the Soongs among their leaders, and a Y.M.C.A. atmosphere began to permeate their modest revels. Charlie even took part in a charity performance at the town hall, acting in the mock new cabinet as "Minister of War." He would naturally want Methodist schooling for his children, and he found it for the girls in McTyeire School. This institution was then on Hankow Road; it had been founded by Southern Methodists and was named for the bishop who had allowed Charlie to be ordained, out of the regular order because of the peculiar circumstances, back in '85.

McTyeire is still the most important foreign-style school for Chinese girls in Shanghai. The old buildings on Hankow Road are gone; the school has moved out to Yuyuen Road. In those days of slow transportation, Hankow Road was a long way from the Soong house in Hongkew, but Eling made its acquaintance through the church next to it on Thibet Road, that which is now called the Moore Memorial Church. Charlie Soong was head of the Sunday school there—he remained a pillar of his Church even though he had given up preaching—and every Sunday he attended service with his wife and those children who were old enough to be brought. The choir was formed of the older McTyeire girls, of sixteen years or thereabouts. Eling, five years old, marked the fact that they had a special place to sit in; she was fascinated. When they sang she was captivated. From that time on her heart was set on McTyeire, which seemed a sort of heaven. Mrs Soong argued that her eldest daughter was too small to start out in the world on her own, but Charles Soong's daughter would not be thwarted.

At last Charlie himself took Eling with him and went to Miss Helen Richardson, the principal, to ask if it were possible to place his five-year-old child in McTyeire. Miss Richardson looked at the child, diminutive in bright-colored trousers, with her hair in a pigtail. In English, jokingly, she asked the baby if she really wanted to join the school; in English Eling replied stoutly, surprising the teacher, that she wanted it more than anything. At last a trial was

[*31*]

settled upon; Eling was to come as a boarder, and they would see how it worked out.

There were still only three children in the Soong household when the little girl started out on her great adventure. For a week she was at a fever heat of excitement over the preparations, the clothes and The Trunk. It was her first private, individual trunk, a beautiful black, shiny one, and her disappointment was intense when it was discovered that with all her new clothes—for it was mild autumn weather in Shanghai, and they were not heavy—The Trunk was not filled to the brim. Eling insisted upon bringing out all her winter clothes too and filling that space, and she had her way.

The day came at last. Eling pestered her father until they were actually setting out for the school, trunk and all, and then—then she didn't feel very well. Her father, quick as always to notice her change of mood, asked her if she wanted to stay home, after all. "No!" said Eling. The family, gathered at the door, had various comments to make: her grandmother kept protesting that it was positively *cruel* to let a small child go off alone like that, and her mother began to waver. It was settled, said Eling, and she was determined to go, but—what about teatime? They had lovely teas at home; would they at the school?

The last thing her mother did for her, then, was to pack a basket of delicacies, with one packet of Gollard & Bowser's butterscotch and one of bitter black chocolate, by special request of Eling. Then everything had been done. The die was cast. The Trunk was loaded. Eling, in a Scotch plaid jacket with green trousers, set off into the great world by her father's side.

In Miss Richardson's study Charlie took leave of her. Then the floodgates broke. Eling made one great leap and clung round his neck, sobbing as if she were being sold into slavery. She cannot remember how he managed to tear himself away, but that afternoon he sent a servant to find out how she was getting along, since he could not bear to come himself. Miss Richardson took the child in her lap and rocked her back to calm.

Because there were no other babies in the school, Eling was the only pupil in her class, under special charge of Miss Richardson, who tutored her privately for two years. The principal of the San Yih Tang, a school for poor children on the Yangkingpang (Avenue Edward Seventh), was a good friend of Miss Richardson, who went every day by ricksha to see her and always took Eling along, sitting on her lap. Chinese in the streets would look at the foreign woman and the little girl and call after them, "Foreign slave! Foreign slave!"

Eling became the mascot of the school, and in a short time Miss Richardson's loving care did a great deal to soften the shock of having left home. Eling still regrets that this wise and kind woman died before she herself was old enough to appreciate her and could thank her, however inadequately. Miss Richardson taught her the old rhyme:

> There was a little girl,
> Who had a little curl,
> Right in the middle of her forehead . . .

"Who is that little girl?" Miss Richardson would say. Eling always replied in Chinese, "Me, of course!" One of the older girls remembers and still chuckles at the memory of Eling's second term, when she was at the awkward age and was losing her baby teeth. Her two front teeth were gone just then, and the older girl said, "Soong Tai-tai [Madame Soong], what's happened to your teeth?"

"Tai-tai," said Eling politely, "the front gates were stolen."

Her desk was too high, and her feet did not touch the ground, and after an hour or so of good, old-fashioned schooling her legs always went to sleep. She suffered horribly from that, and nobody thought of it or of remedying the situation. The Chinese lessons saved her from paralysis, because, as she repeated the words, chanting in proper fashion, she was able to sway back and forth and so to start the blood flowing through her legs again. Also, she never had enough to eat. The bowls of food were put down in the middle of the table, and everybody grabbed at once; Eling's grab was neither so far nor so quick as those of the others, and she was usually left behind.

Another agony was the loneliness at night. While the older students prepared their work in the evening, she lay in bed alone in the great dormitory upstairs, quaking with terror. The evening exercises always closed with the singing of the hymn, "Abide with Me." Even today when she hears those solemn strains a quite special feeling of relief floods her heart.

CHAPTER IV

Boxer Rebellion Days

Eling was ten years old, Chingling seven, Mayling only one at the outbreak of the Boxer Rebellion, which incidentally was not a rebellion at all, but was so called by the Allied Powers as a euphemism, a tactful gesture toward Tzu Hsi when they were all become friends again. Shanghai was not in the area of most disturbance, but anything that affected the Christians, especially the Protestants, of China must affect the Soongs, and Charles and his wife watched the catastrophe with poignant anxiety.

Feng Yu-hsiang, the "Christian general" who has at last joined forces with Chiang's followers, was at the time in the new military training school at Paotingfu, and his record of the period has interest as being written from the viewpoint of a Chinese who actually took part in it:

The Righteous Harmony Fists Society was originally composed of the remnants of the White Lotus Cult. At first they raised their ban-

[35]

ner in opposition to the emperors of the Ming Dynasty and carried on their meetings in secret. Then the extreme hatred felt by the Chinese people for the foreign churches dyed them an anti-foreign color: from inward they turned outward. . . . "With the Manchus to down foreigners" was their program.

The people joined in with this movement from all sides, like the wind and the clouds. Everywhere they burned churches, slaughtered foreigners, destroyed telegraph wires and pillaged railroads. It was expressive of their anti-foreign sentiment, and it showed graphically what deep-rooted and serious hatred was felt by our people against imperialism.

At its high tide, the secondary movement sprang up to mop up the "Secondary Hairy Ones." These were the baptized Chinese, those who with foreigners behind them had always insulted their compatriots . . . foxes who carried on their outlawry with tigers behind them. But the search was not well organized; it had no standards, and any-one was allowed to make accusations without any proof being asked. If a man had a cross in his house he was immediately accused of being a "Secondary Hairy One"; if he used oil lamps, oil or matches, he was again accused. . . .

That year in the First Moon, on the eighth day, the Military Train-ing Corps received orders to put down the Righteous Harmony Fists. At first our troops marched away from Paotingfu along the Baiku River; there we went into action. All the people were silenced and disappeared; the society was completely quenched. But that evening our commander, Chang, a native of Tsinan, Shantung, spoke to us unexpectedly in this fashion: "We must not offend the Hundred Surnames [the citizens of China]. The Righteous Harmony Fists So-ciety is admirable. They fight foreigners, so we must not interrupt them in their work. We were ordered to come here; we cannot help that. We were only compelled, however, *to come here*—but this is a secret. None of you must speak of this outside." . . .

So it happened that when the troops forced them east, the Hundred Surnames who were Boxers drilled in the west. When our troops went west, they went east again to drill there. . . . In the beginning when the society first flared up, the Manchu Imperial Court was a little shaken. The Boxers' program had made it clear that they were both anti-foreign and anti-Manchu. . . . The anti-foreignism could easily develop into civil war. For this reason the Imperial Court hesitated awhile. Should they destroy the Boxers? Or follow the way the wind was blowing, utilize them, lead them, transform them into a purely anti-foreign movement? At last they decided upon the latter policy, and soon the Righteous Harmony Fists were training under the government. Thus a childish movement of the people was utilized by the Manchu Court.

The rest of the story is familiar to most Westerners. Shanghai's part in these alarms was that of a bystander. A false report that all the foreigners in Peking had been massacred on July 14 gave everybody a bad scare. Li Hung-chang, trying valiantly to save China from the Empress' shortsighted policy, came to Shanghai to talk matters over with the consular body, but they rebuffed him, referring him to the envoys, *if* they were still alive, and to the home governments if they were not. Three thousand Indian troops sent to Shanghai by the British from Hongkong relieved the tension somewhat, though the Chinese government protested their landing. Then the French landed a hundred sailors and some Annamite soldiers.

By the time the news came through that the legations had been relieved on August 14, Shanghai was an armed camp. The German offering to peace and order arrived, though a little late, and a splendidly significant military review was held on the racecourse. These foreign troops were not withdrawn until 1902. The protocol was signed in 1901, a year after the relief of Peking. Once again the missionaries in China were safe.

When Eling was ten, and an old resident at McTyeire, her future husband, Kung Hsiang-hsi, was a student in Peking, in one of the colleges that were later to become merged into Yenching University. He was an adventurer in his way, for he had forsaken his family's religious beliefs and was studying foreign culture under constant protest from home.

The Kungs are an old family in Shansi: Hsiang-hsi himself is the seventy-fifth descendant of Confucius. For generations they have been bankers and pawnshop owners, and until Hsiang-hsi's great-grandfather's time they interested themselves in statesmanship. This great-grandfather decided at an early age to try to take an important degree, for which many tried but only one in a great while was chosen. According to the cruelly exacting methods of his day, he studied and studied for his examination, sacrificing his health to this one ambition, and when he was twenty-four the great test came. In the examination hall the pale boy began to write his paper, when suddenly blood gushed out of his nose and mouth. He was taken home a broken man, only one of the many who met their death in this manner. Before he died, however, he called his little son to his bedside and said:

"Swear that you will never enter public life, nor ever allow any of our family to do so."

Hsiang-hsi's grandfather kept the vow and saw to it that his son in turn stayed home and attended to the private family business. Hsiang-hsi himself was raised according to the same precept and might have been in Shansi now but that he was a delicate child with a tendency to goiter. His parents took him to many native doctors, and when their skill failed he was brought to a mission hospital. There an American doctor operated on him and brought him back to health. The influence of this man was responsible for Hsiang-hsi's conversion to Christianity.

Keeping his secret, he merely requested permission to attend school in Peking, and this was reluctantly granted. He was there when the Boxer trouble flared up, and his history at this time is particularly interesting, for Hsiang-hsi was already a revolutionary at heart, though he had not yet made the acquaintance of Dr Sun's Three Principles. As a fifteen-year-old he had watched the troops marching north to fight the Japanese. Most of the men he saw happened to come from Szechwan, and they marched barefoot, as they always did. Now Hsiang-hsi came from Shansi in the north, where the poorest coolie is careful in cold weather to have shoes, and he

was appalled at what he considered the cold-blooded cruelty of the
Ch'ing, to allow their soldiers to suffer in such a manner.

When the Empress Dowager put a stop to the reforms of the
Hundred Days and incarcerated Kuang Hsu, all Hsiang-hsi's dislike of the Ch'ing recurred to him and crystallized in a hatred for
the Empress. Kuang Hsu he looked upon as a tragic nobleman, an
exception to his family. At the university he made friends with a
large number of students who shared his views, especially with a
man named Li who was several years older than himself, though
also in the first-year class. Li's ideas were more practical than those
of the others; he had imbibed a number of revolutionary principles
and liked to proselytize. He was more or less a leader among the
boys, and Hsiang-hsi was his special friend. The group formed a
secret society the chief object of which was to get rid of Tzu Hsi
and replace Kuang Hsu on his throne; they met at night, and each
one swore a solemn oath never to abandon his emperor.

It was Li who came to Hsiang-hsi one day with a fully developed
plan of action. He had made friends, he said, with one of the
Palace eunuchs. He wanted Hsiang-hsi, as the wealthiest boy of his
acquaintance, to finance the venture he had thought of; namely, to
bribe the eunuch to allow him into the Palace, where he could get
close to the Empress Dowager. If only he could accomplish this, he
said, he would manage somehow to assassinate her. The main thing
was to get into the Palace.

Hsiang-hsi agreed and scraped together all his money: book
allowance, railway fare and clothes money. Then the Boxers
started their war and put all other ideas out of the minds of the
students. Hsiang-hsi hurried to the side of his good friends, an
American mission family, and tried to help them to escape. One of
the women sprained her ankle just as they were preparing to get
away, and because she could not go, the others too remained,
knowing that they would be killed. To the Shansi boy they entrusted their last letters home, then forced him to go into the
country. They died; the details of their death are unknown.

Hsiang-hsi, carrying the letters that were practically his own death warrant, made his way through many difficulties to his home, to which his frantic relatives had summoned him. In an inner room he confessed that he was a Christian and said that he could not stay with them for the sake of their own safety. It came as a double shock to the Kungs, but they would not let him go. By night they smuggled him from one place to another, and his grandmother kept the letters, the nature of which he did not dare tell her. Hsiang-hsi and his people survived the Boxer Rebellion, but he was haunted by the thought of his duty to the dead, and as soon as he could he sailed for America with their last messages. He was to stay there for years.

The future Madame Sun was just starting in at school when Sun Yat-sen in 1900 returned to Japan from Europe, where he had been living in prudent obscurity since his flight from China in 1895. His first attempt to overthrow the Manchus had failed, but he was back at the same work, now making friends with the liberal Japanese, consulting with them and listening to their promises of help. Sun, the same age as Charlie, had by this time adopted the foreign style; four years before, he had cut off his queue and now looked rather like a Japanese himself.

Mayling was one year old: Chiang Kai-shek, a fourteen-year-old boy in the country of Chekiang, was looking purposefully toward the new military training school at Paotingfu. . . .

McTyeire on Hankow Road consisted of two buildings, and owing to the haphazard state of growing Shanghai at that time, one was lit by gas and the other by electricity. Chingling, the second little Soong girl (Madame Sun), whose foreign name was Rosamond, did not emulate Eling's Spartan behavior; she appeared at McTyeire at the age of seven. She was a quiet child with a great aptitude for English. Her hair was short and did not make very impressive plaits, and the other girls called her "Little Pigtail." A former schoolmate says that, of the three as she remembers them, Eling had the most sophisticated air; she had great poise for a child of her age. No doubt those early years away from home had something to do with it.

A similar experiment was made when Mayling was five years old. Partly because Eling had survived and partly because they thought the little girl would be better off with her sisters, another special arrangement was made with McTyeire whereby she was to attend the kindergarten that was now connected with the school, and live in the dormitory with Chingling. (She was six years younger than Chingling, remember.)

Mayling was a plump child. In her own words, "I was so fat when I was a little girl that my nickname, 'Little Lantern,' was given to me by one of my whimsical uncles. Mother put me in thickly padded cotton clothes in the wintertime, and I waddled around in them. I remember when I was three or four years old I used to fall after every two or three steps because the clothes were so thick and clumsy, but as I was so well padded, not only with clothes but also with fat, I cannot remember being hurt very much. I had two little queues on top of my head, which were tied with red strings and then rolled into round loops. They were popularly known as 'crab holes,' and were quite à la mode for little girls of that period. Mother always dressed me in flowered designs, a short jacket with the two sides closing one over the other and tied in the back, and long trousers. But my shoes were unique. They were made to look like cats' heads, with two ears sticking out, and embroidered whiskers and eyes. Later when I grew older Mother put me in boys' clothes, presumably because I was such a tomboy and she thought that since I acted so much like a boy and seemed more natural in my older brother's clothes than in my older sister's it killed two birds with one stone. But in reality my brother, T.V., outgrew his clothes so quickly that every two or three months new ones had to be made for him, and I fell heir to his outgrown ones. Up to the time I went to America when I was nine years old [Chinese age] most of the time I wore boys' clothes."

As Chingling's little sister on sufferance, Mayling took her duties seriously. After evening prep Chingling's friends would return to the dormitory to find that "Siao Mei" had prepared tea for them—for Chingling's friends *only*. She waited on them, too.

The passageway between the gaslit building and the electric-lit building was very dark and fearsome for most of the smaller girls, but Mayling was not afraid to walk through it at night, anyway to all outward appearances. "Why can't you walk through there like Mayling?" the teachers used to say to the others. In reality the child was very nervous and was suffering from nightmares and sleeplessness, but it was some time before this was discovered.

Every Thursday night at McTyeire there were religious "discussions" led by important guests. Sometimes the Soong parents took charge, but more often Pastor Li was the leader. There the little girls were encouraged to ask questions and to thresh out in public their doubts and problems of faith. Each question was considered fairly, without criticism from the authoritative people there: the little doubting Thomases met with careful and gentle handling from everybody—except Mayling. She was badly shocked.

"Why do you ask Pastor Li questions?" she demanded indignantly of Chingling one Thursday night after the discussion. "Don't you believe?"

It was one of the teachers who found out that the child was waking up at night in fits of trembling. She would get out of bed and stand up straight, repeating her lessons. Even Mrs Soong could not insist upon further hardening, and Mayling went home, there to be tutored until she went abroad a few years later.

It was soon after this that the kindergarten borrowed Chingling to help in the school play that they were giving at the end of term. Chingling was asked to play a part that was too difficult for the small children. The piece was a fairy story, and just before the curtain, when everybody was going to live happily ever after, the princess Chingling was crowned queen.

The audience was all of Chinese parents in brocaded silk, but save for their costumes and their language there was little difference between them, with their proud, anxious expressions, and the parents gathered in any American schoolroom at an end-of-

[42]

term kindergarten play. Even the uncomfortable little folding chairs were the same, and the preponderance of mothers over fathers. Charles Soong was there. He was a loving father, if a trifle reserved, and he had taken time off from his absorbing business and his still more absorbing friendship with Dr Sun Yat-sen to come and watch his daughter play the lead.

"Aha!" cried Chang Hsu-ho, a friend of his, as, up on the platform, they put a pasteboard crown on Chingling's head. ("I crown thee queen," said the Fairy Prince.) "So, Mr Soong, you are the father of the Queen! King's father-in-law! King's father-in-law!"

They all turned to him and laughed, pleasant Shanghai burghers, founders of families, comfortable honest folk. They all laughed together, and Charlie Soong laughed harder than any of them, as was seemly, for the joke was on him.

CHAPTER V

Charlie Soong's Daughters Get an American Education

THE SUMMER VACATIONS saw the girls all together again, with their little brothers. Their lessons continued, however. An English-woman tutored them in the mornings in her home, teaching them English and Latin (the latter a startling innovation for Chinese girls), and in the afternoon they studied the Classics with the same man who had taught Charlie when he had first returned to China. At noon the three little girls rode home in one ricksha in the sultry blazing sunlight, giggling or slapping one another. After lunch they were supposed to take a nap, but when their mother was asleep they crept out to the back garden to play. Their favorite games were Puss-in-the-Corner and Ricksha Pulling. Eling was playing ricksha puller one day with Chingling as passenger; she pulled badly, her strength failing her, and Chingling was tossed out. She still has a small scar from that accident.

The deep affection that Mayling feels for her eldest sister was born at that time. It is not often that a child so young has any more feeling for the other children of the family than acceptance; sometimes, in fact, large families breed more competition and quarrels among themselves than love. Mayling regarded Eling, however, with a feeling which even today amounts almost to hero worship, because the elder girl was gentle with her baby sister and took her side against the rest of the world, those jeering, nasty little boys and girls who are always ready to bully a baby.

No doubt there was some excuse for them; Mayling was the youngest of the crowd of playmates and was in their way, toddling after them in their games. They vied with one another in thinking of methods to get rid of her. One day her cup of bitterness was filled to overflowing: the children were playing Hide and Seek, and when Mayling clamored for permission to join them they were exasperated. Mayling wasn't much good at Hide and Seek; she was too eager to be discovered when she was in hiding, and no good at all when it came to discovering others. However, they had a plan. With false smiles and honeyed words they told Mayling she could be "It." She must stand in the middle of the garden, they said, and count up to one hundred. She was not to look until she had counted to a hundred.

Patiently Mayling counted, doing her best. She didn't count very well. She went all to pieces, usually, after she had got through the teens, and jumped from twenty to thirty, or even forty, with wild abandon. Naturally she achieved one hundred in record time by this method, but one of the children had lingered to listen and told her she must start all over again. Mayling, her chubby hands clamped over her eyes, obediently started again. This time there was a dead hush, and nobody criticized her counting. "Eighty, sixty, fifty, ONE HUNDRED!" said Mayling triumphantly and looked up. She was alone.

She was deserted. Not a child remained in that garden. From the first second a foreboding of the truth filled her heart, and a long search left no doubt of the perfidy of those others. They had gone, escaped, found some distant place where they were probably laughing at her at that very moment before throwing themselves into a

[45]

new game without her. Mayling was all alone in the world. Nobody wanted her. Vain all her most valiant attempts to keep up with them and to count straight; nobody wanted her. Tragedy engulfed Mayling.

It was then, as she stood crying her heart out, that Eling always came along and wiped her eyes and her nose and comforted her and promised her that someday she too would be a big girl. Eling never failed her, then or afterwards.

The afternoon lessons in the Classics were at home, and Charlie's old teacher felt that he should be particularly strict with the second generation. Eling didn't like those lessons, sitting still and droning away. Her attention used to wander, and the teacher would rebuke her, with dignity but with force. Once when this situation had created bad feeling on both sides, Eling made an excuse to walk behind his chair and there quietly tied his long queue to the chair back. Then she went back to her seat, sat down demurely and began to annoy him again. He leaped up to punish her and was jerked back, falling to the floor with the chair on top of him. That time Charlie did not interfere with the family discipline, and Mrs Soong gave her eldest daughter a good spanking.

Alone she taught us to read and to play music. We encountered innumerable hardships, but she bore them all with good humor. At that time people were only beginning to take seriously the question of girls' education, but our mother had already made up her mind that all of her daughters should go abroad and study in foreign countries. . . . [From the biographical note.]

Eling at fifteen, it was decided, must go abroad, preferably to America. The Soongs were not rich, and in China until this time only the really rich families dreamed of sending their children abroad for their education. Charles Soong, however, had a different reason than theirs for wishing to incur this expense. They looked upon the voyage as something smart, something to be done because the others were doing it: it was an advertisement of their wealth and their up-to-date attitude. Even then, only the sons were sent;

it was unheard of that a daughter should go abroad. But Soong dreamed of that foreign education as he dreamed of the liberation of China; to his mind it was a means to that end. He had not forgotten his own struggle to get away from the shop in Boston; the miracle of General Carr's help was still a miracle to his mind. His children, he had resolved at Eling's birth, should not have that struggle, at least. Life should spare them one trouble, girls as well as boys.

Charles's standing as a Methodist preacher gave him contact with the Southern Methodists in China, and they helped him to arrange the trip. Eling was to attend the Wesleyan College for Women, at Macon in Georgia; incidentally it is the oldest chartered woman's college in the world. Her father, not at all abashed by the criticism he had incurred among his friends by thus indulging a young girl in a mere luxury, went even further: he gave a farewell dinner for her! To us it seems the most natural thing in the world for a father to do. To Shanghai it was a fresh shock. The honest merchants discussed it among themselves and agreed that Soong, always somewhat eccentric, was definitely going mad, or if not he was certainly bringing ruin deliberately into his house. Since he was not a millionaire, he should keep his daughter at home and save this money he was lavishing on farewell dinners, trips abroad and such foolishness that only spoiled her anyway. Thus when she married he would be able to give her a dowry of—let's see, said the merchants, who liked to count every penny belonging to their friends as if it were their own—Soong, a fairly warm man when he kept his mind on business, should be able to settle at least ten thousand dollars on Miss Soong by the time she married. Ten thousand was a huge sum when the Shanghai dollar was at a respectable level. The good men of Shanghai felt as grieved as if Charlie had robbed his daughter outright of her dowry when he persisted in going his own crazy way. Besides, what man would marry the poor child if she went to America and ruined herself with a lot of dangerous progressive ideas?

Meantime it was settled, and Eling started out. She was placed

[47]

in the care of a missionary family, friends of Charlie, named Burke: Mr Burke had been a classmate of Soong's at Vanderbilt. For this voyage Eling was dressed in foreign clothes, with an enormous ribbon bow on the end of her plait; the dresses had been designed and executed according to the advice of certain kindly missionary ladies and were probably not the last word in *chic*. Anyway they were foreign.

On the way to Yokohama, Mrs Burke died, and the family disembarked in Japan. There was little time for rearrangement, but the fifteen-year-old girl could not be sent on without somebody to look after her, and Mr Burke, hastily but conscientiously, found the necessary chaperone. This was another missionary, a Korean woman of the Burkes's acquaintance, who took her trust so much to heart that she became involved in an unexpected quandary. At San Francisco the immigration authorities noticed that Eling's passport was made out as if she were traveling with an American family; her association with a Korean threw them into typical departmental confusion, and for a time all traffic was stopped. Until this involved and suspicious matter was cleared up, Eling could not come into America. She was, however, permitted to remain aboard ship—any ship, evidently, for as time went on, her own ship had to sail away and she was transferred to another. After a few weeks she became quite accustomed to moving from one boat to another, and as a matter of fact she was lucky that they did not put her into the detention house.

The Korean chaperone refused to abandon the child, though she was at liberty to do so and though her father was ill, which was why she had made the trip. She stood by from day to day, from ship to ship. The memory of her kindness and that of Miss Richardson is Madame Kung's chief reason for respecting missionaries today.

When at last things were satisfactorily settled and Eling was set at liberty, she journeyed safely to Macon. She had been courteously treated, in comparison with other Chinese girls, but the memory rankled, naturally. When she visited Washington the next year to see her uncle, Wan Bing-chung, who was heading a committee to investigate educational methods, she mentioned the matter to President Theodore Roosevelt. The future Madame Kung even in those days had a forthright, straight-from-the-shoulder nature that warred with the accepted rules of Chinese politeness, *kutchee*. That word means, literally, "the manner of a guest," but it means much more, actually, than politeness. It is a symbol for all the elaborate ceremony which in old China preceded any discussion of importance; the confusing euphemisms that fill the language; the allusions to poems that are in their turn full of allusions to earlier poems; the intrigue, layer upon layer of subtlety, which is an integral part of the simplest transaction. Charles Soong's reaction to *kutchee* was always that of a blunt, honest American; it was a red rag to his bullish spirit. Eling, from her association with him, had always been incorrigibly sincere.

When she was introduced to President Roosevelt, in spite of her awe of him and the admiration her father had instilled in her for this great man, she felt a burning need to tell him how badly his country was being run. Certain cherished ideals had been rudely broken; the hospitable country that Charlie Soong so loved, of which he had told so many homesick stories to his children, had let her down. Not only her dignity as a Chinese but her sense of right was offended.

"America is very beautiful, and I am very happy here, but why do you call it a free country?" she demanded of the President. "Why should a Chinese girl be kept out of a country if it is so free? We would never treat visitors to China like that. America is supposed to be the Land of Liberty!"

The President said he was sorry.

The younger sisters followed her in 1908. They sailed in the Pacific Mail steamer *Manchuria* in a party of Chinese students bound for America, all under the protection of their uncle and aunt, Mr and Mrs Wan Bing-chung. It was of course too early for Mayling to attend college, but she insisted upon accompanying her sister, blackmailing her parents with the reminder of a promise they had made to her, during an illness, that she could have whatever she wanted. Perhaps her parents thought that since the children had been through McTyeire together, it would be easier for both of them to leave home at the same time.

Chingling, or Rosamond as she was to call herself during the American phase, was at this time a very sober, plain child, the most studious of the three. She gave evidence even then of an interest in moral and philosophical questions; her ideals were high. She was more of a dreamer than were her sisters. Mayling at nine was still the charming child who had been a pet at McTyeire, full of eager questions as to the country where they were going and very sure of her plans for the future. A young Englishwoman traveling home from Shanghai amused herself one day, walking about the deck with Mayling, with asking the child, as one always does:

"And what are you going to be when you grow up?"

Mayling replied promptly, "I want to be a doctor." Amazing ambition for a little Chinese girl at the beginning of the century! The Soongs had assuredly been modern in their training.

The reply shocked the English girl, and she said involuntarily, "A doctor! Oh, my dear, I shouldn't think you would like that, you know. You would have to cut off people's legs, did you know that?"

"Should I?" said Mayling in surprise. "Oh." She thought a minute. "Then I don't want to be a doctor," she decided. "It would be too dirty."

It will be seen that the Soong girls spoke English perfectly fluently at that time; the McTyeire standard was high then, as it is now, but the little Soongs had the added advantage of constant practice with their father. Living for several years in Georgia had a charming influence upon their accents. Today all three of them still bear traces of their Southern training in their speech and particularly in their well-modulated voices. Too many Chinese girls of Shanghai speak English with a raucous Middle West American twang: the pretty speech of Madame Chiang, the liquid low voice of Madame Kung, the gentle sweetness of Madame Sun's words, are due to Wesleyan and the Southern Methodists. Even those who refuse to see good in the Christian missionaries of China should be grateful for this.

The first years of Eling's college life would have been lonely, homesick ones if she had not come abroad very young. She made friends among the American girls, who were vastly interested in this exotic child. For most of them she was the first Chinese they had ever seen, and she fascinated them with her clothes. Now and then a chest of silks would come from her mother in Shanghai, and the whole dormitory would crowd in to admire and envy as Eling unfolded the gorgeous fabrics—supple satin, stiff brocade, heavy poplinlike stuff from the Hangchow looms. In those pleasant days before the invention of rayon, all the silk of China was exquisite, and the American girls of Wesleyan clamored for favor with Eling in hopes that she would "swap" a few yards of the coveted stuff. Sometimes she would exchange a piece for a real American dress: she wore American clothes while she lived in Macon, and with her best friend she divided a certain bolt of blue silk; they made identical party dresses with it. She has not forgotten that blue dress to this day. Those packages from China maintained the Soong girls' prestige at school as nothing else could have done. Other girls, nearer home, received "boxes" every week full of food, cake and sweets and the special tinned foods that schoolgirls used to like. Classmates shared boxes with their Chinese friends who were too far away from home to get such delightful packages, and demanded their company during the holidays when the little Soongs could not go home for a visit.

Mayling was not a regular student; she was not old enough. However, because there was another little girl of her age in the school, the daughter of the president, Bishop Ainsworth, another special arrangement was made, and she stayed on the campus. This worked so well that yet a third child, Claribelle Marshall, the little sister of another big girl, was included in the group, and the three

[*51*]

formed their own unofficial class. Eloise Ainsworth, Claribelle Marshall and May Soong were quite happy, but they had one common longing, the perpetual desire of the little girl to be as important as the big girls.

"The big girls had secrets," says Madame Chiang. "How we wanted to know what they were talking about! But they would never tell us; they would say, 'Run away now, children.' "

The girls' sororities almost drove them mad until they hit on the plan of forming their own. They called themselves the "Tri-puellates" and looked about for a chapter room. Only one room was available, a small one over the big music room, and to get permission to use that they had to swear in Bishop Ainsworth as an honorary member. This worked so well that in a short time most of the faculty were honorary members. The children made up their equivalents to the passwords, secret signs and rules of the big girls' sororities; one of the rules, for instance, was that chewing gum was not to be chewed during chapter meetings. Teachers who in the ordinary way never thought of chewing gum would walk into that room chewing lustily, just to make the founders scream in protest.

Chingling studied philosophy and worked hard. She spent a good deal of time writing long letters, very thoughtful and idealistic, to girls at home. She made friends easily and kept them long. Mayling, who was to specialize in English literature when she grew a little older, was at that time just at the age when she loved to pick up and use long words. She would try them out first on Eling, watching out of the corner of her eye to see the effect on her big sister.

"I've just met the most atter*ac*tive girl, sister," she said one day. "She's my new friend; she's been so nice to me. She's invited me to her box tonight. Oh, she's simply *fanisating*."

The institution of the "box" was responsible for a very dramatic night in the Soong annals. One of Eling's friends had received a fine big one, full of turkey, pickles and other indigestible things. Its arrival was naturally kept as secret as possible among about six of the girls, including the Soong sisters, and they arranged to meet in Eling's room after the hour for going to bed. Boxes were usually devoured in this clandestine and illicit manner. That night the feast was ready on a blanket spread on the floor, when a noise, real or fancied, in the corridor outside sent the visitors flying. The food was whisked out of sight. Chingling and Mayling, who had more or less of a right to be there, went into the bathroom: the other two visitors fled pell-mell into a closet. Eling promptly made confusion worse confounded by tipping two clothesbaskets full of dirty laundry on top of them. She then closed the closet door and opened the one into the corridor.

Nobody was there.

Eling said in a loud voice, "Good evening, Miss Jones," and replied to herself, "I thought I heard somebody in this room. Didn't I hear somebody in this room?"

"Oh no, Miss Jones," said Eling, "there's nobody here."

"Yes, there is," said Eling. "I'm coming in to see."

She kept that up for about ten minues. The only reason she was not choked when at last she liberated her suffocating prisoners was that they were so impressed with her powers of mimicry.

"But I could have *sworn* that was Miss Jones talking. Why, you really ought to be on the stage. . . . How could you have been so *mean?*"

People at Wesleyan say that while the two older girls found it difficult sometimes to learn American customs and idiom, Mayling slipped very easily into the school environment—naturally, since she was so young. Sometimes in the early days her friends, going into her room, surprised her in Chinese dress, but she had always to run into the closet and change before she felt at ease. She was very pert: when one of the older girls said, "Why, Mayling, I believe your face is painted!" she retorted,

"Yes, China-painted!"

She had a quick temper and often quarreled hotly with her two little friends. Mrs Ainsworth once said, "Aren't you ashamed to storm about like this?"

"Mrs Ainsworth," said Mayling, "I rather enjoy it!"

☆   ☆   ☆

Eloise, Claribelle and May started a newspaper. May was literary editor, and the other two divided the jobs of art editor and reporter. It was probably the only paper of its kind in the world, for though there were five copies issued every day, no two of these copies were alike. The society column of one would say:

"Of all the girls on this campus, none is so pretty as Betty Brown. She was seen yesterday . . ." etc., etc.

Another would say, in the same column:

"Dorothy Dell is the cleverest girl in the whole school."

The first paper was sold to Betty Brown, the second to Dorothy Dell, and since each one cost five cents, and since the paper was ordinary school exercise paper, there was no overhead. The Tripuellates had twenty-five cents to spend every day, after their labors. The most trying part of the whole affair was in agreeing how to spend it—on ice cream altogether, or partly on salted peanuts, or on candy. "It must have been priceless," writes Madame Chiang, "because there was one character who appeared every day called 'Madame Telle Storie,' dealing with beauty aids and advice to the lovelorn, comments on campus gossip, and had what I fondly imagined a decided *Tatler* and *Spectator* slant."

A university student in the East heard about this paper and wrote to them, requesting a copy to put on record as the product of the youngest editor in America. He did not include the nickel, and they wrote him scornfully, pointing out this omission. "Especially," they said, "as it is costing us two cents to send this letter." He then sent the nickel, but if he kept his copy it is the only one in existence. The others, unfortunately, are lost.

[54]

Madame Chiang thinks that because of the special tutoring she received during this time, she made much greater progress than she would have done in an ordinary classroom. She learned amazingly quickly, and was to continue to learn quickly, all the way through the university. By the time she was ten she had read every word of Dickens, but she is not prepared to say how much of it she really understood.

Eling was graduated in 1909, at the early age of nineteen, with an enviable record of high "marks." She had attended summer school at various places, during one long vacation at Cornell. In New York at a party she had made the acquaintance of Kung Hsiang-hsi, then a postgraduate student at Yale; she did not remember him, but when they met again, years later, in Japan, he had not forgotten.

From the class prophecy for Eling on her graduation:

Look at that flaming headline on the front page! Greatest Reforms in China that the World Has Ever Heard Of. The wife of the leader is the real power behind the throne. As the result of her sagacity, China has made great strides. We can now understand why Eling felt so insulted once when a Wesleyan professor told her she had become a fine American citizen.

At the graduation exercises she read an original arrangement of *Madame·Butterfly,* wearing a costume of rose brocade of which Charlie had sent her forty yards. That blaze of pink glory was her last experience of America for many years.

She was to arrive in Shanghai just two years before the great Revolution. Eling, coming back to China after so many years abroad in a country where life was comparatively free for a girl, must have had many adjustments to make. In the first place, she had become so accustomed to foreign clothing that it was difficult to change back into the Chinese style. "I always wear foreign dress when I go shopping," she said apologetically to another girl. "It makes me feel less conspicuous." She had brought back with her a wardrobe from America, and her old friends looked enviously at her tailor-made costumes and ostrich-plumed hats. After a little time, however, she gave up her foreign-style dress and adopted the pretty Chinese costume.

Today each of the three sisters has a style of dress that is quite distinctively representative of her character. It is probably an unconscious phenomenon, but very revealing. Madame Kung always wears dresses the material of which is patterned in a small print; she favors blue of the navy or very slightly brighter shades, or black. She likes black lace for evening. Her feet, very small and of exquisite shape, with high instep, are usually in French-heeled slippers.

Madame Sun's dresses are of complete simplicity, and she seldom wears a patterned material, preferring plain colors. For ordinary clothes she uses the bright blue cotton material that is the uniform of the Chinese worker, but even when she is dressed for important ceremonials she maintains a severely plain style. This fashion has developed since her youthful days, for when she returned from America she wore foreign clothes, tailored costumes and picture hats.

It must be remembered that the Soong girls were not exceptional in the use of American dresses. All the women of China's treaty ports during the days immediately following the Revolution had adopted foreign dress, as a part of the general protest against the Manchu-ridden past. For a while the young people of China rapturously welcomed all the appurtenances of Western civilization, and these clothes were as important a manifestation of their spirit as were the factory machines that the new government was ordering in quantity from America. The reaction came, and it speaks well for the esthetic sense of Chinese women that they saw how much better their own dress suited them. Unlike the Japanese women, they evolved a costume of their own, using the old Manchu blouse lengthened to the ankle and slit up the sides for freedom; in a little time the silken trousers, now unnecessary, were discarded. Today it is only the very occasional woman who uses foreign dress; most of them fear, with reason, that any Oriental woman in such clothes will be mistaken for a Japanese, and they continue to use the lovely sheathlike robe, depending for variety upon the length of the skirt and of the sleeve, the buttons, the material and the braid that edges the robe. For some reason a Chinese girl who looks in her native dress like a bamboo or a willow, slender to the point of fragility, becomes a much heftier specimen as soon as she dons foreign clothing. Perhaps it is due to the fact that the Chinese female figure, though hips and bosom are small in comparison with the Occidental woman's, does not have a very pronounced waist. The line from armpit to knee is almost straight, whereas the line along the side of a foreign woman's body is deeply indented above the hips. There, where the waist of a Western-fashion dress is supposed to show slenderness, the Oriental woman is not slender, and the belt often reveals a thickness surprising to Western-trained eyes. Modern Chinese women never use hats, and there too they show their superior knowledge of beauty, remaining free from the tyranny of Parisian designers and their cruel sense of humor.

Madame Chiang, with her characteristic good sense and practicality, started a new style when she began to tour the country with her husband. In the mountain regions of Szechwan and Anhwei she puts aside her silken robes and wears slacks or outdoor pajamas and stout little walking shoes. When she is living in the city she likes dresses of striking pattern, large, colorful flower designs like those beloved of the ancient Chinese makers of brocade and satin; the patterns and the shades set off her vivid beauty and furnish a symbolic picture of modern China, blend of two civilizations, when she makes her public appearances. She used often to wear a fringe over her forehead and draw the rest of the hair back in a knot on her neck; this fashion is a favorite of the young girls in the country. Lately, however, she has worn her hair without the fringe, and Madame Sun uses the same simple style; it is that which most Chinese women have worn for centuries, ever since they abandoned the elaborate coiffure of the Ming Dynasty to which old-fashioned Japanese women are still slaves. Madame

Kung's glossy black hair is pushed off the forehead and worn somewhat high. Chinese women, when they eschew the dangers of the permanent wave, can keep their coiffures miraculously neat, each hair remaining in its place.

It was an effort for Eling to fall again into the habit of speaking Chinese, after six years of practicing English day and night. English had become so natural to her that she thought in that language, and when she spoke in a hurry or inadvertently it was usually English that she used. This habit, common to returned overseas students, disappeared in time.

Adapting herself to life in Shanghai was easier than she had feared. There was plenty of work for a public-spirited young woman in the early years of the century, and her days were more than full. She joined her mother in the charitable affairs of the church, she worked for the civic organizations, she taught English to the other girls of her circle. With the money earned in this way she helped two young friends, a girl and a boy, to begin and complete a university course. The girl is now one of the McTyeire branch principals, and the boy took a degree in law and is now practicing in Shanghai. It was a remarkable thing for a young woman of her age to have done, but Charlie Soong's belief in education had been transmitted to his daughter.

Eling even wrote a play for the benefit of the Famine Relief Fund and directed it herself. It was acted in the famous Chang's Garden: a pleasant little comedy of life in an American girls' school dormitory. The citizens of Shanghai watched in tickled amazement the behavior of these young things of the United States, who according to that clever Miss Soong were always carrying on feuds, freshmen versus upper-classmen, between their lessons. This young group earned a good sum of money for the flood sufferers with her play, which was so successful that a repeat performance was given by request.

"I wouldn't dare do it now," she said recently. "Only an optimistic young girl would have taken on such a task in those days."

CHAPTER VI

Charlie Soong,
Revolutionist

MADAME CHIANG recently wrote to someone (Mr George C. Bellingrath) in Demarest, Georgia, in reply to a request for reminiscences:

My sisters and I spent a summer vacation in Demarest, and when my eldest sister (Madame Kung) returned to China my second sister (Madame Sun) returned to Wesleyan, Macon, Georgia. I was too small then to go to college, being eleven years of age, and as I liked the village and found many playmates among the little girls there, my sister decided to leave me with Mrs Moss, the mother of one of my eldest sister's schoolmates.

I attended the eighth grade at Piedmont, and enjoyed my stay of nine months there very much. It interested me greatly to find that many of the students who attended the eighth grade there with me were in reality grown men and women. They had come from far in the hills, many having taught primary school for years to get the funds necessary to attend Piedmont. All these people were greatly interested in me, and, for my part, I began to get an insight into the lives of those who had to struggle for a living and for even the means to acquire an elementary education. I suppose my contact with these people as a girl influenced my interest in the lot of those who were not born with a silver spoon in their mouths, a contact which I may never have experienced otherwise. It made me see their sterling worth because, after all, they and their kind constitute the backbone of any nation.

I remember that Miss Olive van. Hise taught me physiology and physical culture. I was never so proud in my life as on the day when she announced my average grade in physiology was 98 per cent, and that I was the only pupil who, because of high marks in that course, was exempt from final examinations.

Another teacher was Miss Henrietta Additon, who is now connected with the New York police force, and from whom I received a letter recently. She taught me arithmetic. I must confess that when it came to percentages and discounts I did not acquit myself with any brilliance and only made C grade.

It was at Piedmont that I was initiated into the mysteries of parsing sentences. My knowledge of English then was at best somewhat sketchy as I had only been in America two years and I had many funny little tricks of phraseology which baffled my grammar teacher. To cure me of them she made me try to parse them. Her efforts must have been productive of some success for people now say that I write very good English. If so, I am inclined to think that these sessions of wrestling with rambling phrases and split infinitives may perhaps have had as much to do with any ability I acquired to overcome the intricacies of English grammar and rhetorics as any subsequent training I have had.

The village people used to look upon me as something of a curiosity, but curiosity or not, I thoroughly enjoyed the five-cent gum drops which I used to get at old Mr Hunt's general merchandise store equally as much as any of my playmates enjoyed them. I remember that three or four of us little girls used to consider it a great treat when one of us had a nickel to enable us to invite others to share cheese crackers or all-day suckers, which were displayed so enticingly in Mr Hunt's glass window. We knew little of the dangers of flies and microbes in those days, and cared less about them, even though speckled fly paper shared equal honors with the attractive merchandise displayed in the windows. However, I have lived to tell the tale.

[60]

CHARLIE SOONG, REVOLUTIONIST

Never in my life have I felt such a thrill of righteous charity as when Florence and Hattie Henderson, Flossie Additon and I decided a few days before Christmas that the true spirit of the season demanded the making of someone else happy. We each went the whole hog in our charitable intentions, produced twenty-five cents each, and with that sum of one dollar bought potatoes, milk, hamburg steak, apples and oranges for a destitute family across the railroad. We tried to be modest and keep to ourselves our noble deed, but so great was our excitement that Mr Hunt, at the store, heard us chattering and arguing about the advisability of certain articles of food. I remember—physiology being my favorite subject—that I insisted that we should buy sugar and plenty of it so that the carbohydrate values could keep the puny youngsters warm, and give the mother plenty of energy, whereas one of the other charitably-minded contributors to the great investment was strongly for potatoes as the most filling and warmth-producing foods. Mr Hunt was listening curiously and amusedly to the excited debate, and settled the matter by generously contributing some of each of the articles, but he also gave us and the great philanthropic enterprise away. When we were trudging across the trestle with the parcels in our arms we felt like blossoming Joan of Arcs proceeding upon a sacred mission. However, when we reached the ramshackle wooden shack that the intended recipients called home, and faced the discouraged worn-out mother, with her brood clinging to her hands and peeking out from behind her skirts, we were stricken dumb and none of us could speak a word. We dropped the bundles and fled. When we had run a sufficient distance to feel brave once more one of us dared to shout out "Merry Christmas," and we ran faster than ever.

One of our favorite pastimes was to go hazel nutting. I can see now the long, dusty roads that we used to tramp on Sunday afternoons to get to the woods. Sometimes we were lucky enough to have an obliging farmer driving our way in a wagon pick us up and share with us his lunch of corn bread, occasionally offering us a leg of a frier, but as we were little girls we were too shy to accept the chicken. I invariably came in for quite a bit of gentle teasing. Can't you hear these men of the mountains, trying to confuse the little Chinese girl with such an old chestnut as this: "Where do the nuts come from?" It is obvious that my brilliant answer would be: "From the trees, of course." "And what kind of a tree does a doughnut come from?"

[61]

would be the jubilant retort. That would floor me. "On a pantry," they would roar, and that would floor me. Dropping us at the edge of the wood the kind farmers would go on with the usual admonition: "You girls better start for home before dark." We then would scamper into the bushes to gather hazel nuts, or blackberries. We ate to our hearts' content and probably consumed more than we took home with us.

At Piedmont I used to do a great deal of reading. A favorite place was a wooden bench between two trees beside the house I lived in. It was at Mrs Moss' house. She was the head of the boys' dormitory. I lived with her in a suite downstairs—she, and her daughters, Rosina and Ruby. Rosina initiated me into the intricacies of quavers and semiquavers, chords, and the five-finger exercise. At that time I learned to play little ditties such as "The Little Mouse Runs Around the Field." Every little piece had a story attached to it, "The Little Shepherd Boy," or something. I remember a big, lumbering girl who said the ambition of her life was to be able to play hymns by Christmas time so that she could dazzle her beau. I then thought the object was praiseworthy, but I wondered if the beau was worth all that effort? Most of the boys in the dormitory were twenty years of age or more. Some were country teachers seeking education in the college. Mrs Moss used to invite some of them to dinner each Sunday night. I used to marvel at the plates of hot cakes and blackberry jam that those boys could make away with. The hot cakes disappeared like magic, as did the platters of fried ham, but Mrs Moss and Rosina could produce them with wonderful deftness. In apportioning the ingredients they seemed to know by instinct just how much baking powder and other things to put in, so fast they worked. When Mrs Moss wanted to be very nice to me she used to let me make biscuits. They never came out right. I did not appear to be blessed with the instincts of a cook at all.

In my memory, Piedmont is famous for one thing. It was there that I had the only earache in my life. It was on my twelfth birthday. It was so bad that Dr Lamb had to be called in, and he amused himself with my consternation as he made hot oil to drop into the aching orifice.

I left Piedmont for Fairmont, North Carolina, where my sister had decided to go for summer school. Mrs Moss took me as far as Atlanta, where I met my sister. I never went back to Piedmont, but I remember with pleasure the time I spent in its environment.

☆   ☆   ☆

One summer when the girls were at a northern summer school, the history tutor asked Mayling to describe Sherman's march through Georgia. Mayling said, "Pardon me, I am a Southerner, and that subject is very painful to me. May I omit it?"

A theme of Chingling's, written and published in 1911, indicates an interest in her country's problems—and in her own—unusual in an adolescent.

THE INFLUENCE OF FOREIGN EDUCATED STUDENTS ON CHINA

China, realizing the great need for modern educated men and women, is sending large numbers of boys and girls abroad every year to study in the Western institutions, and assimilate Western ideals, in fact, to acquire whatever is worthy and good for the progress of that ancient contemporary of Egypt, Babylonia, and Assyria. The influence of these students when they return extends to almost every sphere of the Chinese National life, especially in Politics, in Education, and in Social Reforms.

Chinese politics, for many hundred years, have been characterized by nepotism and dishonesty. The government positions have been generally filled by literary scholars, by favorites of the court, and by those who secured these desirable positions by means of "Political Simony." They were entirely ignorant of the science of government, without even a pretended ability for the administration of the country. The miserable conditions of the people, and the frequent riots and rebellions are some of the results of these disgraceful ways of selecting "competent officials." But now the conditions are changing and gradually growing better with the dismissal of these office-seekers, and the promotion of the broadly educated returned students to such offices as they can serve best. Graft or "squeezing" is not carried on in open daylight as it used to be. In fact, the ethical standard of the governors and magistrates is much improved through the exemplary conduct of these foreign educated officials. It is largely through their influence, and untiring efforts, that a National Assembly has been formed and an edict issued by the Regent that China will have a Parliament in 1917.

Education has always held a prominent place in the ideals of the Chinese, but for many centuries education has meant proficiency in the Chinese Classics. But after the Boxer troubles, thinking Chinese began to realize that there was a broader culture than their classics could offer them to be obtained from the more modern education of the West. The Government accordingly invited from abroad eminent professors to lecture in the universities and colleges. Interpreters were employed to translate the lectures into the vernacular, but frequently they proved incompetent, and misrepresented the lectures through ignorance of the subject, and the ridiculous results can be easily imagined. The students returning from Western colleges, competent to present Western ideals to the Chinese in their own tongue, have therefore been welcomed with open arms.

What these men have done for education in China is almost past belief. Realizing that a sound mind should have a sound body, they have introduced Western athletics and gymnastics into the colleges, and now athletics play an important part in the education of the Chinese youths. A new interest in debating has also sprung up, and in the debating societies the students have learned that "Liberty" and "Equality" are not secured by strikes, riots and political disturbances, but by more general education and enlightenment. By the wise counsel of these men, normal colleges are being established all over the northern and eastern provinces for the training of future teachers, with the American and European educated Chinese as professors.

As for their influence in social reforms, it has been and is great. They have been instrumental in establishing organizations in China for the opium-smokers, who wish to rid themselves forever of their habits. In cities, they have organized the Y.M.C. Associations which have become the social rendezvous of the people. The Chinese boys no longer consider deformed feet beautiful or desirable as they used to, and now refuse to marry girls with maimed feet; they even go so far as to break their childhood engagements, which is a serious thing for China. Who infused such notions into the minds of the boys and men? Not the Government, though it has done much, nor the missionaries alone, though they have played such a great part in this movement. But it was the impression and influence of the returned students. The discarding of the queues all over China is another social reform which is widely agitated by them.

Sociological reforms are undertaken by all the foreign educated students. They are trying their best to better the conditions of the slums in the cities. The moral condition of slums is everywhere alike, and China is unfortunate in having this part of the population always presented to Americans in missionary lectures and superficial talks of tourists, who seldom see the life of the better classes. Therefore these returned students are now putting all their energies toward lessening the existing evils and reforming the lower classes.

Thus we have seen how influential the foreign educated students are in China, and what reforms they have already accomplished. China offers a wide field of work, and unlimited opportunities to these returned students, who have proved that they are equal to the task set before them, and are competent to grapple with the great problems of China of today. [From *The Wesleyan,* student literary magazine, November 1911.]

In Shanghai, Charlie Soong was working harder and harder at his chosen task of keeping unbroken contact with Sun Yet-sen and his followers in China. Tension was growing. It was almost an open secret that a revolution was soon to take place, and in Chang's Garden excitement rose to white heat.

Chang Hsu-ho, that same Chang who had once teased Charlie at the McTyeire kindergarten term play, was owner of a large and lovely garden on the Bubbling Well Road. Today this district is a commercial center, and "Ch'ing An Sz" runs by between the Majestic Apartments and the glass fronts of Arts and Crafts, Dombey and Son, and the Chocolate Shop. Then, though, a wall kept Chang's Garden from the gaze of the non-elect, and those who drifted up to lounge about the gate were country folk, for the Garden was on the very outskirts of town. It was the first even almost-public park in Shanghai for Chinese, though it was maintained for their society people. There was an entrance fee of ten cents to keep out beggars and the poor. Every afternoon at four o'clock they began to arrive: men, women and children in their best clothes, driving or strolling along the paths around the lake and through mazes built of spongy rock. Ladies came from the great walled houses, enjoying their escape from the rigid conventions that were at last relaxing. Young men of fashion brought their "express carriages," light pony-carts, to show off their stubby little mongolian animals. Out on the roads beyond the Settlement's residential streets they were accustomed to race one another, treating their occasional arrests and fines by the Municipal Police as a great joke and making the neighborhood perilous for quieter vehicles. But in Chang's Garden the wildest young rake tempered his spirits and behaved himself. Rare flowers and trees imported from foreign countries, pavilions where tea was consumed, curious rocks scattered about to give a "natural" impression, a little pond and famous flower shows: chrysanthemums in the autumn, plum blossoms in spring, lotus in summer, orchids—Chinese Shanghai delighted so much in the Garden that many people lingered within its walls until midnight. On the slightest provocation there were fireworks from a special platform. Occasionally there were lantern slides or sing-songs.

Sometimes even at midnight the gates were not closed. That was when the revolutionists held meetings and explained to increasing audiences the aims and ideas of Sun Yat-sen. As his character gained in reputation, so the crowds of Shanghai swelled, listening to his lieutenants expound his arguments and ideals. By the time Eling returned from Georgia to help her father in the endless work of organizing, collecting funds and tabulating the rapidly increasing roster and resources of the Society, these meetings were an open secret.

It must be remembered that Shanghai is a long way from Peking, and that the Chinese residents of this city were in a peculiarly safe position to contemplate revolution. There were among these merchants and workers few adherents to the Manchu circle. Traders whose livelihood was threatened by the restrictions of the Government, taxpayers from the interior, coolies and petty clerks, and above all the students of China, the eager beginners fresh from their schools and full of confidence and hope—they all listened to Sun Wen's doctrines and fell under the spell of the little Doctor's ideal. Already they had had a taste of reform when Kang Yu-wei had for a short time influenced the Emperor Kuang Hsu. Though the old Empress Dowager checkmated the immediate effect of the Hundred Days, she could not wipe out all memory of that swift and tragic adventure. Sun's men brought more radical hopes to the ears of the Shanghai Chinese, and as they listened they saw how it might be possible to make of their corrupt old country a new nation modeled on the admired United States of America, a government built upon the idea of justice. Most important of all, the poor people heard the Doctor's promise of the equal distribution of land, and perhaps for the first time learned of a past period when the Manchus had not ruled China. A wave of new hatred for the Manchus swept them. For decades Chinese and Manchus together had forgotten that ancient race discrimination and had been merging. Now the old shame was recalled; the old resentment flared up in the hearts of a new generation; people demanded of themselves why this race should monopolize all the positions of influence. Everything wrong in China was blamed on the Manchus. It had happened before; it has happened since; but those who went to Chang's Garden at midnight came home in the early morning with what they thought was a new vision.

For a long time Mrs Soong had remained in peaceful ignorance of her husband's real work, considering Dr Sun merely his very good friend. She had not joined in the hour-long discussions and political conferences that so absorbed these men—night after night. Perhaps she sometimes cast a worried glance at the clock when she felt that they were chatting too late, and that her husband might be overworking himself, but the subject matter of those long talks was outside her sphere of influence and she did not meddle in the world of men. It had nothing to do, she knew, with the family or the church or Good Works, so she did not pursue the matter. Incredible as it may seem, Mrs Charles Soong was taken completely by surprise when it flashed upon the Chinese public—though many people had been expecting the catastrophe—that Dr Sun was considered by the Throne a dangerous revolutionary and a menace to society. There was a price on his head, on the head of that good Sun who was so gentle with the children and such a pleasant house guest.

Further shocks were in store for her. It was not enough that she should have been ignorant of the Doctor's activities, she who was his hostess, while the whole city of Shanghai evidently knew more than she did. The danger came even nearer home. Charles himself, her husband, was threatened. He had not been named in the first list of "traitors," but he watched the reports alertly, and bade her be ready for any emergency. . . . Where an American woman would have stormed and accused her husband of jeopardizing his family, she absorbed the shock in intelligent silence and made plans to follow him if he should be forced out of the country. He, Soong Yao-ju, model citizen, pillar of the church, excellent husband and the best of providers, was actually in danger of being exiled or even—a thought almost incredibly horrible—executed, and for treason!

Fortunately for the Soongs' family life, the Empress had missed his name during the first crisis of 1898. Sun fled to Japan, and Mrs Soong got over the shock and even began to support her husband's cause. In the next years they had been always under the shadow of danger; Mayling and the two younger boys, Tseliang and Tsean, were born into a house where the trunks, figuratively speaking, were never closed and put away. Now these years were perhaps drawing to a close. Soon they would know if the many false starts and alarms, the toil, the endless routine, would mean everything or nothing. There had been such hopes and frights before, many times. . . .

CHAPTER VII
China in 1910

ELING had stepped out of the lazy, pleasant, warm life of a southern United States college into the tense, medieval atmosphere of pre-revolution. To return at all was a terrific change; to come into Shanghai in 1910 was a greater one.

It is always a tragedy for the overseas Chinese student that he must make not one, but two difficult adjustments. Hardly has he adapted himself to an entirely new life far away from his home and family than the years have passed by, swiftly as they always do for the young, and he must go back to a land grown strange and unsympathetic.

Eling had left Shanghai a child in ill-fitting clothes and her hair in a braid; she returned six years later a fashionable young woman. Perhaps she had a chip on her shoulder: there is no doubt that the good people of Shanghai carried chips on theirs. For six years she had been imbibing the ideas of America, and like her father she felt that she must now take up the burden of changing Chinese civilization in order to bring it as near as possible to her heart's desire, which was modeled on the United States of America. She was shocked, too, by the attitude of the foreigners. Just as Charlie had been, she was now subjected to a first sight of their arrogance abroad.

Then too, as a woman she was up against a bigger problem than her father's. Unfortunately for her, most Chinese resent to an extreme degree any attempt to make them depart from their norm. They had no desire to be changed by these young snips. Instinctively they were resenting more and more the returned students with their unspoken criticism and unhappy disappointment in the land of their birth. Eling was face to face with the enormous inertia of the most conservative nation in the world.

Her foreign-style dress, her manner of speaking English, which she used instinctively in the early days following her return, her very record of scholarship made matters difficult: people simply could not understand any girl of their circle becoming so changed. The period did not last long. Eling fought a gallant battle and won it, not only for herself but in behalf of her brothers and sisters who were to follow her home across the Pacific. Ultimately she won over the old neighbors and friends who had been so suspicious of her; to get along with her mother was more difficult, but she managed. The Old Guard, who had decried the new education on the grounds that it makes a girl forward and unwomanly, now retracted their words. They had not even the satisfaction of complaining that Eling had lost the tongue of her forefathers: her Shanghai dialect was clear and fluent.

Some harm had been done, however. Only a small amount of ill-humored gossip came to her ears, but it was enough. Though she was a self-possessed young woman and had developed a magnificent poise, this manner of hers hid a painful shyness, and critcism wounded her deeply, even then. Those who are chosen by fate to act on the stage of public life should be provided with thick skins or with preoccupations that help them to ignore the millions of eyes that are always following every move. Her sisters

[70]

were not to suffer quite so much. Chingling was to be supported by a burning faith and a fulfilled hero-worship as recompense; Mayling was born with a vigorous confidence in humanity, which carried her through. Eling, with her keen intelligence and her unfailing ability to read character, early in her career fell victim to a sort of stage fright that was to accompany her for many years.

History is a progressive simplification and selection. We know that Charlemagne existed, but the color of his eyes, his taste in food and music, his manner toward servants must remain like the song the Sirens sang: matters of conjecture. Abraham Lincoln, unlike Charlemagne, lived yesterday, so these engaging details have not yet been polished away from his figure. We can build up a dozen pictures of him, from a dozen angles, and the ingredients for these portraits all come from the same source—his companions. If it were not for a man's contemporaries we would be forced in our search for his likeness to believe implicitly in his own records, a dangerous proceeding because modesty warps the memory, and mirrors are not so good as human eyes.

Yet History insidiously works her will upon Abraham Lincoln even today. Even today we believe one of his biographers rather than another because he has a more entertaining style, or because he selects his anecdotes with an eye for effect rather than truth. We are still too close to Lincoln to run any grave danger of misrepresentation; his generation is still enough with us to defend his likeness. But who knows what will happen to his name within the next century?

While the Soongs live and themselves mold their statues before the eyes of History it should be a simple matter, one would think, to know what they are really like. Facts exist: the world witnesses their actions, and can compile the records accordingly. But the trouble begins there, since the world is not an accurate witness. In one lifetime the opinion of the public may run the gamut from indifference to black hatred or wild enthusiasm. A man may be without honor abroad and yet a god in his own country, as Hitler's biographers demonstrate. Generalissimo Chiang, considered by the friendly Powers of the West and by his own people the strongest Chinese of the age, is portrayed to the Japanese public as a grasping, stubborn opportunist who plunged his people into a hopeless and senseless war rather than lose his job. Until recently Wang Ching-wei was an honored statesman, and the public was indignant at an attempted assassination of him. Now there is a price on his head. The philosopher knows when he looks down upon a cheering mob how easily those cheers can be turned into bloodthirsty howls.

Regard the Soongs. Today they are recognized as the remarkable family they have shown themselves, even by those of their critics who do not approve of their activities. Madame Chiang is acclaimed wherever she appears, like a cinema star rather than a political figure; Madame Kung is known as a woman of foresight; Madame Sun occupies a unique position, revered even by conservatives for her adherence to her principles and her loyalty to her husband's ideals. China has learned to feel proud of these women. Whereas in the old days the Chinese would have admired the Soong sisters, considering them as interesting manifestations of Nature, they would not have felt any kinship for these women if they were not able to claim blood relationship. The ultimate effect of their careers would have been invisible to the shrewd, kindly eyes of the old-style Chinese subject. Yet it is in large part due to their own efforts that the Chinese today are capable of appreciating the virtues of their compatriots as something of national value, something to be proud of as well as to admire abstractly.

Twenty-five or thirty years ago the Soongs, as young returned students, occupied a different position in the public mind. What did people think of them in those days? Oddly enough this opinion depended in large part upon the fact that they were Christian.

It has already been pointed out that the Chinese are usually tolerant of any kind of religious worship. The Yangtze riots and the Boxer uprising were due to political questions rather than to any hatred for Christianity itself. The mobs who looted mission houses and burned churches were worked up to their frenzy by their leaders' allegations against the foreign teachers of political wire-pulling, and by converts' occasional abuse of privileges obtained through missionary influence. Some of these accusations, it must not be forgotten, were justified, though the revenge they took was not: the more ridiculous charges were made by better brains than those of the mob. There was method in their carefully nurtured madness.

As to the unconverted upper classes of the Shanghai Chinese, many of them were prejudiced against Christians for a special reason. At the time few people among them took religious questions very seriously. For generations under Manchu rule the Chinese had lost hope and integrity, and those who should have been devoting their talents to official work had gone to seed, mentally and morally. It was customary, even fashionable, to quote Confucius' "Virtues," but scarcely anyone tried to live up to the Sage's ideal. They sought influence, money or power, reverting to a completely egotistic philosophy. Among themselves they respected only the wealthy and powerful.

In the beginning, Charles Soong's family was neither. Their only notable quality was that they were Christian, and the fact that Charlie was beginning to make a success in his work was his one recommendation to his associates. Mrs Soong's piety was almost a mystery to the non-Christian women of her acquaintance, who used to say that converts to Christianity had taken this step merely in order to eat at the missionaries' table. A cynical expression was quoted regarding converts: "He eats religion." Mrs Soong's clan had already attracted adverse criticism when the Widow Hsu, of another branch of the family, a Roman Catholic, bequeathed a large tract of land at Siccawei to the Jesuits. It was said that she had cheated her descendants, which according to common belief was as bad a crime as that of neglecting her ancestors.

"Not only do those Hsus forget their ancestors, but their children too!" gasped Shanghai. "And such a good property, too!" The missionaries were widely known as wicked, dangerous, grasping people who attempted to do away with ancestor-reverence, the only cult still taken seriously by the Chinese. It was not easy to shock those good folk, but the Christians succeeded in doing it.

"These converted people," said the terrible old ladies who governed their families with iron hands, "simply have no ancestors, that's the truth of the matter. They have sacrificed their fathers; they look upon foreigners as their ancestors. They have deliberately transformed themselves into bastards!"

So when Mrs Soong and other ladies of the church went calling on their grim old relations and in-laws, they were treated with the exquisite politeness that is only possible when it is intended to chill the heart. As was natural, the moral outcasts began to depend more and more upon one another, less and less upon the old-fashioned conservative element of the town. They formed a tight little circle of the elect, and their old-lady critics promptly said:

"Now they have ruined their children's prospects, just as I prophesied. No man of good family will ever marry those poor girls. No wonder they're sent abroad to school! It's their only chance to get off with some innocent."

The point of view of the Christians was as a matter of fact ludicrously similar. They looked down on the Old Guard as criminally selfish people who cared only for the good of the family group, and who ruined their children's chances in life by spoiling them. . . . "Beasts of burden," said the iconoclasts, "for their sons and grandsons."

Many a growing child had the opportunity to hear such argument, for and against, about it and about, whenever some straying sheep wandered into the fold of the church and elected to stay there. Not all of the families were as unanimous in their beliefs as were the Soongs. Many quarreled and split up on the rock of Christianity. Eling, therefore, was fortunate in that she was supported and encouraged by the most important group of all, her own people. Her mother understood her difficulties, surprisingly well considering that she herself had never been abroad. She was one of the leading spirits of her group, and these people had realized that they must begin to look toward the West. The progressives of Shanghai who admired Charles Soong now watched his children and wondered if they, too, might not make the modern gesture of educating their daughters. After all, if you ignored the croakings of the older people and took a fair view, it hadn't seemed to hurt Eling a bit. . . .

Only Charles himself protested.

"Don't send your children abroad," he said to a friend, in whimsically rueful tones. "Nothing's good enough for them when they come back. They want to turn everything upside down. . . . 'Father, why can't we have a bigger house? Father, why don't we have a modern bathroom?' Take my advice; keep your children at home!"

CHAPTER VIII

The Revolution

A FLUKE brought on the Revolution too early. Sun Yat-sen counted this effort as the eleventh attempt, and as the successful one—for two years. Actually it was not the Revolution of his first plans; it did not overthrow such tyrants as those he had inveighed against, years before. The old Empress Tzu Hsi was dead, having expired the day after her unlucky nephew Kuang Hsu departed this earth—helped on his journey, it was said, by his grim old aunt, an intrigante to her last breath. The new Emperor was a child.

Since 1900 the Ch'ing, realizing the inevitability of change, had been trying to reorganize their government to meet those demands, at least, which they could not ignore. Yuan Shih-kai, an experienced statesman, headed this last-minute reform; the Army organization was changed and the civil service examinations abandoned, just as Kuang Hsu had tried to do during the Hundred Days. The Ch'ing government also drafted a new code of laws that were never carried out, and even planned to introduce representation by popular vote in the Palace. Given time and a little common sense these compromises might have saved the Ch'ing; as it was, they were overthrown. It was too late.

Most of the preparation for the eleventh revolt was made in Szechwan, that distant wild province that had been misgoverned for so long. A local rebellion broke out there in September, 1911, but it was the Hankow incident that brought matters to a head. In readiness for the Revolution and against the return of Sun Yat-sen, bombs had been stored in various places in Hankow; one of these in a house in the Russian Concession went off by accident, on October ninth. Foreseeing embarrassing complications, the conspirators decided on the bold course and allowed everything to blow up prematurely. The Revolution began, officially as it were, the next day.

The district troops, already prepared, threw in with them; in a short time Wuhan (Wuchang and Hankow) fell to the rebels, and the revolt spread quickly over tinder that had long awaited the burning. Peking sent government troops, hoping to crush this manifestation as they had the preceding ones, but the fire had spread beyond their sphere of power. The Imperial forces did indeed recapture Wuhan, but on the eve of this triumph came news of the Revolutionists' occupation of Nanking.

In Shanghai, Chen Chi-mei was one of the leading spirits among the rebels, and Chiang Kai-shek returned from school in Tokyo to report to him for service. Chiang had made Sun's acquaintance in Japan at the meeting of Chinese students there; as soon as he heard of the Revolution he had slipped out of Tokyo and come back to China. Chen detailed him as Chief of Staff to take care of matters at Hangchow, and himself started operations in Chapei, a district of the native city of Shanghai, on November third. They captured the arsenal and then the Woosung forts, and on the fourth Shanghai was declared in the hands of the reformers.

In the International settlements, the foreigners were frightened or blasé, according to their natures and their individual experience. It was just another war to the old hands. There was some frantic talk of helping the existing Government, on general principles, with man power, but everything went quickly and from their point of view harmlessly: they accepted the *fait accompli*. A couple of shells did fall into the Settlement, but no important national was harmed.

One American confesses to a moment of realization only when he saw the changing of the flags on the Custom House. When the Dragon Flag came down and the Five-Barred Flag went up, "This," he said to himself, "is probably important." That was all.

Among the Chinese there was more excitement. The men who had worked for so long under cover now came into the open at last and proudly hung out their flags. Flags were everywhere, fluttering from windows and over the fronts of shops.

Meantime Sun Yat-sen, father of the Revolution, was not to be found. He was in America, and happened at that time to be traveling through Colorado, working as usual to collect funds for his cause. On his way to breakfast in a Denver restaurant he first saw the news in a headline:

WUCHANG OCCUPIED BY REVOLUTIONISTS

Alone, thousands of miles from the scene of his success, he made a characteristic decision: his friends still needed money, no doubt, and he could do best by continuing to canvass for money. Sun continued toward New York. In St Louis he read in the newspapers that he was to be first President of the Republic. He decided to go to England and work for recognition of the new state; he was fairly sure of the friendly attitude of Japan and America, but England was not such a simple proposition.

He did not disclose his identity until he reached London. There he received a telegram addressed to "Sun Wen, London," formally asking him to accept the Presidency, and it had been delivered at the Chinese Legation! A foreign friend to whose house the telegram was taken had prudently copied it out and then sent it back, saying that Sun was not with them. Thus it was from a copy, stolen out of the official correspondence of the Ch'ing Legation, that Sun learned of his country's invitation.

[*78*]

THE REVOLUTION

The Four-Power Consortium group had already paid over one sum to the Imperial Court for railway construction in the East; Sun arrived in London in time to stop a second loan. His actual request was that this amount be paid to the new Republic, and the Consortium did not refuse outright, but said that a recognized government would receive consideration. Sun was satisfied with this. He sailed from Marseilles for China, at last. In Hongkong he landed freely and under his own name for the first time in sixteen years of hiding and wandering. He arrived in Shanghai on Christmas Eve.

Meantime, as might be expected, there had been a lot of discussion and arrangement between the Imperialists, under the direction of Yuan Shih-kai, and the Revolutionists. Yuan, frantically summoned by the Peking Court to assist them, had taken his time about replying, which is one reason that the war had dragged on as long as it did. He was now working as liaison officer between the opposed factions, trying to persuade the Court to come to terms. The Peace Conference opened in Shanghai six days before Sun's return.

In Nanking on January first, 1912, Sun Yat-sen was inaugurated the first President of the Provisional Government of the Republic. The Soong family, all of those who were in China, attended the ceremony; Charlie had been in a pleasant state of excitement and happiness ever since the return of his friend. He and his daughter Eling were in Nanking most of the time at this period.

In Georgia, the news of the successful Revolution inspired Chingling to write a paper about it. The article was published in the school paper in 1912. Mayling was not quite so stirred; she was still so young that the school limits were the boundaries of her universe, but Chingling's paper is interesting.

THE GREATEST EVENT OF THE TWENTIETH CENTURY

One of the greatest events of the twentieth century, the greatest event since Waterloo, in the opinion of many well-known educators

[79]

and politicians, is the Chinese Revolution. It is a most glorious achievement. It means the emancipation of four hundred million souls from the thralldom of an absolute monarchy, which has been in existence for over four thousand years, and under whose rule "life, liberty, and the pursuit of happiness" have been denied. It also signifies the downfall of a dynasty whose cruel extortions and selfishness have reduced the once prosperous nation to a poverty-stricken country. The overthrowing of the Manchu government means the destruction and expulsion of a court where the most barbaric customs and degrading morals were in existence.

Five months ago our wildest dream could not have been for a republic. To some, even the promise of an early constitutional government was received with skepticism. But deep down in the heart of every patriotic Chinese, were he a politician or a laborer, there was the anti-Manchu spirit. All the sufferings, such as famine, flood, and retrogression in every phase of life was traced to the tyrannical Manchus, and their court of dishonest officials. Oppression was the cause of this wonderful revolution which came as a blessing in disguise.

Already we are witnessing reforms that would never have been accomplished under a despot. We read in the papers of the queueless movement in China, and how thousands and thousands have sacrificed their appendages—the Chinese national disgrace. To appreciate this fact, which seems so commonplace to the matter-of-fact foreigner, we must remember that the queue is a trait or a characteristic of centuries, and that the Chinese are the most conservative people in the world. They love to adhere to old customs, and up to six months ago the queue, which was their most striking mark of distinction from the rest of the civilized world, was carefully cherished. Ten years ago, the number of queueless heads could be counted on the fingers. No one who expected to hold governmental offices dared to cut off his queue. Such an act was regarded as being anti-Manchu, therefore it was revolutionary. But now the anti-Manchu spirit is the order of the day and in China the number of heads with queues can be counted on the fingers. There are innumerable other reforms that are now taking place in China; among them are the social, educational and industrial reforms. Since order is restored, the Currency Problem and the Taxation Question will be the next problems to be solved. We are firm in our belief, with the knowledge of the glorious success of other important reforms, that the Chinese are capable and efficient to deal with these intelligently, to the prosperity and integrity of that ancient empire.

The Revolution has established in China Liberty and Equality, those two inalienable rights of the individual which have caused the loss of so many noble and heroic lives, but there is still Fraternity to be acquired. Dean Crawshaw of Colgate University said in one of his lectures that Fraternity is the yet unrealized ideal of humanity, and that Liberty has no safe foundation except human brotherhood, and that real Equality can never be anything but a dream until men feel towards each other as brothers. In fact, he said Fraternity is the basis of both Liberty and Equality, therefore it should be the purpose of the 20th century to foster that ideal.

And it may be for China, the oldest of nations, to point the way to this Fraternity. In other ways, too, China will take her place in the effort to uplift humanity. Napoleon Bonaparte said, "When China moves, she will move the world." The realization of that statement does not seem to be far off. A race amounting to one-quarter of the world's population, and inhabiting the largest empire of the globe, whose civilization displays so many manifestations of excellence, cannot help but be influential in the uplifting of mankind. China was the first possessor of a criminal code; her philosophers gave to the world some of the noblest contributions to human thinking; while her extensive literature which has delighted and won the admiration of those learned Europeans who spent their lifetime in the exclusive study of China and her exquisite code of Social and Moral Ethics are hardly paralleled elsewhere. For centuries the Chinese have been a peace-loving people. To them the pen is mightier than the sword. They have esteemed the arts of peace, and neglected the arts of war, worshipped the scholar and slighted the soldier. Sir Robert Hart said: "They believe in right so firmly that they scorn to think it requires to be supported or enforced by might. These qualities are not to be found simply in isolated cases, but are characteristic of the race as a whole." Mr Conger, the United States ex-minister to China, has said that "If civilization means, as it should, the highest sensibility of the conscience of man, there is in China the highest civilization to be found in the world." China, with its multitudinous population, and its love of peace —love in the real essence of the word—shall stand forth as the incarnation of Peace. It cannot but be instrumental in bringing about that humanitarian movement—Universal Peace—when Rights need not be backed by armies and "dreadnaughts," and all political disagreements will be, at last, settled by the Hague Tribunal. [From *The Wesleyan*, April 1912.]

When Charlie sent Chingling the new Five-Barred Flag, she climbed up and pulled down the Dragon Banner from the wall and stamped on it, crying, "Down with the dragon! Up with the flag of the Republic!"

Sun formed his Cabinet and began to organize his duties. Years of canvassing had given him a talent for such matters that was to be useful to him now; the new Republic was totally without any working capital, and it was impossible as yet to borrow from foreign governments because of that awkward word "Provisional." Nobody in those sedate days was willing to lend to a temporary organization. The President therefore borrowed a considerable sum from the Japanese, using for security the iron works at Hankow.

It became evident to him very soon that he was not the person for the job of the Presidency. He had never had the slightest experience in administration, and to a man of his detached attitude it seemed, no doubt, that the most direct and sensible thing to do would be to resign in favor of somebody with better qualifications. His work had all been collecting, enlisting and teaching.

Besides, there was much dissatisfaction among the lesser fry because of sectional jealousy. Sun was a Cantonese, and they accused him of putting too many Cantonese into important positions. They forgave him his Christianity, and they forebore to complain that most of his leading supporters were also Christians, but they could not, anywhere but in Kwangtung, forgive him for being Cantonese.

Then too Yuan Shih-kai was obviously anxious for the job himself, and he was the only person who could manage the abdication of the Manchus. Sun was eager to push the matter through, and he thought Yuan would be a good leader if he were watched. Yuan had promised to persuade the Ch'ing to recognize their fate and bow to it, but he allowed it to be understood that he would be more successful if he himself could be the heir to their power. Therefore the President telegraphed Yuan and invited him to be President—on condition the Emperor abdicated. It took almost another month, but Yuan persuaded the Ch'ing at last, and on February twelfth the Empress Dowager, in the name of the young Emperor, issued an edict by which the Ch'ing gave up the throne, to all appearances graciously presenting their sorrowing country with a ready-made republic. She ordered Yuan Shih-kai to organize this new government on certain conditions; namely, that the Republicans permit the Emperor to retain his title until death, that they give him an annuity, that they complete Kuang Hsu's tomb, and that they allow the abdicating monarch the right to his palace. The five races—Chinese, Manchus, Mohammedans, Mongols and Tibetans—were promised absolute equality.

Sun Yat-sen objected to the form of the edict, arguing that the Ch'ing were in no position to speak of "conferring" any government, even a republican one, upon China, but Yuan reassured him as to the wording of the pronouncement, and an agreement was reached. Yuan was elected President and Li Yuan-hung, a hero of the Revolution, was Vice-President.

It might at first thought seem strange that the Chinese were willing to take as their President a man who had until a few days previous worked for the archenemies of the republic, the Ch'ing. It was not really unreasonable. Until the Revolution was successful there was no chance for any official to be trained in the work of administration unless he was connected with the Imperial Court; there were no other men fit for the task. There was only one practical way out, and that way was followed by the essentially practical Chinese; they assumed tactfully that all these officials had been unwilling slaves of the Ch'ing until they were set free by the Revolution. From this point of view, Yuan was quite eligible for the Presidency, and the most able man they could find. Above all, he had given them the Ch'ing abdication. He was, indeed, the most popular man in China, next to Sun himself.

It looked now as if all the chief troubles were swept away. There was great rejoicing in the homes of the idealists who had toiled and worked and risked their lives for this end. A new energy filled the tired middle-aged men who had been dissatisfied with the old regime, and for every reactionary who trembled with rage and fear of the dangers ahead there were plenty of students who were blissfully confident of their ability to construct Utopia.

☆   ☆   ☆

It is the fashion nowadays in China to paint Yuan Shih-kai as a deep-dyed villain who planned from the first to undermine all Sun Yat-sen's work. Probably this is not true. Yuan had gained his training, that training which made him a passable President where Sun felt sure he himself would fail, in an exacting school; he had learned his ideals in the same school. One fault of old China, which is the same fault that we find in our democracies today, is that the man who goes in for politics and who makes a success at the game is usually the man who works first and foremost for himself. He has no conception of any other service. Yuan had the mentality of a Dictator. He wanted to manage the country because he was sure he knew what was best for the country. *He* was best for the country, to begin with. He proceeded on that assumption.

The new party of the revolutionists, the Kuomintang (People's Party) wanted to maintain the government capital at Nanking. Yuan preferred Peking. He was used to Peking; he was a Northerner; his friends were all there. He made good excuses for postponing the move South. Moreover, he knew that the Kuomintang stood in his way.

This obvious fact did not impress itself upon Sun's consciousness. He was still confident that all could and would go well. He visited Yuan in Peking and was charmed by the statesman's easy manners; he came away vowing that in all important matters they were of one mind.

The first friction between north and south was felt over the question of financing the Republic. Sun's action in borrowing from Japan had tided them over for a while, but money was needed again, and Yuan saw that he must get it from the Powers. He applied to the Consortium for that loan which Sun had stopped when he was in London; the bankers, realizing that they had China by the short hairs, proposed exorbitant terms. Immediately the Kuomintang began to grumble threateningly. While Yuan waited and haggled, syndicates secretly lent him money on various Chinese securities, against the whole original intention of the Consortium; the revolutionists grew more suspicious. One of the Consortium's suggestions was that they supervise the salt taxes in much the same way that the Customs were being managed: the Kuomintang members pointed out that such a bargain was a typical Manchu deal, and that at this rate China would have no resources left.

Yuan Shih-kai persisted, for he could not imagine any other way to get the money (nor, probably, could the Kuomintang). He had appointed Sun Yat-sen Director of Railway Development, thinking that this honor and the large salary attached would keep the doctor out of mischief. Sun, however, took his work very seriously and kept at it; as Director he went to Japan and there began to negotiate another loan, without asking the President's opinion of such an undertaking. Yuan did not trust anybody so much as Sun did, and especially he did not trust Japan. He preferred to risk the Consortium. Relations became strained.

By the end of the year the Consortium had offered nine million taels, and Yuan was willing to accept the terms attached to the offer. The Kuomintang's resentment flared out when President Wilson announced the withdrawal of the United States from the bargain, basing his action on the belief that the terms agreed upon would touch nearly on the independence of China. Yuan insisted that the loan was already authorized. Sun Yat-sen cabled the Powers, requesting them not to carry on. The agreement was put through but the break between Yuan and Sun was complete.

To a man of Yuan's mentality the actions of these Republican people, whom he considered hopelessly impractical, must have been maddening. In his own opinion he was doing the best he could and the only thing he could. His natural Dictator's impulse was to put his house in order, as directly as possible, and the higher-handed the method the better.

If Sun and the Kuomintang seem in retrospect to be something of what Yuan accused them, if they were hypercritical and offered no alternative to the actions they decried, let us remember the terrific problems that they faced. China in overthrowing the Emperor had leaped a gap of centuries. Her Republic was not the natural outgrowth of years of development. Most democracies, though they result from revolution, are still the children of the monarchies they displace; monarchies that are part of yesterday, not of many years ago. The men upon whom the Chinese government now depended had to learn overnight the lessons of generations. The wonder is that Sun Yet-sen himself did not fall victim to temptation, that he did not try to take complete control just to hurry things along, as Yuan Shih-kai did. It was his exceptional attitude that saved Sun Yat-sen from China, and China from Sun Yat-sen.

CHAPTER IX
Eling's Marriage

"I SHALL soon be on my way home," wrote Chingling, after her graduation in the spring of 1913, to one of her teachers. "I am taking a box of California fruit to Dr Sun from his admirers here, and I am also the proud bearer of a private letter to him."

On her arrival in Shanghai she found her family absorbed in the troubled politics of the day; Eling was acting as Dr Sun's secretary and also helping her father, who as treasurer of the Railway Commission was still consulting with Sun, still making plans, still hoping for further reform, in spite of the glorious First Revolution that was to have settled everything and left China to live happy ever after. The Soongs were living in the French Concession in an Avenue Joffre house, though they traveled back and forth between Shanghai and Nanking most of the time. Sun in Shanghai made his home with them.

Chingling's meeting with the Leader, the first since she was a small girl and he an obscure revolutionary, must have meant far more to her than to him. She had long been hearing of him as a national hero and her father's best friend. Her ardent enthusiasm for China and the great struggle the country had undergone was quickly transmuted to a personal hero worship; after all she was barely twenty and of a strongly idealistic nature. Sun had married at a very early age, according to Chinese custom, and his children had grown up in the care of his wife while he lived and traveled abroad. Like many another leader of men, he had sacrificed the best part of his home life to his public duty. Now, though he and his wife were reunited, he may have felt that they had grown apart. The appearance of this lovely young girl, however, could not have seemed particularly significant to him at first. His wife was very friendly with the Soongs and had even traveled with Mrs Soong and Eling to a hot-springs resort in Japan.

For a little time Chingling's life was the normal one of a girl just returned home from college. She wrote to a former school-mate,

Our life here is exactly like yours. We live and dress à la European, even to the decoration of the rooms, so you can sometimes picture me not as a friend of far-away China, soaked in oriental atmosphere, but as one of your American friends in the busy city. For Shanghai is really very modern, more so than Atlanta in many ways. Our house is nice and big, and has all the modern conveniences. There are plenty of bedrooms and tubs and lavatories, so you must come for a visit some time.

And again, "What of the old maids in our class? What are they doing—'waiting' or 'baiting'?"

She accompanied Sun's party on one of his Northern trips, before the break with Yuan became inevitable. The outward forms of respect toward the father of the Revolution were still observed, even in far-off Peking; as Director of Railways he traveled where he would, and Chingling saw him as a conquering hero. Perhaps if he had remained in that position, a strong man without need of reassurance or comfort, the romance would never have developed further; Chingling would have transferred her respectful adoration to some other hero in the course of time. In China, however, people in the public eye do not usually rest in peace. Sun's triumph was soon to be eclipsed for a period.

The Reorganization Loan from the Consortium went through, and in June the trouble started when Yuan dismissed three Provincial Governors, who had protested his actions, from office. He had first taken the precaution of strengthening his army and of placing troops where he thought they would do most good. In July the Southern provinces all declared independence of the Northern President, and the second revolution began. Shanghai was in the power of Yuan's troops: the movement was quickly crushed. Sun went to Japan; so did the Soongs; so did Chiang Kai-shek.

Charlie Soong took with him all of the family that had returned to China, with his household staff and everything he owned. It looked as if the second period of reorganization would be a more arduous affair than the first one, and he was safest in assuming that he would be a refugee for a long, long time. They traveled under a false name, and lived first in Kobe, later removing to Tokyo and Yokohama, where they rented a house on the Bluff and settled down for almost two years.

In China, Yuan declared the Kuomintang a seditious organization and ordered it to be dissolved; then appointed a Political Council to advise himself and organized a Constitutional Council, supposedly made up of freely elected representatives. He also began to think of the advantages of monarchy over republicanism; a few people shared his views. From Japan, the exiled revolutionists watched the destruction, as it seemed then to be, of all their work, and began with patient industry to build it up again.

In Tokyo one day Charlie Soong was introduced to Kung Hsiang-hsi. Kung had returned to the East from Oberlin and was at this time working with the Chinese Y.M.C.A. in Japan; when he met Soong he told him of having made Eling's acquaintance at a party in New York, and Charlie promptly invited him home to dinner. When Eling consented to give up her work as Sun's secretary in order to marry Kung, she thought that she was entering upon a completely domestic career. There was nothing about Hsiang-hsi in those days to indicate what a position he was later to hold in the government. He was absorbed in his Y.M.C.A. work.

The "Y" was having a difficult time in Japan, where the Chinese students were reflecting in miniature the turmoil in China. Dr C. T. Wang was secretary of the organization, and because of some political upset he was attacked by certain of the students, and had to leave. John R. Mott, head of the "Y," asked Kung Hsiang-hsi to take on the job, which needed a young man with a strong personality. Kung consented, stipulating, however, that he should stay only one year at the work.

A good deal had happened to this young man since he had gone to America. Like many other Chinese students he came into contact with Sun while he was abroad, first through some of the Doctor's followers and later through his writings. He did not meet Sun Yat-sen himself until the big student rally in Japan, but long before that he had accepted the new revolutionary dogma in lieu of his youthful loyalty to Kuang Hsu. No Ch'ing whatever would be better for China, after all, than even a fairly good Ch'ing.

When the Revolution took place, Hsiang-hsi was back in Taiku trying to found a school that would educate people for the job of carrying on a democracy. He had refused all offers of diplomatic posts, though young men with foreign educations were at a premium just then. The uprising did not take him by surprise; owing to his position in the town he was respected by his neighbors, and they asked him to take charge of the Shansi volunteer revolutionary troops. His province had never been very warlike, and these troops were made up mainly of policemen and the bodyguards of business houses. Such as the army was, however, Hsiang-hsi whipped it into shape in his new capacity as Commander-in-Chief, and he insisted against all precedent upon handing it back to Yen

Hsi-shan when that leader returned from his wanderings during the war. It was suggested that Hsiang-hsi become governor of the province, but he was stubbornly faithful to his idea of a school.

"You can't carry out a revolution overnight," he insisted. "The military turnover, yes; that can be done all at once. But where are you going to get the men for the government afterwards? It needs training to govern a country, and education is the first and most important step in a revolution."

The death of his first wife and the march of events in Peking—he had reason to dislike Yuan Shih-kai—persuaded him to take a year from home, and that is how he happened to be in Japan.

At the end of this term, the young people were married in Yokohama by Christian ceremony, in a little church on a hill. Eling's wedding dress was of pale pink satin (a Chinese bride always wears pink or red); it was embroidered in a design of deeper pink plum blossoms and fashioned into a jacket and skirt. Her hair was bound with a fillet of plum blossoms. It was a small wedding, with only the Soongs, Dr Kung's cousins and a few intimate friends as guests.

The morning dawned gloomily, with heavy rain, but before the party started for church the sun came out. After a wedding breakfast at the Soongs' house, the Kungs motored to Kamakura, Eling wearing an apple-green satin dress embroidered with little golden birds. The captious Japanese sun shone all the way to Kamakura, through the branches of trees that lined the road. Just as they entered the Kamakura Hotel the rain fell again, in a torrent, but Eling's delicate dress had escaped injury. Dr Kung was much pleased by these convenient manifestations of Nature, who had treated their wedding so kindly. "They are very happy omens," he said.

When Mayling was left alone after Chingling returned to China at the end of the spring term of 1913, she went to Wellesley and was enrolled there as a freshman. Her brother Tse-ven, known as

"T.V.," had already come to Harvard the year before, and was taking the academic course. Mayling recorded him as her guardian, and at least once she found an opportunity to go over to Cambridge to see him. He was living in a private house there, with three or four other Chinese students; a tall, very quiet, slender young man, he showed the same tranquil disposition he retained during his early success in the financial world of China, when he was the aim and admiration of every marriageable girl in Shanghai.

One of the other students caught a glimpse of Mayling once as she was going into the drawing room to wait for T.V. Homesick for China, he stared at the young girl and dreamed romantically for days thereafter. Mayling was plump in those days, with a high healthy color, and her hair was still in a plait down her back.

"She was at that time," says a friend, "a graceful, charming young woman with easy manners, a delightful hostess and popular with her college mates. She had been in America so long that some of her friends felt a great deal of apprehension about her return to China, fearing that she would not be happy in her own land."

Her career at Wellesley has been described in the college magazine of February, 1938:

A brilliant student, she majored in English literature and minored in philosophy. It is said that she particularly loved the fiery conflicts of Arthurian Romance, a course then taught by Professor Emeritus Vida Scudder. She studied French and music (theory, violin and piano) all four years, and also took astronomy, history, botany, English composition, Biblical history and elocution. She also received credit for a course in education taken in the summer of 1916 at the University of Vermont.

In her senior year she was named a "Durant Scholar," the highest academic distinction conferred by the college.

She did not go out extensively for athletics, but enjoyed swimming and tennis. During her junior year she was elected a member of Tau Zeta Epsilon, one of the six local Wellesley societies, open only to upper classmen, and devoted to semi-social, semi-serious pursuits. T.Z.E. spends its serious hours studying music and art. Still a loyal "sister,"

Meiling recently sent the society a de luxe first edition of her book, *Sian: a Coup d'Etat,* printed in China and autographed by herself and her husband, the Generalissimo.

She wrote and spoke beautiful, idiomatic English with a flavor which was Southern rather than Oriental. It is told that, not liking Wellesley on her first day, she walked into the office of the late Edith Souther Tufts, then Dean of Residence, and said, "Well, I reckon I shan't stay raound here much longer."

Her Wellesley friends remember her as sometimes vivacious, sometimes sober and sombre, but always an individualist. Professor Annie K. Tuell, who lived with her in Wood Cottage, writes, "She kept up an awful thinking about everything. She was always questioning, asking the nature of ideas, rushing in one day to ask a definition of literature, the next day for a definition of religion. She thought about moral matters and discovered for herself some of the standards which people more conventionally brought up take ready-made, without inquiry. She was a stickler for truth, and resented any discovery that she had ever been fed conventional misinformation. . . .

"We all liked her and took her for granted as one of ourselves, quite forgetting any foreignness in her. . . . She was, of course, much admired, not for beauty in those days, as were her sisters; but there was a fire about her and a genuineness, and always a possibility of interior force. . . .

"As the years went on, the return to China presented to her very hard problems, as she and T.V. both felt, and she wondered at difficulties ahead, when she should return to a world and domestic standards from which she had grown away. She was, with all her sociability and considerable popularity, a little remote, watching us, questioning, criticizing or liking, feeling herself a bit of an alien."

One alumna confesses that classmate Meiling was responsible for getting her through Wellesley. They sat next to each other in philosophy class taught by Professor Mary Whiton Calkins, and the American girl found herself hopelessly at sea in the subject. Meiling took her in hand. "Buy Miss Calkins' book (*Persistent Problems of Philosophy*)," she said, "study it, and come to me every night with what you do not understand." The American girl passed the course and got her B.A.

Another classmate remembers that Meiling had a large Oriental scimitar hanging decoratively on the wall of her dormitory room. It was a weapon which so terrified one freshman with notions about the "heathen Chinese" that she was never able to pass the door without breaking into a run.

Meiling was very popular with the Oriental students at Harvard and other colleges throughout the East. As one friend put it, "there always seems to be some nice Chinese boy or other on the doorstep of Wood." Apprehensive of a family-made marriage when she returned home, she became engaged at one time while she was in Wellesley. It was later, of course, broken off.

As a college girl she wore the sturdy American shoes and skirts common to her fellow students, but often had a bright silken Oriental touch about her blouse or jacket.

A former teacher of music, Miss Hetty Wheeler, who taught Mayling for two years, said that she had been most impressed by her pupil's consciousness of Oriental culture and its heritage. This feeling seemed to grow stronger in Mayling as she grew older, as it usually does: at first, says Miss Wheeler, she seemed completely Westernized, but gradually she became more and more proud of China's art and literature. Miss Elizabeth Mainwaring of the English department agrees with this; she did not teach Mayling herself, but once had a talk with her. Mayling at that time was eloquent about China's contributions to civilization, and expressed regret that the Western world should neglect them.

The emotions of an exiled student must at all times be very complex. Mayling had come to America while she was still a young child, and it is a child's impulse always to imitate as closely as possible his near companions. There are children who are afraid to admit that they know more than their playmates do, and some who deny that they speak any language but the one of the country where they live. As she grew up, she probably felt drawn to her own land, especially after her sisters had left her to go back. That yearning, however, must have been mingled with fears as she thought of the codes and traditions that held China so firmly in thrall, and from which she had escaped for so many years. Even those of us who do not go abroad for our schooling are conscious of misgivings when the time comes to go home. It was perhaps some such feeling, a sudden resentment against the fate that was to call for another great effort on her part, another major feat of adaptation, that caused the young girl to write to a friend,

"The only thing oriental about me is my face."

Certainly she told the truth—for that time. According to a photograph of herself taken with two other Wellesley students, in sailor blouses and soft coiffures, not even her face was very Oriental. She looked the perfect type of pre-war American college girl back in the days of banjos and fudge, pennants on the wall, and pride in the privilege of being still a lady, although learned.

CHAPTER X

Chingling Weds Her Hero

Sᴜɴ Yᴀᴛ-sᴇɴ made Japan his headquarters in the ensuing two years, but he again adopted his old habits as a refugee and traveled incognito, slipping into China when his presence was needed for the new plans. Canton and Hongkong were the safest places for him now. With Chen Chi-mei and Chiang Kai-shek he discussed ways and means for the new campaign; Chiang was by this time very close to the Doctor. On one occasion, in 1914, he was entrusted with a trip to Manchuria to spread the revolutionary gospel and to see what chances there were for an uprising in that district; after a journey full of danger he returned to Tokyo to report that there was small chance of success for such an enterprise.

In the meantime, Eling's marriage and departure had left Sun without a secretary, and he took her advice and asked Chingling to do the work. The younger girl was thus thrown into the daily company of her hero, and matters took the course that was to disturb her family so greatly. One day to the horror of the Soongs she announced her intention of marrying Sun Yat-sen. Nothing could possibly have shocked her mother more. Both Sun and his wife were Christian; there was no chance to excuse the suggestion on the ground that Chinese marriage ties are not necessarily binding. Besides, the first Madame Sun was a woman of the Doctor's own age, having married him in his youth and borne him three children; she was his rightful wife, according to every tenet of Mrs Soong's Spartan philosophy. Any proposal on the part of the Doctor to abandon a faithful spouse, and for a young girl's sake, would have met with the sternest disapproval from Mrs Soong, but that the young girl should be her own daughter was the cruelest blow of all.

Chingling was determined, and she needed all her determination. She had taken on a difficult task. Not only was she opposing her mother's strong will, but she was going against the conventions of both the Christianized and the non-Christianized society of China. According to the old-fashioned customs of China it may be proper for a girl to become a second wife, but only when the arrangement has been approved by her elders of both families: indeed, the convention is that such a marriage is *proposed* by the family leaders; she herself according to the rules of propriety must pretend only to submit to their decision. Certainly she is not supposed to arrange her disposition for herself—and against the will of her people.

In spite of everything, however, that could be said to dissuade her, Chingling persisted. In the end she ran away and formally joined Sun. It was the first sign of her strength of character, that strength which has held her to the pathways she has chosen and has governed her slightest action.

She wrote an American school friend of her wedding:

It was the simplest possible, for we both hate surplus ceremonies and the like. I am happy and try to help my husband as much as possible with his English correspondence. My French has greatly improved and I am now able to read French papers and translate by sight easily.

So you see marriage for me is like going to school except that there are no "exams" to trouble me.

Marriage to the busy Sun must have been very much "like going to school" for a twenty-year-old girl. The fact that she worked so hard at foreign languages in order to help her husband accounts for one notable difference between herself and her sisters. Madame Kung did not leave Shanghai for America until she was fourteen years old; her Chinese is fluent. Madame Chiang set to work earnestly to learn Chinese as soon as she returned to Shanghai, as we will see later. Chingling speaks English by choice, even with Chinese people.

It is interesting to compare the attitude of Chingling's family after she had made her decision with the behavior of a Western clan in similar circumstances. Americanized as the Soongs were, their Chinese background had an effect on this situation. An American father and mother might have cast their daughter out of their lives; they would certainly have blamed the man, and cut off relations with him. The Soongs were unhappy about it, but made no public sign of their feelings. If the sisters did not see one another for a period of time, if Mrs Soong continued to disapprove, nobody outside the intimate family circle knew of this. Nor did Charlie Soong allow his lifetime's devotion to be affected by his daughter's action. He continued to work as before for Sun and for the China for whose future he had given his life.

Japan's presentation to Yuan of the Twenty-one Demands in January 1915 was at once a blow and a stimulus to the revolutionists. At the same time that it stirred them to greater efforts, it proved to Sun that this ally was one that would bear watching in future, even when the present Northern government was overthrown. Any bargains made by a dispossessed ruler would not be binding to his successor, but Japan was an embarrassingly near neighbor, and the threat would remain.

Toward the end of 1915 the exiles struck again in Shanghai, managing to win over to their cause the commander of one of the warships in the Whangpoo, the *Chaohu*. Chiang was with Chen Chi-mei at the time, and they made an unavailing attack on Nantao, outside the Settlement. Later Chiang captured Kiangyin fortress near Nanking and held it for several days, but the troops rebelled and the revolutionists were forced to retire.

It was fairly obvious that Sun's followers needed firmer organization. To this end the Doctor made a tour of the Southern provinces of Kwangtung, Kwangsi and Yunnan, speaking wherever he went and cementing the Kuomintang by strengthening the spirit of the people against Yuan Shih-kai. He then transferred his headquarters to Shanghai, where within the Settlement he was reasonably safe from Yuan, though several attempts were made on him and his lieutenants by assassins. Chiang Kai-shek was very nearly killed in one of these incidents.

Up in Peking, Yuan's ambition had been growing, and in December of 1915 he had himself declared Emperor. The prompt protest that came from Yunnan, Kwangtung, Kweichow and Kwangsi, which provinces immediately declared independence, frightened him into canceling the project, but he could not quiet the turbulent South. His supporters deserted him, and he chose this appropriate moment to die. The figurehead of Sun's opponents thus disappeared, but his work remained; China was once more plunged into civil war.

It was possible, however, for Charles Soong to return to Shanghai, and he came back, bringing his family with him. Kung Hsianghsi went to Shansi to prepare his home for his bride; he felt free, now, to realize a long-cherished ambition and to found a school in his own province. What is now Oberlin-in-China Junior College was begun with nine students; the school today has spread into a chain across the entire province, and numbers thousands of students of all ages. Dr Kung is still president. At that time, however, all of this had still to be started. Madame Kung stayed with her parents in Shanghai until he came back for her.

It is a long journey into the interior, even today. In those days there were no roads to Taiku, Kung's own city. The young couple went as far as possible, to Yutse, by train, and the rest of the journey was done by sedan chair, with sixteen bearers, for Madame, and by horse for Dr Kung. It was Eling's first experience of life in the interior of China, and she was awed and fearful of what awaited her. She had heard stories of the primitive conditions under which people lived in the country and she had steeled herself to find unknown tortures of discomfort.

The Kung family house was a complete surprise to her. Taiku was known as "The Wall Street of China," because it was there that most of the important bankers lived, and her husband's home was one of the biggest. It was immense, a palace built with thick stone walls, standing in an estate of eighty or ninety mow. Five hundred people made up the household. The furniture was of heavy teak and had been brought by caravan from Canton. She had never dreamed that such luxury was to be found in far-off Shansi.

Those early days were busy ones for her. Dr Kung's school was organized at last and he was about to realize his hope of modernizing his province. Everything there was ready except for the faculty, which was still shorthanded. They had been depending upon the arrival of a certain teacher from Oberlin, but at almost the last moment he sent word that he could not keep his promise to come. The staff was short of teachers, also of the time and money needed to bring a substitute from the China coast, which appeared to be the only alternative. It was then suggested by some daring free-thinker that Eling was quite well qualified to teach.

Today we might consider this solution to the problem a most obvious and natural one, but this was twenty-five years ago, and in one of China's most backward provinces. Shanghai had at last accepted Eling with her foreign education, but Taiku, Shansi, had yet to be convinced that a young woman could actually usurp the position and duties of an honored schoolmaster. In a man's school, moreover—a school in which many of the pupils were older than the teacher! Still, it was a foreign school and thus a new departure anyway, and Eling was protected by her position as a member of the Kung family. She taught the usual subjects, with emphasis upon English, also hygiene and sanitation.

"I had no right to attempt it," she said later when speaking of this phase of her life. "I didn't know enough to teach in any ordinary school, I'm quite sure, but this was an extraordinary case of necessity. . . . I remember that one of the students asked me some question in English class, as to why one sometimes doesn't repeat the noun in a compound sentence, and I answered, 'Oh, that's understood.' It seemed to me a most satisfactory reply for many questions that puzzled me as well as the students. After that I said, 'Oh, that's understood' whenever I thought I was getting into deep water."

CHAPTER XI

Mayling Comes Home

GENERAL YEN HSI-SHAN was governor of Shansi at the time of Eling's marriage, and after the Kungs were settled down in Taiku Dr Kung accepted the position of his High Adviser. This was a chance very much to his taste, for he could now go further in his ambition to modernize the province. He was responsible for many reforms in the educational and transportation systems of Shansi.

It was in Taiku that the first Kung child, Rosamonde, was born, in 1916. Madame Kung had not been in good health during her first year in the interior, and the birth was not an easy one. Upon her recovery she found herself thinking, as we so often do after narrow escapes, about her religion and the real state of her belief. Before this experience Eling had not been what she herself considered a real Christian. She had examined the state of her mind now and then and had even written a thoughtful paper upon missions in China when she was at Wesleyan, but on the whole she had rejected the formalized methods of worship beloved by her mother. Mrs Soong and her eldest daughter had indeed discussed the subject many times, and the mother was sadly worried about Eling's state of grace. The more they talked, the further from her mother's religion did Eling feel herself to be.

For the first time, after Rosamonde's birth, Madame Kung discovered within herself a desire to thank God in person, as it were, for her recovery and her baby. She thinks that she became a genuine Christian at that time, and not before. Even today she is not much inclined to profess her feelings on this subject, nor does she in her rare public speeches use God's name overmuch or appeal to Him with many demands. Her friendly feelings for missionaries are due rather to her admiration for their goodheartedness and bravery than because she is particularly eager to Christianize China. Madame Kung's religion takes the form of a quiet, sure faith in which there is no desire to force her convictions upon others. It is something, she believes, that comes to each person individually in its own good time, sometimes early and sometimes late.

The year 1916 was a significant one for her brother-in-law Sun Yat-sen. It was in January that the monarchy was declared and then forsworn by Yuan, and in June he died. Sun's opportunity was at hand and he began once more to campaign for his constitutional government. The situation, however, was even more chaotic than it had been while Yuan was alive, and Sun had many foes, gangsters and small party-leaders who were quite as eager for power as the President had been. Meantime the Vice-President, Li Yuan-hung, had succeeded to the Presidency, and the North seemed hopeless as a headquarters for Sun. He looked again toward Canton.

Early in the next year the World War began strongly to affect China's confused politics. In Peking, Parliament was against the suggestion, proffered by England, that China break off diplomatic relations with Germany and Austria, but the Premier was in favor of this action and made himself so unpopular by advocating it that he was ousted. The militarist group, whose man he was, thereupon promptly persuaded Li Yuan-hung to dissolve Parliament. The dying Republic was now dead, and the monarchist party slipped into power long enough to restore the child Emperor to the throne. He stayed there only a fortnight; then the militarists rose up and took over the capital, on July fourteenth. They re-restored the republican government, though Li refused to take on his former job of the Presidency; the Vice-President took his place, and the militarists had their way. China declared war on Germany, August fourteenth, 1917.

Sun was in Canton at this time, leading the outcry against China's participation in the war. The country's first need, he insisted, was a *working* government; if Asia entered the struggle over in Europe, both China and England would probably suffer from the aftereffects. Many were of his opinion, but their advice was unavailing.

It was in 1917, too, that Mayling came back after spending ten of her most formative years in the United States. Chingling had written, "Just think, little May-ling will graduate this June and return to China in July. How time flies! She is a popular lassie and enjoys her college life immensely."

Few Americans can say that they know their country as well as Mayling does. In her own words, "I have been all over the United States, in practically every single State. I spent my summers either with friends of my father or visited my American schoolmates." In the eight years that had elapsed since Eling's return, Shanghai had become hardened to the idea of the feminine overseas student, and a few years later these girls formed a club in the city. Mayling had still a few shocks to administer to the public, however. She was then as she is now immensely energetic, and she threw herself into public and social service work. She was a slender, vivid girl, and her vitality was an immense contrast to the regulation *jeune fille* of the time.

At first she too used foreign dresses, until the strangeness of Chinese clothing wore off for her and her eyes became accustomed to it. Then she adopted the native dress again. She has always, however, retained certain touches of foreignism in her clothes; in cold weather she wears hats, for example, and her jackets and jerseys are shaped at the waist, though custom today decrees that Chinese girls use the straight cardigan style in their overgarments. She did not hesitate, either, to wear riding clothes of modern cut, with a smart broad-brimmed hat. Many Chinese women today ride in breeches or jodhpurs, but Mayling was the pioneer.

One of the first things she did was to find a Chinese teacher and set to work with lessons. Her childhood memories would have been sufficient to bring back the Shanghai dialect after a very little practice, but Mayling would not have been satisfied to speak and understand Chinese. She wanted to read and to write. Her teacher was a scholar of the old style, and she studied the Classics as if she were a child at school again, chanting and swaying in the proper fashion. (Most returned students disdain Chinese literature.) Daily she studied with her instructor, and she kept it up for many years —fortunately, for today a large part of her work is in public speaking, and her fluent Chinese has gone further than have any of her other accomplishments to quiet the criticism of the old-fashioned die-hards. They may still grumble that Madame Chiang is "completely foreign," but they cannot add that common complaint, "Why, she doesn't even speak Chinese!"

Mayling joined the Y.W.C.A. and helped them with their social work; she also became a member of the National Film Censorship Committee. When the Shanghai Municipal Council asked her to join the Child Labor Commission they were breaking all precedent; no Chinese had ever before been offered such an appointment. Her experience on this Commission was to have strong influence upon her career in later life; the resulting contact with Shanghai's shameful labor conditions in the factories was by way of an initiation for the girl whose training had until then been purely academic.

Today Madame Chiang has much to do with the new educational methods of China. She is particularly interested in the intensive training, primitive but efficacious, that is given to girls taken from the small towns and the countryside and then sent out in their turn as teachers to the peasants. Madame plans the classes and tries to visit them every day, giving lectures and addresses. She shows an obvious talent for teaching; she speaks clearly, choosing her words with a nice judgment as to the capacity of the listeners to absorb ideas, and her patience is inexhaustible. She has never taught, however, as a regular teacher, nor even taken a few pupils, as did Madame Kung when she first came back to China: many Shanghai schools did invite her to join their faculties, for they were eager to learn from an American-university graduate, but the Soong parents thought that her own Chinese lessons were of more importance.

Her social activities too were considerable. Shanghai was a pleasant place for prosperous Chinese families such as the Soongs and their friends. They added to the Western luxury of the city their own Chinese comforts, and when the European war came to an end there was a business boom. All the friends of the Soongs, like themselves, had motor cars. Parties were very lavish; people vied with one another in entertaining. Those were the days when families would celebrate birthdays with enormous feasts that lasted several days, importing famous actors by the troupe and having their private plays for the benefit of their relations. China proper seemed very far away. The Soongs were still outstanding in their friendships with foreigners; the other Chinese still kept themselves to themselves. Mayling's American contacts were kept up, however.

Often, though she was so busy, she felt the same impatience that her father and sisters had experienced in dealing with the community in which she lived. A childhood friend retains a characteristic memory of the girl. They met in the street, and as they strolled toward the Soongs' house Mayling invited the Englishwoman in for a cup of tea.

They went into the living room. Mayling rang the bell and gave the order, then as she glanced around she made an impatient little sound. "Dust!" she said in explanation. "These servants simply don't know how to clean a room." She called one of the women, pointed to an offendingly dusty table, and told her to clean it again. Shamblingly the *amah* went and fetched a cloth with which she began to flick the surface of the table. Mayling waited for as long as she could endure it, then she took the cloth herself. "No, that's not the way," she said. "Here, like this. . . ." She began briskly dusting the room, rubbing wherever it was necessary to rub, and speaking rapidly over her shoulder to her guest:

"You can't expect them to know how until they've been taught. . . . I suppose most people would say I'm losing *face*"—she spoke with tremendous scorn—"by doing this. But I can't stop to think of those things."

Many a visitor to China can recall similar experiences of his own when he has seen Madame at work in hospital or training school. Twenty-three years have not given her more love either for dirt or for misplaced dignity.

That summer the Suns went to Canton, the Doctor determined to re-establish the true constitutional government of China. He invited the members of the Parliament that had been dissolved by Li Yuan-hung, suggesting that they convene again in the South. A number of them responded. Then Li himself was asked to come down and take his old place as President. He never did come, as a matter of fact, but for a time he considered the possibility, and things looked hopeful. Sun Yat-sen himself was appointed "Generalissimo" of the provisional military government.

For the past two years Madame Sun had been with the Doctor at all his appearances in public, and his followers had long since accepted the situation. Among the Chinese people opinions, where there were any opinions at all on the subject, were sharply divided. The old-timers still stood by their guns and declared the matter disgraceful, but most of the young people, those with revolutionary sympathies, were heartily in favor of the marriage. News of Chingling reached even into Szechwan; the students there heard tales of a beautiful young girl from an American school, the daughter of Soong, Sun's first and most faithful friend. They hailed their Leader's action in marrying this fabulous girl. She would help him with his progressive program and his reforms, they agreed among themselves: moreover, his defiance of the old-fashioned notions of propriety appealed to them simply because they were young and iconoclastic.

"You know how I dread publicity!" wrote Chingling to America. "But since my marriage I have had to participate in many affairs which I'd otherwise escape. The Chinese are not like Europeans. They always thrust greatness and honor, not upon those who deserve them, but upon the timid. I see people every day; in fact I'm simply pulled out of my shell by circumstances. I was dumbfounded at some of the reports that have been manufactured about me in Macon. For instance, I learned that I was once a spy of the revolutionists before my marriage! And the various exciting and thrilling incidents that I have gone through must have been my nightmares, though I'm sure I *never* told about them!"

Sun Fo, the Doctor's son, had been in America at the time of the marriage of his father and Chingling. Evidently no one had told him of the domestic rearrangement in his family, and he was incredulous. He gave an interview to the press of San Francisco, denying that there was any truth in the story. Now, however, he did not allow his natural sympathy for his mother to keep him away from what he considered his duty, and he came back to China to offer his services to the new government, returning from Columbia University, where he had been doing postgraduate work in journalism. He was appointed Secretary to the National Assembly.

The inevitable cliques soon made trouble in Canton and managed to take control out of Sun's hands. His opponents created an Administrative Committee and made him one of the members instead of placing him at the head; even as a member he was comparatively powerless. Sun went back to Shanghai in disgust. For two years thereafter he and Chingling lived quietly in their house in Rue Molière, seeing their friends and producing books of his addresses and articles.

It was in 1918 that Charlie Soong died, on May third, of cancer. The three girls and two of his sons were with him at the time. Soon after this the Soongs removed to another house in Seymour Road; Mayling had already begun to carry most of the responsibility of housekeeping, and now there was the added duty of helping her mother with business, winding up Charlie's many affairs. Mrs Soong elected to give up most of his interests, and busied herself more than ever with church work.

In 1920 Chingling returned to Canton with her husband. Things had taken a turn for the better in the South; Chen Chiung-ming, one of Sun's older friends, had managed to drive out the "Kwangsi faction," which had edged the Doctor out of their political game two years before. Once more the remnants of the old Peking Parliament were brought together, and this time they elected Sun to the title, if not the deed, of "President of China." The new President immediately appointed his friend Chen Chiung-ming Governor of Kwangtung Province, which was the only province controlled by his government, and also made him head of the troops. It was a natural appointment for Chen in consideration of his services to Sun's group, but it led to trouble. That system of reward-for-services-rendered, that which is called the pork barrel and which the English know as the Old School Tie, can develop as awkward complications in China as it does in the West.

The first thing Sun set out to do was enlarge his domain. As President of China, even of Southern China, it behooved his people to get at least one more province under their control, and Chen Chiung-ming promptly took Kwangsi, the twin-province to Kwangtung, in July of 1921. Sun Yat-sen then proposed a Northern Expedition. General Chen did not think the idea a very good one, but the President overruled his objections and himself started out the following winter, leading the army. Chen thereupon refused to supply his troops with either money or arms; the expedition promptly collapsed, as he had known it would, and Sun returned to Canton, where he dismissed Chen from the Governorship in punishment for his non-co-operation.

Up in Peking, important things were happening. Wu Pei-fu took control of the Northern government in 1922, announcing that he intended to restore the constitutional form of legislation. He went so far as to replace Li Yuan-hung in the now familiar Presidential chair, and actually invited Sun Yat-sen to come to Peking and help him unify China.

Sun refused to go. He was suspicious of the invitation, quite naturally. But Chen Chiung-ming, still smarting under his dismissal from the post of Governor, seized his chance to criticize the Doctor; he demanded that Sun resign, claiming that there was no reason for carrying on with an extra President in the South, now that the Peking group was behaving itself and forming a Republican government. Sun did not resign, and Chen felt that he had been given enough excuse to start a revolt.

The Suns did not suspect until the last moment that the dispossessed Governor would really carry out his plan. It is an interesting point that up until two days before the climax, Eling had been visiting them with Rosamonde, her baby daughter. Everything in Canton seemed quiet. Sun had suggested that Kung come South to help him, and had offered him a portfolio, but Dr Kung was absorbed in his educational program for Shansi and was not eager to take part in public life. His wife, however, had been in Canton for seven weeks, and when she was leaving there was a sisterly argument as to whether she should take little Rosamonde back to Shanghai with her. . . .

"Leave her here," Chingling urged. "I'll take good care of her."

Eling almost weakened. If she had left the child, history would have been changed; the Suns would never have been able to manage their escape with a baby. But Madame Kung was not philosophical enough to separate herself from her child. Rosamonde went back to Shanghai in time.

The flight of Sun and Chingling from Canton is now an important and exciting part of China's history, but nowhere has it been told more vividly than in Madame Sun's own words, published in a Chinese magazine.

THE ESCAPE FROM CANTON

Seizing his opportunity while Dr Sun and his troops were at the front conducting the Northern Expedition, Chen Chiung-ming had marched his men, without giving us any notice of his intention, into the city of Canton. His troops behaved badly, trying to disrupt communications and destroying peace and order. Dr Sun at last resolved to return to the capital.

As soon as we arrived, Dr Sun commanded the army to withdraw to their original quarters. Chen promised to carry out these orders, and we had no reason to doubt his sincerity, for to all appearances he was retiring to Hweichow, and all this time he continued to give us assurances of his fidelity. He never ceased corresponding with us. Only a week before the insurrection he telegraphed us, congratulating us upon our victory at the front. He had been co-operating with our Party for years. Certainly he can trace all his own power and position back to his work in the Party.

Chen's troops, which numbered about twenty-five thousand still living in the city, were now completely demoralized. Looting went on quite openly, and every day the situation became more aggravated. We had only about five hundred men in the capital; all the rest of our troops were at the front. The disparity between the forces was obvious, and Dr Sun tried by open attack to persuade Chen to remove his men to beyond the city limits.

About two o'clock on the morning of June sixteenth Dr Sun roused me from my sweet dreams, telling me to hurry and dress, that we were in danger and must escape. He had received a phone call to the effect that Chen's troops were about to march on us. We must leave immediately for a gunboat, from where we could direct our men in resisting the rebels.

I thought it would be inconvenient for him to have a woman along with him, and urged him to leave me behind for the time being. There couldn't, I said, be much danger for me as a private person. At last he saw the sense of my argument, but he would not go even then until he had left all fifty of our bodyguard to protect the house. Then he departed, alone.

Half an hour after he had gone, at about half past two, rifle shots rang out in the vicinity. Our house was half way up the hill, connected with the President's Residency at Kuang Ying An by a passage about a li in length, which stretched over the streets and houses like a bridge. It had formerly been the private mansion of Lung Chi-kuang. The enemy fired downhill at us from two sides, shouting, "Kill Sun Wen! Kill Sun Wen!" Pitch darkness covered them completely. Our small defense corps therefore kept quiet. I could just discern the crouching bodies of our guards in the darkness.

As day broke out men began to reply to the fire with their rifles and machine guns, while the enemy employed field guns. My bath was smashed to bits. One third of our handful of troops had been wiped out, but the remaining men resisted with more determination than ever. One of the servants climbed to a high place and succeeded in killing quite a number of the enemy. By eight o'clock our store of ammunition was running low, so we decided to stop shooting and preserve what was left until the last possible moment.

There seemed no use in remaining, now. Our Captain advised me to leave and the troops agreed with him, promising for their part to stay there in order to halt any possible pursuit by the enemy. . . . Later, all of the fifty were reported killed.

Four of us, Colonel Bow who was a foreign attendant of Dr Sun's, two of the guards and myself, taking with us only the most necessary supplies for every day, crawled along the bridge passage to make our escape. The enemy soon concentrated fire on this passage and flying bullets whistled about our ears. Twice bullets brushed past my temple without injuring me, however, for at that time we were quite well protected by solid rails on both sides of the bridge. Soon, though, we came to a place where the rails had been smashed by the fire, and we were obliged to make a wild dash for it. Suddenly Colonel Bow cried out, and blood began to flow down his leg. He had been shot through the thigh; a large artery was broken. The two men carried him on.

We were several hours in the passage before we could manage to attain the back garden of the Residency. Half an hour after we had got there we saw a flash of fire, and one section of the bridge was completely demolished. Communication therefore was completely cut off. The enemy's fire was now concentrated on the Residency, and we could not return it because the building was surrounded by private houses.

We took Colonel Bow into one of the bedrooms and dressed his wound roughly. The sight of his agony greatly affected me, yet he never stopped consoling me, saying, "The victory will be ours some day!"

From eight in the morning till four that afternoon we were literally buried in a hell of constant gunfire. Bullets flew in all directions. Once the entire ceiling of a room I had left only a few minutes before collapsed.

At four o'clock Division-commander Wei Pang-ping, who had until then been neutral, sent down an officer to talk peace with us and to offer conditions of surrender. The first demand made by our guard was for my safety, which the officer refused to guarantee, saying that they had no power over the troops of another man. Even the enemy officers could do nothing with these soldiers, who had by this time gone completely mad. Our iron gates were soon smashed and we were confronted by the bloodthirsty bayonets and revolvers of the soldiers, who rushed, however, not for our persons but for the bundles in our hands. Quickly we seized our chance, and ran toward two currents of wild crowds of troops, rushing into each other's paths; one was a group of escaping soldiers and the other a batch of enemy looters. I succeeded in making an escape, wearing Colonel Bow's hat and Dr Sun's raincoat.

A rush of enemy troops flashed by, attempting to loot the Ministry of Finance and the Customs Superintendent's office. We picked our way through the crowd in the savage mob, finding ourselves at last in a small lane, safe so far from the looters. I was absolutely exhausted, and begged the guards to shoot me. Instead they dragged me forward, one on each side supporting me. . . . Corpses lay about everywhere, some of Party people and others of plain citizens. Their chests were caved in, their arms slashed, their legs severed. Once we saw two men squatting face to face under a roof. Closer observation revealed that they were dead, their eyes wide open. They must have been killed by stray bullets.

Again our way was cut off by a group of the mob running out of a

[*113*]

little passage. The whisper ran through our party that we should lie flat in the street, pretending to be dead. In this way we were left unmolested; then we arose and continued our journey. My guards advised me to avoid looking at the corpses lest I should faint. Half an hour later, when the rifle shots were thinning out, we came to a small farmhouse. The owner tried to drive us out, fearing the consequences of sheltering us; his attempt was forestalled, however, by a timely swoon on my part.

I woke up to find the guards washing me with cold water, and fanning me. One of them went out to see what he could of the way things were going, when suddenly there came a tattoo of rifle shots. The guard indoors rushed to shut the door; he told me that the other one had been struck by a bullet and was probably dead by this time.

While the firing subsided I disguised myself as an old countrywoman, and with the guard in the guise of a pedlar we left the cottage. I picked up a basket and a few vegetables on the way, and carried them with me. At last we reached the house of a friend which had already been searched that morning. To go on was absolutely impossible, so we spent the night there. Shelling never ceased the entire night, and our relief was enormous when we heard cannon shots at last from the gunboats. Dr Sun, then, was safe. . . .

Next morning, still in my countrywoman outfit, I arrived at Shameen with the others, and there another friend, a foundry worker, arranged for a small motorboat for me, by which we got to another house in Linnan. The river was thronged with boats full of booty, both girls and goods. They were being sent away for safety. It was reported that two women unfortunate enough to answer to my description had been thrown into jail. That same afternoon I left Canton, the house in which I had stayed the night was searched again.

At last, that night, I succeeded in meeting Dr Sun on board ship, after a life and death struggle. We soon went to Hongkong, disguised.

Chingling managed to reach Shanghai soon after the escape. Dr Sun, however, stayed aboard the ship for almost two months more, waiting for a possible revolution among the troops and hoping for help. Chiang Kai-shek stayed with him, looking after him; the Generalissimo has himself written a history of that period, and his biographers record how he worked, devoting himself to the

Doctor and doing all the necessary jobs, from those of a servant to the work of a common sailor, trying to mitigate the trials of life on a Chinese gunboat under the tropical Cantonese sun.

After waiting as long as they could they gave up hope. Dr Sun also returned to Shanghai, to Rue Molière.

CHAPTER XII

Death of a Leader

I<small>T WAS AT THIS TIME</small>, after the escape of the Suns from Canton in September of 1922, that the Doctor's friendly relations with the Soviet became publicized. Sun had naturally been deeply interested in and sympathetic with the Russian Revolution when it took place in 1917, and many of the Chinese who followed him had already gone further than he had in declaring their approval of the direction of events in Russia. Joffe had been sent over by the Russians that summer as ambassador, to see what he could do in the way of cementing friendship between the two countries, and in Peking he promised Russian aid if China should, under certain circumstances, desire it. Many people listened to his promises and made their plans accordingly. The Hongkong strike of 1922, combined with Joffe's visit, was enough to make the most shortsighted of the "imperialist" tradesmen on the Coast become somewhat nervous of the Russian bogey.

[*116*]

After his visit to the North, Joffe came to Shanghai in January, 1923, and there he saw and "cultivated" Sun Yat-sen. They soon reached an agreement as to policy, though at that time nothing was done save on a personal basis. Together they published a statement to the effect that Sun believed the Soviet system "cannot actually be introduced into China because there do not exist the conditions for the successful establishment of either communism or Sovietism. This view is entirely shared by Mr Joffe. . . . he has assured Dr Sun Yat-sen that China has the warmest sympathy of the Russian people and can count on the support of Russia." The Russians moreover, Joffe said, were willing to give up their special privileges in China, inherited from Tsarist days, which accrued to "extra-territoriality." It was a gesture that went straight to the hearts of a people who for years had been resenting the status of the foreigners trading within their boundaries. Sun's sympathizers were over-joyed at this concrete proof that he was raising the country to a position of international dignity.

Enemies of Sun had been grumbling that he was a tool of the Soviet and was now coming into the open with his Communist policy, which he had, they alleged, been pursuing in secret for many years. The statement made jointly with Joffe took the wind out of their sails: Sun had declared himself frankly, and his declaration proved that he was not nearly so extremely leftist as the critics had avowed. A wave of approval for himself and of friendship for Russia swept the Doctor to Canton yet again, the following month. Civil wars had gone round the old circle, war lords fell out, and Canton was leaderless. Sun took his opportunity. His third journey South was successful, ultimately, as the other two had never been.

Ultimately. In the meantime he was up against the same old problems: uncertain power, threats from war lords and lack of money. Russia came to the rescue. To begin with, he was appointed "Generalissimo," and there was no doubt that he was leader. Chiang Kai-shek, aided by military advisers from the Soviet, began to remodel the army, and the first time a war lord tried to dislodge the new Government they managed to beat him back. Then

Borodin came from Russia to help the Party with reorganization, with advice, and most of all with funds. Once he had arrived, the affairs of the Kuomintang went more smoothly than they had ever done before. It was the real turning point of Sun's career, though success came almost too late for the old warrior.

Part of the vigor of this new regime was due to the number of bright young men with whom Sun surrounded himself. Chiang was becoming known as one of the Doctor's hopes; he was sent to Moscow for a year to study Russian military methods, but even before this he attracted attention with his ability as a commander. He was still young as army officers went in the old Chinese fashion, but the Soviet people had introduced the cult of youth, and it fitted in well with the spirit of reform that permeated Canton.

Another rising young man was Chingling's brother, T.V. He had returned to China in 1917, but in all these politically troubled years he had worked in Shanghai as secretary and general adviser to a large coal company there. Now that the Nationalist Government had been formed in Canton, when they saw that they would need expert aid in the practical details of reorganization, they sent for T.V. and made him Director of the Department of Commerce. He was very good at his job, and later when he became General Manager of the Central Bank the most aggrieved protestants against the influence of the Soongs, the most jealous of commentators, were never able to complain that T.V. had not been a most happy choice.

Madame Kung's four children were born in rapid succession; David, Jeannette and Louis all first saw daylight in Shanghai. It was an easy journey between that city and Peking, though the times were troubled, and Eling often visited her mother, though her home was in Tientsin at this time. Since T.V. and Chingling were in Canton with Sun, Mayling divided her visits fairly equally between North and South.

She thus found plenty of opportunity to contrast the milieus and to watch the rival governments at work—the seething excitement of the South, where all development, according to the optimistic Russians, was a thing of the future, and the old order in the North, which meant periods of stagnating calm interrupted now and then by civil war. It was an intensely interesting period. Only a Chinese family could have maintained a safe position in both camps, and only in China could Mayling have traveled about in this manner.

It was in Shanghai, in Dr Sun's house, that Chiang Kai-shek first saw her. He made up his mind very shortly that she was the girl he wanted to marry. He had divorced Miss Mao of Fenghua, and one day he informed Dr Sun of this.

"I have no wife now, Teacher," he said. "Do you think Miss Soong could be persuaded to accept me?"

Dr Sun did not, but he consulted his wife. Chingling replied with some heat that she would rather see her little sister *dead* than married to a man who, if he was not married, should have been to at least one or two women in Canton. Gossip had been very busy with Chiang's name.

Sun Yat-sen did not bring back this unqualified refusal to Chiang, because he liked the younger man. "Wait a while," he counseled, and Chiang understood, and waited.

He was to bring the matter up twice more before Sun's death, and each time he was told to wait. He did wait, for almost ten years.

Chingling at this time was finding it necessary to watch the Doctor carefully, for his health was failing and he would not pause to take care of himself. He knew from hard experience how important any detail might be at this period, and he had never been very good at delegating duties to other people. Having worked alone so much of his life, he could not accustom himself to his position; he still carried out many duties in person, not because he did not trust his lieutenants, but because he was sure he could do these things better than anyone else.

The picturesque General Morris Cohen, who was with him at this time, recalls an incident when he found himself, as he says, in an embarrassing quandary. It was the only time in his life that he was forced to disobey Sun Yat-sen. The Doctor had decided impulsively to go in person and interview a certain war lord whose intentions, he feared, were not strictly honorable. This man, though he kept making the conventional protests of love and loyalty, persisted in keeping his army within the city walls, embarrassingly close to the government headquarters. Sun wished to see him, to persuade him by sheer force of personality to remove his troops to the outskirts of the town. It was a dangerous mission, especially as he wanted to go alone. He ordered General Cohen to stay with Madame Sun in order to protect her if occasion should arise.

Obediently the General took up his post.

The Doctor started off on his errand.

"What's this?" demanded Chingling. "General Cohen, you must go with Dr Sun."

The General hesitated. Madame Sun stood firm. He had to make up his mind quickly, and with her eye upon him he had only one choice. He hurried after his leader, catching up with him at a distance. The Doctor scolded him, but did not again send him back. And anyway the expedition was successful; the war lord decided to be tactful and to withdraw, so Chingling did not, after all, need any protection for that time.

Though Sun was now working in close co-operation with Russia, he did make one last attempt at persuading the Western Powers to take a hand in China's reconstruction program. He suggested to the American Minister at Peking a plan by which Western foreigners might train the Chinese in the technique of legislation, but nobody responded to this proposal. Sun thereupon decided once and for all that Russia was his only friend: the Powers, he said, in continuing to recognize the Northern government were hindering China's development. Borodin was in Canton when the Doctor, on New Year's Eve, 1923, stated in a public address,

Dr Sun Yat-sen and wife with officers of the President's Army
on their Northern Campaign

"We no longer look to the Western Powers. Our faces are turned toward Russia."

☆   ☆   ☆

The Kuomintang was reorganized along the same lines as the Soviet party; this method is still in use in China. Under Chiang's head the Whampoa Military Academy began to turn out a new type of officer, well trained in warfare methods and possessing a clear conception of the State and the soldier's duty toward it. Until this time, a Chinese soldier had been a sort of legalized bandit, feared and detested by the people; Chiang with Borodin prompting him spoke to them of a united China and of their work in building it. The army improved enormously, and in record time.

Dr Sun showed how his backbone had been stiffened when he took a firm stand against the Powers by demanding for the use of his government the receipts of the Customs in Canton. America and England had a nasty surprise. They had become accustomed to the smooth working of China's Customs Service; nobody had made trouble about it for many years. For a while both countries resisted, landing men in Canton and putting up a show of force, but Sun did not back down and in the end they compromised, granting him a part of the Customs receipts. The Chinese became more enthusiastic than ever over Sun; this was a real victory against the world.

Following the Russians' advice, a Congress was called for the new Central Executive Committee at which all members were supposed to discuss their work as it had been done in the past and was to be done in the future. It was an opportunity for general helpful criticism, chiefly educational in intent. Even at this time, however, Sun did not declare outright for Communism in China, nor did Borodin try to hurry him to a decision. Sun never did commit himself. He took pains at the Congress to reassure the reactionaries as to his intentions. At one of the meetings, Party members entered the room to find Sun at his table with a large placard in front of him. He was working with a Chinese pen, drawing a large circle,

[*121*]

which he labeled with characters at the top: "Kuomintang." Within this circle he drew, with silent deliberation, a number of smaller circles and duly labeled them too—"Communism," "Capitalism," "Socialism," "Marxism," and all the other "isms" of current discussion. Then and not until then did he stand up and address the meeting. Pointing to his diagram, he said that China was not bound to accept any one of these philosophies *in toto*. China, he declared, had her own problems peculiar to her history, and she must make a careful selection from the methods of other governments and from their experience, without pledging adherence to any one of them. Out of their mistakes and their triumphs, China must build a new structure suitable to herself.

Borodin showed no desire to hurry Sun or to force him to go more obviously to the Left. His own work progressed smoothly; as director of political education in China he realized that he could do, ultimately, as he thought best. Sun's last days were devoted to public explanation of his policy, speechmaking about the new program and the Party principles. Some of these addresses were collected and published under the title San Min Chu I, which serves today as the Kuomintang's Bible. As a good Bible should, it furnishes ideas, enough for anybody who refers to it, varied enough to suit almost any political argument. Dr Sun is quoted today by almost everyone in China, by Chiang Kai-shek, by Wang Ching-wei, by the Japanese themselves, who all dip into the San Min Chu I for some phrase or conception which they can interpret to suit themselves.

Since the death of the Doctor, Madame Sun has naturally fallen heir to this confusion and the argument that used to swirl round her husband's person. Did he mean this? Did he not mean that? Surely Wang ought to know; wasn't he closest to the Doctor? What does Madame Sun say? Only Madame Sun can tell. Make Madame Sun tell. . . .

Madame Sun, like her husband, has never accepted Communism publicly, nor has she declared a religious faith in all its precepts. She became a champion of all the principles that seemed to her best for the people, and that is as far as she will go. After Sun's death she had the opportunity to see the working of the Russian plan; she visited Moscow and perhaps at that time she was almost convinced. Her experience, however, has been similar to that of young Left-wing radicals in many other parts of the world. Later developments in Russia may have destroyed some of her faith in their program, but she had made no public statements, and there was nothing to retract when she changed her mind. She is still strongly pro-Russian.

The autumn of 1924 brought trouble to Peking. Wu Pei-fu could not continue to keep the peace, and in September another war broke out in the North, in Peking and the Yangtze Valley. Sun organized an expedition and himself set out with Chiang to take part in the struggle; he announced that he would even join forces with his old opponent Chang Tso-lin if it could mean a unified China in the end. Before he had got very far, however, the Christian General Feng Yu-hsiang double-crossed his friend Wu Pei-fu by occupying Peking while Wu was away at the wars. Feng tried to set up a President on his own, but the attempt was unsuccessful, and then he invited Sun Yat-sen to come to Peking in order to hold a conference with himself and the friends who were now in power.

Dr Sun when he had been invited by Wu Pei-fu had refused to accept. This time, however, his position was stronger, he had more self-confidence, which was justified by the support of the Soviet, and he trusted Feng more than he did Wu. He was very ill now, but the idea seemed good in relation to his own projects, and so he set out with Chingling on November thirteenth, 1924. It was a very leisurely journey, for he stopped at many places on the way to make speeches and grant interviews. They reached Peking on December thirty-first, but by that time the Doctor had collapsed. He was taken to the Union Medical College Hospital, where the doctors discovered that he was dying of cancer of the liver, and that it was too late to do anything for him.

Dr Kung, who lived then in Peking, did all he could to comfort the Leader during the last days. His service was so devoted that

Chingling has never forgotten it, and even at moments when she was most bitter, later on, against Chiang's government, she never allowed a word of criticism of Dr Kung to escape her lips. He was her elder brother in those days when she needed help the most.

Sun Wen died in Peking, in Dr Wellington Koo's house, at the age of fifty-eight. It was March twelfth, 1925. His son Sun Fo, his daughter, and Chingling were with him at the end.

CHAPTER XIII

Chiang Breaks with Moscow

Sun Yat-sen was dead; Charles Soong was dead; the work they had tried to do was unfinished. According to the Russians, it was still all to do from the very beginning. The second generation of revolutionaries was left with the heritage of his will, a rapidly growing hero worship for him and the friendship of the Soviet, for which the price was still pending.

Of the present generation, Kung was Commissioner of Finance of Kwangtung and Minister of Industry for the government, besides being a member of the Kuomintang Political Council. He is today the only one of the Ministers associated with Sun who is still in the national government.

T.V. remained in Canton, where Chiang Kai-shek, still President of the Whampoa Military Academy, was polishing and preparing the army, and reforming spoiled cadets. Mayling continued to live with her mother in the Seymour Road house in Shanghai.

Chingling, whose shyness had since her marriage been at war

[*125*]

with her position as Sun's wife, was not permitted by her conscience to retire to Rue Molière, the house which with his library were all the private fortune her husband had left her. As his widow she must go on with the plan, particularly of political education, that he had started under Borodin's advice; Borodin too remained, and Chingling worked at revolutionary schools and in the bureau of propaganda. In 1926 she was offered a place on the Central Executive Committee, which she accepted.

Like her elder sister Eling she had always been shy and sensitive, more like the Chinese ladies of past dynasties than the Americanized Mayling. This trait was noticed even when she was a schoolgirl; the Dean at Wesleyan tells how Chingling was worried that her gown would not be ready for the graduation exercises, and when the older woman said that in any case there was always her own son's gown, ready for use, the girl cried, "Oh, but I couldn't use a *man's* gown!" Seven years of an American school during that period of life we call "formative" had not cured her of a super-sensitivity; it is unlikely that her married life with all the attendant publicity did more than intensify her dislike for showing herself. But just then it was not only her own spirit of loyalty to Sun, it was the enthusiasm for him that was being fostered everywhere by the Soviets which made it imperative that his widow should do as much as possible in his plan, in his memory.

As soon as Sun died, in fact even before his death, while he lingered in Peking, Chiang found that he had his hands full in quelling aspirants to the headship of the government. Hu Han-min was acting as generalissimo, but it was Chiang who defeated three war lords, one after another, who attacked the army. He too was given a place on the Central Executive Committee, and in a short time, by the end of the year, all of Kwangtung was quiet.

The Russians in the meantime were pursuing their plan, unchanged by the death of Sun Yat-sen, of political education. Chiang saw that their influence was rising steadily. It was then that he began the policy he has followed ever since—tedious as it must at times have been—that of waiting and learning from foreign nations, of overlooking attempts, however patent, to usurp power until he can wait no longer, stretching his patience as far as possible so long as he can still receive the help that in his judgment the country needs. The propaganda of the Soviets affected the cities of Shanghai and Canton, so that a strike took place in Shanghai, beginning at some Japanese mills where there was labor trouble, and spreading through the ranks of the students. The now famous incident in which Municipal Police shot and killed some of these students during a demonstration of sympathy brought on the general strike. Then in Canton more trouble was brewed; French and British troops fired on a parade of strike sympathizers, killing many people, and the anti-British boycott began.

Following the advice of the Russians, the revolutionaries in Canton now announced that their government, reshuffled and reorganized, was national and representative of the entire country. The Peking government had abandoned its attempt to restore the constitution, and the Canton government was ready to fight and to spread its doctrines wherever necessary. Wang Ching-wei was chairman, Chiang Kai-shek commander of the student corps, Hu Han-min foreign minister. Soon, however, Chiang found that Hu was trying to get rid of him, fearing his mounting influence. In August, on the twenty-fourth, Hu and his friends were rounded up in a general clean-up by the Whampoa cadets under Chiang's direction. Hu was sent abroad. After that Chiang became general military commander and had now to deal only with enemies from outside and—the Russians.

Chiang Kai-shek led an expedition against the North, with the intention of unifying the country once and for all, in June 1926. The Central Executive Committee placed him in command of the Nationalist army and left the entire enterprise to him. The ground had already been prepared, and with the propaganda methods taught the Nationalists by the Russians, many of the petty war lords in the intervening territory were ready and waiting to welcome the Southerners. In Shanghai, Dr Kung received word of this plan by way of a request that he take on double jobs as Minister of Industry and Acting Minister of Finance. T.V., the actual Minister of Finance, was to travel with the army. They would need him in Hankow.

The Kungs made preparations to leave, and their children watched anxiously, begging to be allowed to come along. Their parents said, as parents often do,

"Not this time. Next time you can come."

After a few weeks in Canton, Dr Kung and his wife returned to Shanghai to wind up matters there in preparation for a long stay in the South. The children hung about again, trying to make up their minds who should be first to remind the elders of their promise. Finally they disappeared for a space and produced a petition which went like this:

Dear Parents:
Last time we wanted to go with you to Canton you said we could come next time you went. Now you are going. Please let us come with you.

This document was signed by a circle within which the four children had written their names along the circumference. Thus no one of them had run the risk of offending his parents by being the first to sign. . . . They went to Canton, too.

On the way down, the first night out, Madame Kung was studying the evening's menu card. The usual "musical programme" was listed; she read it aloud, and suddenly called to Louis, the youngest.

"Look at this, Louis," she said. "This must be a telegram from Uncle (the Generalissimo). It's about you, and what do you think it says? 'Don't—bring—Lulu.' What do you know about that?"

"It's a mistake," said the five-year-old Louis anxiously. "It *must* be a mistake. He meant to say 'Don't bring David.'"

By the middle of July, Chiang's troops occupied Changsha. There the army was split into three parts; one went into Hunan, one into Kiangsi en route for Nanking, and the third to Chekiang by way of Fukien. By September eighth they had occupied Hankow.

David Kung, the second of Madame Kung's children, had accompanied the army all the way as mascot. He had his uniform all complete, but to make himself look more terrifying he drew enormous black brows over his eyes, like the villain on the stage.

While Wu Pei-fu lost ground even in his own domain, the Nationalists went on rapidly from one victory to another. The campaign had been carefully planned beforehand and it proceeded smoothly. In many cities it was not necessary to strike a blow, for the leaders had already been given the opportunity to understand what was afoot, and had been persuaded in one way or another to join the conquerors. Kiukiang fell to them, and Chiang occupied Nanchang after a siege of two months. Chang Tso-lin, the Old Marshal, was now virtually in power in Peking.

The Nationalist government moved from Canton to Hankow and began to function there, with Borodin as much in evidence as ever. In January 1927 a Chinese mob overran the British Concession; the foreigners escaped in the gunboats that always guarded their interests, and shortly afterwards England gave up her concessions both in Hankow and Kiukiang to the Nationalist government. In February, Chiang met and defeated the army of the North at Hangchow. The Northerners then occupied Nanking, whither Chiang's army followed and besieged them. Soon afterwards the Nationalists took control of the Chinese cities around Shanghai, and two days later, on March twenty-fourth, they marched into Nanking. Some of the troops got out of hand and began to loot and riot, attacking foreigners and their possessions. Some foreign nationals were killed, more were wounded, and much property was destroyed before British and American boats could come to their rescue. This was done by shelling the city and then evacuating all foreigners.

Chiang, in Shanghai, heard of this incident, which might well have been disastrous to his cause. He hurried to Nanking and

started an investigation. He himself made no hasty claims of innocence for his men, but the Hankow government, which was by
this time very much under the influence of the Soviets, announced
quickly that the Nanking trouble had been caused by Northerners
to put the Nationalists into the bad graces of the Powers. It was a
thin story, and as diplomacy it was bad. Chiang perceived that the
time had come to call a halt with the Russians, and the first step
in this program was to break with Hankow. He prepared to set
up another government, with the many other people who feared
that China might become completely Communistic. He had the
backing of most of the banking set in Shanghai, among whom
was numbered Dr H. H. Kung.

In the meantime, both Chingling and T. V. Soong were on the
other side, with the Hankow government. T.V. later came down
to Shanghai, but Chingling remained with the radicals, feeling
that the Hankow group was carrying out the intentions of Dr Sun,
and that to be disloyal to these people would be to desert his
precepts.

Madame Kung's views were directly opposite. From what she
saw in Canton, she decided that the Communists and those who
worked with them were far too apt to take the intention for the
result. It is a failing common to the Chinese anyway, she reflected,
and though Communism may have had a chance in Russia, it was
bad rather than good for China. What her country needed and still
needs, she believes, is less theory and more practical action than
the Russians offered. The business sense she inherited from her
mother caused her to interest herself in the question of China's
industries rather than her politics, and she could see little hope
for these in the near future of Communism.

The anti-Red movement started simultaneously in Shanghai,
Nanking and Canton, with a campaign against all alleged Communist sympathizers. Chiang did not employ the Nationalist army
for this work, but turned the job over to secret societies, the members of which arrested thousands of suspect agitators and executed
many of them. It was a bloody time in the cities of Central and

South China. Hankow repudiated Chiang and he was voted out of the Kuomintang. The new government was promptly set up in Nanking, and the two cities carried on a verbal warfare while the Northern Expedition remained in abeyance, waiting for the dispute to cease. Peking's troops were stationed ominously near Nanking, at Pukow.

For a few months in 1927 [writes Vincent Sheean in *Personal History*], a little more than half of the year, Hankow concentrated, symbolized and upheld the hope for a revolution of the world. Delegations came there from all over Europe, Asia and America to see for themselves what constituted Hankow's success, the surprise and delight of a generation of thwarted Communists. . . . French Communists, German Communists, Hindoo Communists, British I.L.P. people, and numerous agitators responsible to the Komintern gave the place a fine mixed flavour of international revolt. The fact that many of these revolutionists preferred not to appear in public, and liked to conceal their comings and goings as much as possible, made the phenomenon more significant. . . . The numerous foreign revolutionists were only the froth of the brew, but they caught the eye. Other immediately visible phenomena: frequent strikes, mass meetings and demonstrations; the workmen's place (the New World, it was called, a centre in the Russian and Italian style), and the conduct of students or trades unionists, gave the illusion of a highly organized social-revolutionary movement that might, at any moment, seize the machinery of production and proclaim the dictatorship of the proletariat.
But it didn't happen.

As Sheean points out, Borodin could not declare a Soviet because of the strong influence of the British and American interests in Hankow and on the river, quite aside from the fact that most of the Chinese had not as yet been educated in Communist ideas to the necessary pitch. The Hankow government also had trouble with civil wars; Canton seceded under the leadership of Li Chi-sen, and Hunan and Szechwan became restive. Chiang could have dealt with these matters, but Chiang was no longer with them. He was on the other side, suing as was Hankow for the favor of Feng Yu-hsiang.

Feng was encamped in Honan, having scattered the army of his old opponent Chang Tso-lin; he and his troops lay between Hankow and Peking, in a most strategic position. Although he played both sides for a long time, it became fairly evident toward the middle of the year that he was casting in his lot with Nanking.

Then many of the Chinese in Hankow were shaken from their adherence to the Left wing by the evidence that Borodin and his associates had the intention of setting up the Soviet. Many of these people had not realized that they had committed themselves to such an extreme program, and even members of the Kuomintang were horrified at the idea of communizing all private property in China, including their own. The Hankow government was very shaky indeed. Feng's decision was a death blow to their hopes, at least for that time. At last on July fifth the blow fell, though without warfare or bloodshed of any sort; the Communists and the Kuomintang were divorced. Borodin and the other Russians went back to Moscow by way of Mongolia. The chief among those Chinese who had remained loyal to the Left-wing program went shortly afterwards. Chingling returned to Shanghai, where she remained in Rue Molière for a time. Her farewell message was printed in the *People's Tribune,* Hankow, July fourteenth, and was responsible for the suppression of that paper. It began:

We have reached a point where definition is necessary and where some members of the party executive are so defining the principles and policies of Dr Sun Yat-sen that they seem to me to do violence to Dr Sun's ideas and ideals. Feeling thus, I must disassociate myself from active participation in carrying out the new policies of the party. In the last analysis, all revolutions must be social revolutions, based upon fundamental changes in society; otherwise it is not a revolution, but merely a change of government. . . .

She went on to state her belief that Dr Sun's third principle, "the livelihood of the people," was in danger of being forgotten. The working classes, she said, and the peasants

become the basis of our strength in our struggle to overthrow imperialism, cancel the unequal treaties that enslave us, and effectively unify the country. These are the new pillars for the building up of a free China. Without their support the Kuomintang, as a revolutionary party, becomes weak and chaotic and illogical in its social platform; without their support, political issues are vague. If we adopt any policy that weakens these supports, we shake the very foundation of our party, betray the masses and are falsely loyal to our leader. . . . We must not betray the people. We have built up in them a great hope. They have placed in us a great faith.

Madame Sun did not stay in Shanghai. Her friends in Hankow were all going, by various roads, to Moscow. Those of her sympathizers who were in touch with her urged her to consider that it was dangerous to remain in the treaty port; if not dangerous bodily, her relationship with T.V. and Dr Kung might still be used as an argument by the Nanking faction that her sympathies were divided, and that she might yet come over to their side.

It was decided that she too go to Russia, to visit Moscow. Her sympathies were with the Hankow government, which she felt was the legitimate interpreter of Sun's ideology. She left the city secretly and with her American friend, Rayna Prohme, who had worked for Borodin in Hankow, she went to Vladivostok and from there to Moscow.

Eling was living in Shanghai, as were T.V. and Mayling. Even though it now seemed that Hankow should become reconciled with Nanking and the two governments combine, the Soongs had separated.

So began the situation which, added to the political positions of their three husbands, has made the three Soong sisters famous. It is piquant and it makes an excellent story, one that has not lost its fascination in twelve years. Here we have one family in which

[*133*]

the two extremes of policy, one would say, and the middle way are all represented.

Indulging in poetic license we relegate Madame Sun to the Left, Madame Chiang to the Right, because of her husband's anti-Communist activities, and Madame Kung to the Center; the Communist, the Capitalist and the—Liberal, shall we say? There is no good term for the middle way. It is a good story, and we imagine the details that must accompany the situation, the stresses and strains of such a family group. Such a divergence of opinion simply must lead to a split, one would think; we have always assumed that such a split has taken place. Any foreign resident of a treaty port a year ago would have declared that the Soong Family had divided into three camps; Madame Sun repudiated her family, and the other two sisters were supposed to have parted ways over a squabble that had to do with the Ministry of Finance. . . . But in China it seldom happens like that.

Indeed, in the whole world it seldom happens like that. Seldom do the myriad facts and influences of a human relationship arrange themselves into a form convenient for story-telling; that is the chief reason fiction must always mislead its readers. When you put everything in, the story becomes too complicated. It is easier for us to imagine a dramatic family quarrel, the dissolution of the group, the three paths taken thereafter by the three sisters, and so without realizing it we have made that story up, or rather followed the furrows already plowed by our trained imaginations. We have gone wrong, and it is not entirely our fault. Not understanding it, we have failed to make allowances for the family system in China.

The word "instinct" has been misused so often that one is tempted to misuse it again and to say that the Chinese has a strong instinct for his family's unity. But since we are probably all born with our individual proportion of instincts, and since it has never been proved that the clan spirit is instinctive beyond certain limits —who ever heard of an instinct to make a will, for instance?—it is safer to say that most Chinese are trained from birth by precept and example to present to the world an unbroken family front.

This does not mean that family members do not quarrel, but it does mean that they do not allow their quarrels to go to the limit. They have not developed the carefully unsentimental attitude of the English, who do their earnestly best to ignore, if not to outrage, family ties. The Chinese pays his mother, even when he is furious with her, every courtesy and kowtows to the family head on New Year's Day; the Englishman conceals his natural affection and speaks roughly to his wife, and slangs his father, and his wife understands and is pleased thereat, and his father slangs him back, glowing with pride. Both attitudes are simply matters of convention, but they are also matters of fact.

If Chingling had been thoroughly American she might really have flounced off to Russia as she is supposed to have done, and her American family would have sat back on its shameful moneybags and never expected her to darken the door again. She did not flounce. She departed because her principles were involved in this threatened compromise, and she did not wish to appear to countenance it. The struggle in China for unity was not then and it is not now a family affair, nor could it have appeared so to her. No doubt the other members of the clan disagreed with her; even T.V., who had worked with her friends in Canton and Hankow, was now inclined to prefer Chiang to the Russians. This personal disagreement, however, could not affect the strong structure of the Soong family any more than it could affect China's destiny. To puff it up into a melodrama is false, whether it be Communist or reactionary propaganda. It is not true that Chingling cut herself off from her people, or that her people left her to suffer in poverty in Moscow. We might imagine such a situation, wherein the political ideas of a young woman would lead her family to take such drastic measures, but a representative Chinese would stare in amazement at such a suggestion. Yes, there are ancient plays in China where the righteous Princess kills herself because her husband is a traitor to the Emperor, but such things do not happen now. The Princess of today publicly may disapprove of her husband's actions, but he is still her husband—in private life.

This extremely humanitarian philosophy of the Chinese is partly responsible, no doubt, for the difficulties encountered in China by sociological agitators of all kinds. A Trotzkyite once told me in despair that he had never dealt with such people in his life, and was convinced he could do nothing with them. "They have no capacity," he said, "for sustained indignation *en masse*. They are hopeless."

CHAPTER XIV

The Generalissimo Takes a Wife

WHEN THE twogovernments agreed to make it up, one of the compromises suggested was the resignation of Chiang as commander of the Nationalist army. Chiang promptly walked out, announcing that he was completely willing to sacrifice his post for the general good of the Party. The other two of the old guard from Canton, Hu Han-min and Wang Ching-wei, who had gone in opposite directions on the subject of Communism, also departed; Hu resigned and Wang went to Europe, while Chiang himself departed for Japan.

These departures left the combined government without a real leader, and the Northern Expedition, once started, had to be carried on. Troops from Peking began to threaten Nanking, and war lords were beginning to make trouble again. The Nationalists begged Chiang to come back.

He came, but not before he had won a victory of another sort, over Mrs Soong. For five years he had been proposing marriage to Mayling, and her consent might have been given sooner save that her mother was very much opposed to the idea of Chiang as a son-in-law. He was a soldier, to begin with, and the educated Chinese of the past generation classed soldiers very low in the social scale. He had been married, too, and though the marriage was a family-arranged affair that took place when he was a boy of fifteen and he was supposed to have been divorced, Mrs Soong was not satisfied that he was clear of this relationship, nor of others that were rumored. Most important of all, he was not a Christian. That fact in itself was enough to set Mayling's mother firmly against the Commander-in-chief.

She was intensely prejudiced against him. After his hope to marry her youngest daughter became known to her she went to immense trouble to avoid any discussion of the subject, and refused for many days to see him. This behavior was obvious enough; it was the Chinese way of saying No. Any other suitor would have recognized his fate and bowed to it, since Mayling would not have married him without her mother's consent. But Chiang Kai-shek was determined. He continued to besiege Mrs Soong without ceasing, and in the end he ran her to ground—in Japan.

She had been in the West of the island when she heard of his arrival; she fled immediately to Kamakura, all the way across Japan, at the threat that he would come to call on her and once again ask for Mayling. Chiang followed. He had hopes of success, for Mayling had at last given him reason to think she would consent. It would not be fair to Madame Chiang to say she married the Generalissimo because she thought it her duty; she has never been such a prig as that. But there is no doubt that she did look forward to helping him in his work of unifying China, and that this was one of her reasons for accepting him. Mayling would never have made a marriage in which she would not have the opportunity to do constructive work; she had refused a large number of men, and would have remained unmarried rather than enter the selfish life of the ordinary upper-class Chinese women of the time.

On this occasion, urged by Madame Kung, who was sympathetic

to Mayling, Mrs Soong did at last grant an interview to her daughter's persistent suitor. Chiang had provided himself with proof of his divorce from his childhood wife, and had settled the other complications of which the gossips had made much. There remained, however, the matter of his religion. Mrs Soong asked him if he were willing to become a Christian, and fortunately his answer pleased her. He would try, he said; he would study the Bible and do his best, but he could not promise, sight unseen, to accept Christianity. Mrs Soong began to waver in her prejudice, and after a short time the engagement was announced.

They were married on December first, 1927, with two ceremonies, the Christian and the orthodox Chinese. The first and Christian wedding took place in the Soong home, on Seymour Road; it was very quiet. Dr David Yui, secretary of the Y.M.C.A., officiated. Afterward the party went to the splendid Majestic Hotel, which in those days was at the height of its glory and is still remembered affectionately by Shanghai residents. There, guests awaited the couple—everybody of importance who was within traveling distance of Shanghai had come to see this union between the Soong family and China's foremost strong man.

From the *Shanghai Times* of December second:

It was a brilliant affair and the outstanding Chinese marriage ceremony of recent years. It unites on the one hand the former all-powerful leader of the Nanking armies, and on the other the family of Dr T. V. Soong, brother of the bride, in addition to the family of the late Dr Sun, founder of the Kuomintang.

Fully 1,300 persons were present in the ballroom of the Majestic Hotel yesterday afternoon when the ceremony took place. All chairs at tables were filled and scores were standing when Generalissimo Chiang Kai-shek made his appearance with his "best man." Hand-clapping greeted the appearance of the former military leader.

Gathered there were prominent foreigners and Chinese of Shanghai and many parts of China. The Senior Consul, Mr Edwin S. Chunningham; Sir Sidney Barton, HMS Consul-General; Mr N. Aall, Norwegian Consul-General; Mr S. Yada, Japanese Consul-General; M. Naggiar,

French Consul-General, and Consul-Generals of various other nations were present. Admiral Mark L. Bristol, Commander-in-Chief of the American Pacific Fleet; Major-General John Duncan, Commander of the North-China Command, and other high foreign service officers were present in civilian clothes.

At the entrance to the Majestic Hotel Ballroom stood Mr. T. W. Kwok, secretary to the Commissioner of Foreign Affairs, serving as head of the reception committee; invitations were shown to Mr Kwok, after which guests were ushered in to the ballroom.

Upon entering the ballroom, gaily decorated for the occasion, one was immediately struck with the imposing array of flowers, arranged by the Lewis Nurseries. On the platform, if such it may be called, was a large and lifelike portrait of the founder of the Kuomintang, Dr Sun Yat-sen. On one side of the portrait was the flag of the Kuomintang and on the other the flag of Dr Sun.

On the orchestra platform a Russian orchestra impatiently tuned instruments and awaited orders for the playing of the Mendelssohn wedding march. At 4:15 neither the bride nor the bridegroom had put in an appearance. Outside the ballroom, a crowd of approximately 1,000 Chinese had gathered and were standing by quietly hoping to glimpse the former Generalissimo and his bride.

Inside the hotel and surrounding the premises were scores of foreign and Chinese detectives, carefully guarding the premises and on the alert to prevent any disturbances. At the door of the ballroom it was necessary to show invitations and to sign a register before being admitted. After signing the register the signer was presented with a small pin bearing the name of the Generalissimo and Miss Soong. Signers of the register were also presented with a programme printed in Chinese.

The Programme divided the ceremony into ten parts, as follows:

1. The arrival of the guests
2. The arrival of those officiating and of the witnesses
3. The arrival of the bridegroom
4. The arrival of the bride
5. Three bows to the portrait of Dr Sun Yat-sen
6. Reading of the marriage certificate
7. Affixing the official seal to the certificate

8. Bride and bridegroom face each other and bow once
9. Bride and bridegroom thank those officiating and the witnesses by bowing to them
10. Bride and bridegroom bow to guests and thank them by bowing once.

. . . The civil ceremony at the Majestic was performed by Dr Tsai Yuan-pei, ex-President of the Peking National University, and at present Minister of Education of the Nanking Government.

Before the ceremony began the foreign orchestra played foreign music. There was an expectant hush, a craning of necks, and Chiang Kai-shek, accompanied by the best man, entered the ballroom and the cameras began to grind.

Another hush, another craning of necks and mounting of chairs by those in the road, and to the time-honored music of "Here Comes the Bride," Miss Soong entered on the arm of her brother, Dr T. V. Soong, former Minister of Finance. The cinema cameras by now were grinding furiously.

Miss Soong carried a huge bouquet of white and pink roses. Both she and the bridegroom posed for the cameraman before the ceremony. Then came three bows to the portrait of Dr Sun Yat-sen, which occupied a central position on the platform. On the right of his portrait was the flag of Dr Sun and on the left the flag of the Kuomintang. The portrait was in the center and the bows were first to the right, then to the left and then directly in the center.

A calm Chinese voice was then heard reading the certificate of marriage, following which the official seal was affixed to the certificate. The bride and bridegroom then faced each other and bowed once. Then came the thanks to the "witnesses" which were made with one bow. A final bow was made to the guests.

The orchestra was playing and hand-clapping was heard as the new Mrs Chiang walked from the platform with her husband and the two posed under a huge bell of roses while pictures were taken.

Contrary to the Christian custom, the bride was not embraced or kissed by the bridegroom, minister or others. The ceremony itself was brief and simple. The bride was given away by her brother, T. V. Soong. The best man was Liu Chi-wen, Chief Secretary to Chiang.

A feature of the wedding was the singing of "O Promise Me," by

Mr E. L. Hall. Following the ceremony tea was served in the ballroom and the Venetian Room.

The *China Press*:

The main ballroom and sides had been hung with wedding-bells of white massed flowers, and the aisle leading from the east side, down which the wedding party proceeded, was also lined with flowers. . . . The altar . . . was composed of a Chinese table fronting an alcove made of green and white foliage, on either side of which were gigantic white shields of massed flowers, the character for long life and happiness worked out in red geranium on them, and the back of which was a photograph of Sun Yat-sen below crossed the flags of the Party and Government—the red, white and blue, and the blue and white. . . . The couple left tonight by special train for Hangchow.

The *North-China Herald*:

The bride looked very charming in a beautiful gown of silver and white georgette, draped slightly at one side and caught with a spray of orange blossom. She wore also a little wreath of orange buds over her veil of beautiful rare lace made long and flowing to form a second train to that of white charmeuse embroidered in silver which fell from her shoulders. She wore silver shoes and stockings and carried a bouquet of palest pink carnations and fern fronds tied with white and silver ribbons.

She was followed by four bridesmaids, Miss Pearl Kwok, Miss Yoeh E. Wang, Miss Pauline (Rosamunde) Kung and Miss Jessie Nyi, the two former wearing peach charmeuse beaded with diamante and peach coloured beads, and with sleeves of the charmeuse to the elbow, where they blossomed into bells of georgette, also of peach shade. The two smaller bridesmaids wore dresses of the same but trimmed with frills of georgette at the neck and having sleeves of frills. After the bridesmaids followed little flower girls, the Misses Chow and Chan, dressed in ribbed peach taffeta and carrying little baskets laden with flower petals, and the train was ended by two small pages, Miss Jeannette Kung and Master Louis Kung in black velvet suits with white satin vests.

The bride's mother wore wine-colored chiffon velvet and black shoes and stockings.

. . . The bride and bridegroom returned by their crimson path to two chairs under a huge bell of flowers from which hung ribbons which when pulled swung the bell, which released a shower of rose petals on the pair beneath. After many photographs had been taken, the bride retired with the bridesmaids and tables were set ready for the bridal party to take tea under the bell of flowers. However, while this was being arranged, the bride escaped from the retiring room and neither she nor the bridegroom were seen again by the guests.

The honeymoon will be spent in Hangchow and Mokanshan, though it is not known how long Generalissimo Chiang Kai-shek and his bride will be away.

They were away, in fact, little more than a week, for the Nanking government asked Chiang to take his place again as Commander-in-chief and finish the Northern Expedition. Nobody else was able to do it, and things were in a bad way for the Nationalists. There were quarrels and threats from the ubiquitous war lords, and the Communists in Swatow were waiting.

Chiang agreed to see the war through, but he said that he wanted to resign the military post when it should have been brought to a successful close. Feng Yu-hsiang had promised to support him, as had also Yen Hsi-shan, which took care of Hunan and Shansi. The Government called a meeting of the Central Executive Committee, and Chiang was made chairman of the Central Political Council, and also of the National Military Council. On January tenth Chiang announced that he intended to suppress the Communists.

Nanking, which by 1937 had achieved the dignified beauty of one of the world's capitals, was at this time a sad mixture of ancient, crumbling glory and new raw ugliness. The Ming tombs and the famous avenues of animal statuary, the walls surrounding lotus-choked pools, a number of old houses hidden jealously away, and the purple mountains that guarded the valley were the only compensations for filthy crowded streets and low-lying huts. Factory conditions were appalling, and the local government had gone its way without attempting any reform.

The Nationalists set to work to build a permanent city of which China could be proud. To begin with and for many months they camped out, living in what buildings they could find, while the streets were prepared for the Government houses. Whole rows of houses had to be pulled down; they were clustered thickly about the highways and on the bridges. It was to this mixture of raw, scarred emptiness and yet untouched squalor, surrounded by the distant beauty of the Nanking mountains, that Chiang brought his bride. They were to make their home here until he began again to lead the army North.

Mayling had traveled much in China, but her experience was limited to the cities of Tientsin, Peking and Canton. Life for her until her marriage, in her own words, had been "easy and comfortable." Nanking was a change for her, a change that most of the women of her class were unwilling to undergo; none of the other wives of the Nanking officials came up to live there, preferring to remain in Shanghai, where their husbands could visit them occasionally. This state of affairs continued for several years. There was no social life of the usual sort, but the Generalissimo was of course very much entertained by his colleagues, attending dinners and receptions constantly. He insisted that Mayling accompany him and act as hostess at his own dinners; she was the only woman present at these parties, and at first she felt very uncomfortable.

"I think the officials themselves were also very conscious of me as a woman," she said, "but later on I forgot about myself in my interest in helping my husband in his work, and they also began to regard me not as a woman but as one of themselves.

"Nanking was then nothing but a little village with one so-called broad street from the station to the Bridge House (a hotel near the Bund). Even then the street was so narrow that if two motor cars were coming in opposite directions one of them had to back off on a side street until the other passed. The houses were all very primitive, cold and uncomfortable. The exceptions were those on the missionary compounds."

Anybody who knows Nanking can testify that of all places in China, it probably touches the two extremes of discomfort in climate, in midwinter and midsummer. Mayling left the ultramodern steamheated houses of Shanghai in January and settled down in one of the icy barns of China's interior. It was a poor substitute for a honeymoon. Yet there were compensations. Nanking had a spirit of joyous endeavor and hope that even Canton had not possessed during the period of Sun's Presidency, for it was obvious to everyone that there was at last a chance of bringing some order out of the sixteen-year chaos that followed the Revolution. She threw herself into the work of construction, and soon found several outlets for her energy.

It was at this time that she started the Schools for the Children of the Revolution. Many of the revolutionists had died in battle, and others had lived on to make more sacrifices; the children of these people were left without anyone to overlook their education. "These children, I thought," said Madame Chiang, "would be the most valuable material if they were molded right, as they all had revolutionary blood in their veins." It was a natural woman's adaptation of the program Chiang had taken and developed from the Soviet, that of political education. Mayling had here an opportunity to put into practice some of the theories of teaching that she had unconsciously developed. "What I have learned," she says, "about the training of students has come mostly through observation of how students should not be taught. In other words, I saw that there were certain discrepancies in our system of education and the life around us. For example, book knowledge alone was emphasized and no attempt was made to point out the necessity of assimilating learning with practical living or to prepare the students for their future by teaching them how to live as citizens of a community.

"In the Schools for the Children of the Revolution, my children were taught to use their hands and their bodies and to reason out

[*145*]

why such and such a thing should be done in a certain way. In so far as possible, I tried to get away from the idea of regimentation by emphasis upon the necessity of developing initiative in co-operation with observance of school discipline in self-discipline. Also, I organized rural service clubs in the Schools so that the students could help the farmers in the community, and, at the same time, put into practice the theory of learning by doing.

"I do not claim to be a born teacher or even that I am a good teacher now. I am still experimenting with educational ideas. Each training class that I have had since the war I have learned a little more myself and the subsequent class benefits from the experiences I have had with the previous classes."

The Officers' Moral Endeavor Association (it does not take nearly so long to say this in Chinese) had already come into existence, though in a slightly different form, during the early days of the Nationalist Government in Canton, while Chiang was still President of the Whampoa Military Academy. In those days it had been known as the Whampoa Officers' Moral, etc., and had been merely another club in the Academy, formed for the purpose of morale and extra-curricular political education. Now, in Nanking, Mayling noticed that the young officers had rather a dreary time of it. They had no homes and no companionship, with few chances for relaxation after work. Nanking could not offer the usual wartime distractions to her warriors; no cabarets lit up those dreary streets, and there had been no time in which to organize private clubs. The lazy, dissolute officer of pre-Canton days had disappeared; Chiang's iron regime had produced lean, self-denying, serious youngsters who made excellent soldiers but had no talent for leisure.

Many of the Generalissimo's former students from Whampoa would come to visit him, and Mayling talked to them. She heard the same complaint from all of them—there was nothing to do in Nanking while they waited for their orders for the front. Here was another job she could do. Out of these talks the Chiangs developed the new Officers' Moral Endeavor Association, or, as most people inevitably call it in English, the O.M.E.A. J. L. Huang, an experienced Y.M.C.A. worker, was persuaded to come up from Shanghai and to see what he could do to build up the organization.

"It was just a little low shack at first, in the middle of a lot of other shacks," he said. "Near by was the Y.M.C.A. building, a fine new house. I admit it was a temptation to stay with the 'Y' when I contrasted those two buildings, but after I had looked around and asked a few questions I realized that this might be a big thing, and it could do more good for the army than the Y.M.C.A. in a different way, because it was something that had been planned especially for the officers. We could influence the men directly with an organization like that. So I agreed to take it on. The first few months were exciting. A lot of the cadets were prejudiced against us, feeling that the O.M.E.A. was a new method of foreign propaganda and a hidden way of forcing them to become Christians even if they didn't want to. They used to throw things at me when I was out walking in the street, and sometimes they talked of burning down the building. But little by little they began to like coming up and using the place. Now all the officers belong."

Today the O.M.E.A. is responsible for most of the musical entertainment in the army, and its art department is an important center in Chungking, supplying posters for propaganda, paintings in general, backdrops and scenery for plays and decorations for public buildings. It all dates back to those first days of feverish energy on Mayling's part.

There were three months of preparation for the resumption of the expedition, and during that time Mayling and her husband worked hard but quietly, taking walks in the country and reading and discussing the Bible—for he kept his promise to his mother-in-law and studied Christianity with all the concentration of which he is capable.

The war proper began again in April. From that time on, Mayling went with the Generalissimo on all his campaigns, living wherever they could find quarters, in thatched huts and railroad stations and farmhouses. It was an initiation for her into the true living conditions of China; some of these places were a greater departure from the houses of Nanking, chilly and comfortless as they were, than Nanking had been from Shanghai.

Wherever she went, whatever she saw strengthened her desire to clean it all up. The energy with which she insists today upon scrubbing the floors and tables, washing the linen, cleaning the windows of any place where she is in charge represents more than a personal foible. For Madame Chiang, that cleanliness where age-old dirt reigned before her coming is a symbol of all that must be done for China. Her spirit, inherited from the redoubtable Charles Soong and encouraged by her American training, was never cast down by the magnitude of the task she set herself. The more she saw of her country the more energetic she became. It is no delicate and feminine gesture when she takes curtains and flower bowls with her to the front and decorates the house in which she is to live with the Generalissimo, no matter how poor a hut it may be. It is an outward sign of her defiance, the war she is continually fighting against sloth and *laissez-faire*.

CHAPTER XV
Victory for Chiang

IT TOOK less than a month for the Generalissimo's troops to get as far as Tsinan, the capital of Shantung. The Old Marshal's army had not resisted for long; Chiang, with Feng and Yen to help him, seemed in a fair way to get to Peking without too much trouble. The Japanese, however, did not relish the success of the Southerners, for they were in possession of Tsingtao and wanted to retain control of Shantung. Therefore they sent men up to Tsinan and barred the way of the Chinese along the railroad. There was an outbreak of fighting on May third.

Chiang had no desire to be interrupted again in his Northern Expedition, or to be tricked into a war with Japan before he had unified his own country. He therefore tried to quiet down the trouble, and negotiated with the Japanese General, agreeing to suppress anti-Japanese propaganda and to move his men seven miles away from Tsinan—for the Japanese had excused their actions on the grounds that their people in Shantung needed "protection."

The Generalissimo insisted, however, upon a right of way along the railroad in order that his army would have a clear path to Peking.

The Japanese would not agree to this compromise, and on May eighth there was a battle between the forces, in which the Chinese were driven out of Tsinan and seven miles away. Feeling in China ran high, and there was more evidence of what the Japanese called "anti-Japanese propaganda." Evidently aggrieved and astonished by this reaction, the Nipponese warned both Nanking and Peking not to make any more trouble, or they would begin to "maintain order" in Manchuria; to begin with, they suggested that the Old Marshal retire then to his own domain, north of the Great Wall.

Chang Tso-lin agreed to this with unbecoming alacrity, and began moving out of Peking with his troops. On June third, as his train approached Mukden, it was blown up by a bomb, and he was killed. This left his son, the Young Marshal, Chang Hsueh-liang, in charge of the Manchurian troops, and he continued to move them north. Yen Hsi-shan's army took possession of Peking on behalf of Chiang, who was still on the other side of Tsinan, held up by the Japanese: the Northern Expedition had at last arrived at its destination. Chiang Kai-shek came to Peking on the third of July.

He had promised to resign as Generalissimo as soon as the expedition should be at an end, and now he did so, but the Central Executive Committee refused to accept his resignation. Chiang was named chairman of the Committee, the highest post in the Government, at the next session in August. On the "Double Tenth" —October tenth, the anniversary of the Republic—Chang Hsueh-liang announced that he was willing to stand by Nanking, and was appointed to the State Council. Manchuria had joined forces with China. The powers recognized the Nanking government before the end of 1928; China was evidently unified at last. It was even more of a triumph than Sun's had appeared to be in 1911, at the close of the Ch'ing Dynasty.

The Generalissimo had become famous in an incredibly short time. In America and Europe he was discussed everywhere; the conservatives called him China's Strong Man, and the others considered him a dictator. As Madame Chiang said somewhat bitterly, in later years, "If a man changes with every wind he is called weak and spineless. If he is firm, he is called a dictator."

He had need of all his firmness, for he was now faced with a bewildering number of problems compared to which the Northern Expedition had been simple and easy. Victory, as he was to find out, is often more arduous than the contributory struggle. With Mayling at his side, acting as his secretary and interpreter, he had to deal with the generals who had aided him in his campaign; many of them, chiefly Feng and Yen, were demanding the rich rewards which the traditional spoils system led them to expect. There was also the matter of the army; now that the war was over, the obvious thing to do was to disband a large part of it and relieve the nation of the expense of keeping all these men. But this program, though it sounds simple, was almost impossible to carry out. China had been torn by civil wars for many years. Each leader had built up his army, which he had later contributed, still under his own leadership, to the general cause of Chiang Kai-shek, in the hopes of having his reward after victory. Now from the point of view of the leader the Generalissimo was trying to double-cross him. Not only was he trying to hog all the power, but he wanted each general to give up his personal army, the only weapon he had with which to maintain his threatened rights! The country seethed with suspicion, and months went by while the soldiers in their millions continued to be kept and idle, eating and sleeping and waiting for the civil war that Chiang was trying to avert. The quarrel reached such proportions that Chiang resigned, but everyone became frightened at this and urged him to come back. In the end the generals reached a temporary compromise.

The same problem arose in regard to political control. Chiang wanted to centralize the government, now that China was unified, and he tried to do away with the outlying "representatives" of the central body, who because of the nature of China, geographically and psychologically, too often were rather free in their interpretation of central governmental orders. Immediately, as was natural, the leaders of these outlying centers accused him of arbitrary methods. He was, they said, betraying the original idea of the Republic. He was trying to become a dictator. The first openly to revolt were Pai Chung-hsi and Li Tsung-jen in Kwangsi, two generals who had greatly helped Chiang when he first moved against the North. There was a quarrel about their manner of managing Kwangsi, particularly over the governor of Hunan, who was loyal to Nanking and who had because of this been discharged from his post by Li and Pai.

The Generalissimo started a punitive expedition against the Kwangsi leaders, sailing up the Yangtze toward Hankow. In a short time he had routed the troops from that city. The commanders quickly capitulated to Chiang, and Pai ran away. The clique attempted more resistance, first in Canton and then in Kwangsi itself, but the Generalissimo followed them and at last the province was quiet.

Immediately thereafter, Feng Yu-hsiang, who had in all probability been helping the Kwangsi leaders secretly, came out into the open and rebelled. The Government announced his expulsion from the Party and demanded his arrest, but Yen Hsi-shan was on his side, and Feng, though he was defeated because many of his people went over to Nanking, was not punished.

According to one story, Madame Sun first heard of her little sister's marriage when she was in Moscow, and the news was such a shock to her that she took to her bed. As we have seen, this is not true, but the marriage, if not a shock, was still most distasteful to her, and no doubt she felt it keenly at the time. Chiang Kai-shek had been, in her opinion, directly responsible for the downfall of the Leftist government in Hankow, though Sun Yat-sen had trusted him and singled him out as a favorite, by not carrying out the Doctor's wishes and cutting himself off from Russia and the

Soviet advisers. Now this man was to be her brother-in-law. Chingling, after her visit to Moscow, had no desire to return home to see the triumph of Nanking: she journeyed to Berlin and stayed there for months.

Meantime the little sister was developing into a hard worker, and many of her duties were similar to those of Chingling's herself when she was a bride. Everybody who interviewed the Generalissimo found her with him, interpreting if need be; she and her husband discussed everything, from the foreign policy to the Bible, and she began to teach him English. A girl who had known her before her marriage said that in those earlier days she had always had the impression that Mayling's life in Shanghai, the ordinary social routine of a girl of her class, did not satisfy her. She had her other interests, the clubs and the Child Welfare Association, but all of that was extra-curricular; it did not fulfill her need for action. Her superabundant energy and intelligence made her seem impatient and unconventional at times: during the interminable sessions of mah-jongg, for example, with which many of the Shanghai women kill great quantities of time, Mayling after a few hours of it would stand up and take her leave abruptly, though custom decreed that a player must not go away until she had gauged the exactly polite moment for departure according to the score, or until the entire party broke up. It was as if she was overcome, all of a sudden, with a sense of the futility of what she was doing.

Now there was no more boredom and no sense of futility. She had not yet begun to take an active part in the work of administration, but she was very busy as her husband's helpmeet. Then too the house was often overrun with Eling's children. Dr Kung was Minister of Industry, Labor and Commerce, and kept two houses, one in Nanking and one in Shanghai, in which city he had to spend a good deal of his time. The children attended school in Shanghai, but there was a good deal of visiting back and forth, and their aunt was very fond of them. Although Eling was concentrating all her efforts upon raising them in the way they should go, the children's characters were developing at an alarming rate, and sometimes both mother and aunt found themselves baffled by the diversity of problems that were offered by these young personalities. One afternoon in Nanking when the Generalissimo was holding an important meeting with some of his staff, a furious row broke out from the sun porch above his study. He hurried upstairs to find Jeannette and Louis squabbling loudly; Louis, alleged Jeannette, had struck her, and she wanted revenge. She talked about it so much and so indignantly that her uncle reprimanded her, saying that it could not have been so bad, after all, since she was the elder and bigger. He then turned to go out, satisfied that he had settled the matter: at the door he happened to glance back over his shoulder, and saw Louis in the act of striking Jeannette again for being a tattle-tale, while Jeannette, too frightened to complain again, meekly accepted her fate.

Madame Kung at the beginning of her children's lives made a resolution not to be so strict with them as her mother had been with herself and her brothers and sisters. She had not forgotten the Spartan regime that had governed the little Soongs. *Her* children should be strong and self-reliant without suffering quite so much during their tender years. In one respect she failed to invest Louis, at least, with complete courage, but she hopes that this early influence will be forgotten. It happens that Madame Kung is one of those people who fear dogs. She is afraid of cats, too; in fact, she is afraid of "anything furry," and the family pets were kept out of her way. One day when Louis was a baby she left him alone on the veranda for a moment, and was indoors when she heard him shriek with terror. She rushed out and found a large dog poking its nose inquisitively into his pen. Mother love triumphed over her fear, and she seized her child and confronted the dog until he trotted off the veranda. It was, she thinks, the bravest deed of her life. She was quite willing to face the Japanese in 1937; their army had no terrors for her, but she has never forgotten that dog. It is to be hoped that Louis has, but a later development makes this doubtful.

One afternoon Madame Kung was taking him to see his grandmother, and in preparation for the visit, as was her usual custom, she telephoned before starting out and told her mother's servant to tie up the big watchdog, Carrie, before they should arrive. Louis scorned her for her cowardice.

"Let Carrie alone," he protested. "There's nothing to be afraid of in a dog. I'm not afraid of the dog, and she's bigger than I am. You're bigger than she is; why should you be afraid?"

Shamed by this logic, Madame Kung revoked the order, and when they arrived at the Soongs' house Carrie came to meet them. Louis promptly shrank back behind his mother's skirts.

"Why, Louis," she said, "I thought you weren't afraid of dogs. Why don't you go and pet her?"

"It's not Carrie I'm afraid of," said Louis; "I'm not afraid of anything about Carrie except only just her mouth."

It was Louis, too, who boasted to David one day that he knew a lot of English. "I can say anything in English," he said proudly. "I know it all. Ask me something."

"All right," said David. "Louis, how would you like to be a bachelor all your life?"

The word "bachelor" stumped Louis. He hesitated, then decided on a safe course. "Not very much," he faltered.

On the day Jeannette was to go to kindergarten for the first time she objected strenuously and kicked the servant who carried her out of the house. She was still upset and frightened when she arrived at McTeiyre, though Rosamonde was there. The teacher asked her name.

"Mei-mei [Little Sister]," she replied.

"That's what they call you at home," said the teacher, "but you have another name, haven't you?"

Jeannette hesitated, then remembered a name she had heard somewhere: "Ling-yi," she suggested.

"That's *my* name," cried Rosamonde. "Yours is 'Ling-wei'." (There are ten characters in the Kung family, one to be used for each generation in the names of all the children until the last has been used up, when it begins over again. The Empress Dowager bestowed this right upon the Kungs in honor of Confucius. Dr Kung's generation were all "Hsiang," and his children are all "Ling.")

It was too much for Jeannette, who burst into tears. "Can't I even borrow a name?" she sobbed.

The young Kungs, as it turned out, needed a certain amount of discipline, and Eling found herself developing a strong if belated sympathy for her mother's methods. One of the family rules that had to be brought into existence, for example, dealt with the matter of after-dinner fruit. The dish was piled high with apples, pears, oranges or whatever was in season, and passed around the table; to avoid a general grab for the best piece, Madame Kung decreed that each child should take the fruit that happened to be on top, no matter how big or small it might be. One day the top fruit was a pear with a bad spot on it; the dish was placed first before David.

"I don't think I'll have any fruit today, thanks," said that young man indifferently.

The dish passed on to Rosamonde, who obeyed the family rule and took the spotted pear without a word of complaint. The fruit dish traveled farther, made the rounds, and was placed again in the center of the table with a nice unspotted pear reposing on top. . . . David glanced at it and said, "I think I'll have some fruit, after all." Calmly he reached out, appropriated the pear, and began peeling it. The other children clamored shrilly; unfair, unfair, David had cheated!

David lifted his eyebrows as he peeled his pear. "Fruit politics," he explained.

☆   ☆   ☆

Nanking was growing. Among the many foreign advisers whom Chiang Kai-shek had invited to the capital, military and financial and aeronautical, was the American architect Henry Killam Murphy, who designed the government buildings. These were planned as a blend of modern comfort and the ancient spirit of Peking; one traveled along straight wide streets between the tiled roofs of noble buildings, and out of the city toward the carefully restored Ming tombs. Most elaborate of all was the mausoleum built on the Purple Mountain for the body of Sun Yat-sen, which was removed from its temporary grave in the Western Hills near Peking and brought down to Nanking for an impressive ceremony and burial. The Purple Mountain's side, covered with pine trees and flowering gardens, looked down on Nanking in the valley; a long triple flight of glittering white steps led up to the crypt.

It happened that this same year Sun's old friends the Russians fell out with the Young Marshal's government in Harbin over the Chinese Eastern Railway. The Manchurians had seized the management of the line, which had always been administered by Russians, in June; Russia immediately issued an ultimatum. If the offices were not returned to Russian control in three days, she would start to make war. Chang Hsueh-liang, who had pledged his allegiance to Chiang Kai-shek, turned the matter over to the Nanking government, to Foreign Minister C. T. Wang. Nanking through Wang stood by the Young Marshal, and Russia moved on Manchuria.

Chiang offered to help Chang and his generals, but they were suspicious of his motives and preferred to carry on their own fight —to their cost, because the Russians were winning all along the line. There was possible danger, also, from the Japanese, who had spoken before of their desire to "maintain order" in Manchuria. C. T. Wang was appealing to the League of Nations, but this procedure got no more quick action than usual, and the Young Marshal could not afford to wait. On the advice of Wellington Koo, he agreed to the proposals made by the Russians at the beginning of the quarrel, and restored control of the railway to the original arrangement.

In the meantime Madame Sun had come back to China, to attend the services for her husband when his remains were transferred to the crypt at Nanking. She had announced in Berlin, on May Sixth, "I am proceeding to China for the purpose of attending to the removal of the remains of Dr Sun Yat-sen to the Purple Mountain where he desired to be buried.

"In order to avoid any possible misunderstanding, I have to state that I emphatically adhere to my declaration made in Hankow on July fourteenth, 1937, in which I announced my withdrawal from active participation in the work of the Kuomintang, on account of counter-revolutionary policy and activities of the Central Executive Committee. . . .

"It must therefore be abundantly clear that my attendance at the burial will not mean and is not to be interpreted as in any sense implying a modification or reversal of my decision to abstain from any direct or indirect work of the Kuomintang so long as its leadership is opposed to the fundamental policies of Dr Sun; namely, the policy of effective anti-imperialism, the policies of co-operation with Soviet Russia and the Workers and Peasant policy. . . ."

When she arrived in Harbin she made several statements to the same effect. There was to be no misunderstanding whatever as to Chingling's attitude toward her brother-in-law's government. . . . Yet she remained on the best of terms with Mayling.

Randall Gould, in "Madame Sun Keeps Faith," an article in the *Nation*, January twenty-second, 1930, wrote:

Upon her arrival in Peiping to start the long funeral journey from the Western Hills to the new mausoleum just outside the city walls of Nanking, Madame Sun made it abundantly clear that she had no intention of lending her name and reputation to the government or party. Keeping herself apart even from members of her family, she went through with the long and trying ceremonials, saw the casket safely deposited in its million-dollar resting place, and returned to her house in the Rue Molière in Shanghai. For some time she maintained silence. Then, on August 1, she fired a shot which would have echoed throughout the country had not suppression intervened.

It was a telegram to the Anti-Imperialist League in Berlin on an International Anti-War Day. An excerpt:

While the oppressed nationalities today form a solid front against imperialist war and militarism, the reactionary Nanking Government is combining forces with the Imperialists in brutal repressions against the Chinese masses. Never has the treacherous character of the counter-revolutionary Kuomintang leaders been so shamelessly exposed to the world as today. Having betrayed the Nationalist revolution, they have inevitably degenerated into imperialist tools and attempted to provoke war with Russia. But the Chinese masses, undaunted by repression and undeceived by lying propaganda, will fight only on the side of revolution. . . .

This message was at first ignored in China. At last one British paper in Shanghai printed a distorted translation from the Japanese, though the editor ignored a proper version when it was sent to him in correction. The Chinese press simply avoided all mention of it, though Government officials heard of it and were furious. One man who tried to distribute leaflets containing a Chinese version was arrested in Shanghai, but somebody threw handbills with the same message from the roof of the Sincere Company in Nanking Road, in the heart of the city.

Madame Sun's house was kept under observation, and the sound of her typewriter gave rise to rumors that she was sending secret messages by wireless to Moscow. Her own comment was:

"I feel good inside since I sent that telegram. It was necessary to express myself. What happens to me personally as a result is not important."

Nothing happened to her, however, as a result of this message. She stayed on in Rue Molière, though there were many reports of her departure—for Moscow, for Berlin, for many places. Rumor ran wild about Madame Sun, but she stayed where she was, in quiet seclusion.

CHAPTER XVI

Rebels and Reds

In October, on the 1929 "Double Tenth" anniversary, a number of generals in the Northwest, members of the People's Army, rebelled against Nanking by denouncing the Government and the Generalissimo. This development was the outcome of Feng Yu-hsiang's plotting. At the same time there was trouble in Hupeh, fomented by General Hu. Chiang drove back the People's Army from Loyang, Honan, but two generals who had been Feng's men before rebelled and looted Pukow, across the river from Nanking, while he was busy at this. He attempted to bring Yen Hsi-shan over to his side without signal success, though Yen did not quite come into the open and refuse. However, when Chiang tried to follow the two generals who had looted Pukow, sending troops after them along the Tientsin-Pukow railway in February, 1930, Yen objected and begged the Generalissimo to give up his command. This meant that the Shansi governor had declared for Feng.

Chiang nevertheless prepared for a real campaign against Feng, and Yen then joined forces openly with the Christian General. Chiang called on the Young Marshal for aid, but the Manchurian leader hesitated for a time. The rebellion had become the most serious war since the beginning of the Nationalist government: Chang Hsueh-liang hesitated to bring his troops south of the Great Wall and involve himself in such a melée. One of the reasons for Feng's and Yen's confidence in their prospects was Wang Ching-wei, who had become their ally. Wang since his retirement in favor of the Generalissimo had made quite a name for himself as the "true heir to Sun Yat-sen," and there was a good deal of sympathy for him, while Feng had been associated enough with the Communists (though this association was occasionally interrupted, as for instance in regard to Hankow) to play politics as a common man for the common people. As for Yen, he was deservedly one of the most popular governors in China: Shansi was famous for its prosperity. The three decided upon another Peking government with Wang at the head. They accused Chiang publicly of military dictatorship and of ignoring the rights of the democracy.

By the first of April, their troops were moving south and Chiang was in the midst of preparations to meet them on the way. There was some fighting in Shantung and in Honan. Chiang's army moved up the Lunghai railway and met Feng's troops, the People's Army, and was beaten back. Then in June another wing of the rebel troops captured Changsha in Hunan, though Chiang took it back later on. In the meantime Yen on behalf of the new government appropriated the customs revenue at Tientsin. In Peiping, the name the Nationalists had given the old city of Peking (Northern Capital), Wang Ching-wei duly instituted his government, which was of course to be the most truly democratic body yet seen in China.

Chiang's retort to this action was to open a large-scale offensive campaign. In a big battle on August fifteenth he took Tsinan, beating Yen's troops back across the Yellow River. Until this moment Nanking and Wang Ching-wei had both been trying to tempt the Young Marshal to take sides with them; now he came out for the Generalissimo, and Yen gave up the game completely. He was confronted by the enemy and another enemy waited at his rear; there was no good in going further in any direction. Chang brought his troops into North China and Wang Ching-wei moved out of Peiping with his friends to Shihchiachuang. There was no fighting near Peiping, but Chiang Kai-shek in the meantime captured Kaifeng and Chengchow in Honan. The civil war, a severe and bloody struggle, ended on October sixth. Once more China was at peace and in a unified state—until the next spot of trouble.

Only comparatively at peace, however. The Communists had begun a sort of guerilla warfare upon the breakup of the Hankow government. Those people who had been "converted" by Borodin's men, and even by Chiang Kai-shek himself while he was working under Sun Yat-sen and learning the science of propaganda from the Soviet, had not been willing to abandon all these carefully nurtured ideas when the Generalissimo went to the Right. First they had been let down, they felt, by Chiang, and then the Kuomintang itself betrayed them by disagreeing with Borodin and compromising with Nanking. A number of them fled because they were in danger; others joined in the flight as protest and from principle. The massacre of Communists in the treaty ports did nothing to convince them that they had been wrong. They traveled in the wilder provinces of China, making war on Government troops and persuading country people to join them. After a time they constituted an important force, with concentrated armies of men who were trained in their particular kind of warfare, and set up a center of government too near Nanking for that city's comfort. Chiang knew that as soon as he had settled the Feng-Yen combine he would have to deal with them.

Nevertheless, during the breathing space that followed the Young Marshal's entry into the quarrel, the Generalissimo took time off to do a very significant thing. He became a Christian. It was not quite three years since he had married Mayling, after promising her mother that he would study his Bible and do his best to understand and accept her religion. He had kept his promise faithfully. He had read the Scriptures and discussed them with his wife, he had found comfort in the Bible during his trials, he had come to depend more and more upon this new philosophy, and now he felt honestly ready to become a son of the Church. One of the reasons he gave when he was questioned by the pastor was typical; he had found, he said, that the best of his officers were Christians! Certainly a large number of the generals and officials of the Government were members of the Church. This marked a definite difference between the new Nanking and the old Canton; in the three years since the Generalissimo had introduced his bride to the capital there had been a vast change in the sentiment of the public towards Christianity. It was suffered and even approved, save by the die-hards. No longer need Colonel Huang dodge flying missiles when he walked in the street, and the O.M.E.A. and Y.M.C.A. buildings were now in no danger of being burned down.

The Chiangs came to Shanghai quietly, without any advance publicity of the event, on October twenty-third. Chiang Kai-shek was baptized in the home of Mrs Soong, by the Reverend Z. T. Kaung. Everyone in the family was present save Chingling. Madame Sun was not in Shanghai, but even had she been there it is doubtful if she would willingly have attended this ceremony. She had taken on the ideas of her husband in regard to organized religions, though as a child she had been, of course, quite as much a Christian as had the rest of her family (Lyon Sharman, in her excellent book on Sun Yat-sen, has gone deeply into the matter of his Christianity. It seems to have fluctuated with his years and his political opinions. When he first returned to China as President he was sternly in favor of Christianity, to the detriment of the older religions of his countrymen; he called most Chinese forms of worship "superstition." Some people hold that his father was a pastor in the Church, and his home environment may have bequeathed to him his earlier ideas on the subject. Later he seems to have added Christianity to his list of superstitions, though he was not definite about it, nor did he denounce it in any way. Madame Sun likewise has never made a public pronouncement as to her state of grace. Her sympathies, however, are not with the missionaries.)

Since his baptism the Generalissimo has been as regular as his duties permit in his attendance at church. He finds comfort and guidance in prayer, taking refuge in a period of quiet on his knees whenever he has an important decision to make. Every day when he rises at five-thirty he says his prayers as unfailingly as he writes in his diary, and that is a part of his daily routine that he never forgets. . . .

The anniversary of his wedding day was usually the occasion of a celebration of some kind, and in 1930 something happened which Madame Chiang still considers the most remarkable escape of their lives. They were living in Nanking, in a remodeled Chinese bungalow that Mayling had done her best to make habitable. She was not satisfied with the result, but she knew better than to expect too much comfort in those early days.

The Generalissimo, several days before the anniversary, suggested to her that they cross the river and spend a little time in the country, for a holiday. Madame Chiang consented, but as the time drew near she felt uneasy, though she did not know why.

"I really don't want to go very much," she confessed to her husband. "I promised, and I'll go if it would disappoint you to stay here, but—I don't know what it is, but I'd rather stay home."

"You're tired," said Chiang. "Of course we'll stay at home."

On the evening of the day they had planned to leave, he had reason to regret his wife's whim, for he had several long interviews to get through, and saw no signs of being free until late at night. Mayling went to bed early, but she could not sleep. It was very cold, as it can be in Nanking, and the builders had laid the floor directly on the earth beneath, so that there was always a clammy dampness in the house. She lay in bed wide awake, wondering why she felt so nervous. There was nobody near the bedroom; her *amah* had retired to her own quarters. Madame Chiang lay there in the darkness until she could not bear it any longer, then she turned on all the lights in the room, in the bathroom and in her husband's study near by. She got up and put on her dressing gown with the idea of asking Chiang to come in if only for a moment, but then she realized it would look silly and hysterical, and she contented herself with standing near the door, finding some comfort in the sound of voices from the other room.

The first interview finished; she heard the Generalissimo say good night. Then to her dismay someone else was shown in. It was a General Hsi, who had come to protest, against rumors to the contrary, that he was loyal to his leader. Madame Chiang could not face the idea of another long wait; she knocked on the door and asked her husband to come in.

"Something terrible is going to happen," she insisted. "Please, please be careful. I know that something terrible is going to happen."

"But what could happen?" he said reasonably. "Everything's perfectly peaceful. You're nervous and overtired. I'll call the *amah* to stay with you, and I'll try to get rid of this man as soon as I can."

A little pacified, Mayling refused the company of the *amah* and went to bed again, and in a little while she fell asleep. But when at midnight Chiang came to bed, she sat up in terror.

"I had a dream," she said. "I dreamed there was a big stone or a boulder [Chiang's name means "stone"] in the middle of a stream, and the moon lit up the water, and all of a sudden the water turned to blood. Rivers of blood!"

Again her husband reassured her, and they went to sleep. At three in the morning someone knocked on the windowpane to report the troops of General Hsi, who had just paid a special visit to assure Chiang of his loyalty, had mutinied and were making trouble across the river, in the region where the Chiangs had planned their holiday. At the moment their General was at the bungalow, they were changing their armbands and announcing that they were breaking loose from Nanking.

There was no more sleep for the Chiangs that night. For several hours Mayling was too busy to think, and then she remembered

[*165*]

that her sister Eling was arriving by steamer from Shanghai that day.

"She's not due until the middle of the morning," she thought with relief, "and by that time the ship's company will probably have warned the captain; he'll turn back."

At six that morning, however, Madame Kung walked into the bungalow, surprised to find everyone already up and about. Madame Chiang cried out when she saw her:

"Go away! Don't you know what's happened? You're in terrible danger!"

Nobody on the boat had heard anything about the rebellion. When Madame Kung understood the situation, however, she refused to leave. Instead she telephoned her mother in Shanghai, on the new long-distance line. It was impossible to talk plainly over the phone, for the city had not yet heard of the crisis and the Generalissimo was trying to postpone the inevitable panic as long as possible. Madame Kung therefore said:

"Mother, something very bad is happening. I can't tell you what it is, but May and I want you to pray for us."

Two hours later they had a telegram from Mrs Soong, referring them to a verse in the Bible that said, "The enemy shall retire of its own accord."

It was late in the day before they heard that Hsi's troops had thought better of their rebellion and had gone away.

It was now time for the Generalissimo to turn his attention to the godless Communists, and he began work in December. The main concentration of the Red troops was very near to Nanking. Chiang first, following time-honored procedure, called upon them to give in; he promised freedom and protection to all those who would return to his fold. To those who refused he declared his willingness to fight to the end. At the beginning of the campaign, however, he was hampered by the fighting methods of the Communists, unusual at that time but familiar now to anyone who knows their technique. It has been used since in the Sino-Japanese engagements. The Communists, by means of signs and posters and persuasion and field work among the noncombatant farmers who communicated with both sides, managed to bring many of Chiang's men over to their way of thinking.

In the cities, too, especially those large ones under the control of Nanking, there were plenty of people who remembered wistfully the visions of Sun Yat-sen when he collaborated with Borodin. It had been only five years since those hopeful days, and not everyone was convinced, as was the Generalissimo through personal experience, that their Russian friends should have been cast out so completely. Centers of this dissatisfaction were the universities; both professors and students openly discussed their criticism of the Government at Nanking, and several periodicals demanded modification of Chiang's "dictatorship." Chiang declared his intention of dealing sternly with such people, going so far as to threaten to incarcerate students who might cause riots and disturbance.

The campaign against the Communists did not go well until the Generalissimo himself led his forces into Kiangsi, where the enemy was strongest. He drove them out of the province; the Reds retreated to the South, out of Central China. At the same time trouble of a different kind was brewing in Canton.

It was a different kind of trouble, but it bore relationship to the old trouble in that Wang Ching-wei was again mixed up in it. There were also Feng Yu-hsiang, Yen Hsi-shan and Hu Han-min, all of whom had come together, bound in a common cause—to defeat Chiang. Wang's persistence inevitably reminds one of his name, or vice versa: the Ching-wei is a mythical bird that works its whole life endeavoring to fill up the ocean in order that he may walk across it. All day long, life long, it picks up pebble after pebble in its beak and drops it into the sea.

CHAPTER XVII

Eling Gets a Taste of Public Life

IN MAY 1931 the group of dissatisfied leaders in Canton interrupted the people's convention that was being held at Nanking with a telegram of denunciation. Sun Fo showed that he was in sympathy with the critics by walking out. Kwangtung announced that its differences with Kwangsi were patched up, which meant that the South was united again, and against the Government. It looked very much like another civil war; but Chiang did his best to avert it.

Before the month was out the Southerners had demanded his resignation, and when he paid no attention to their ultimatum they set up a Cantonese Central Executive Committee, and then a government of their own. Chiang still tried to avoid war. This time it would be more than a mere punitive expedition; so many of his erstwhile friends were on the other side, and the nation had been so weakened by the constant fighting of the past four years, that it would have been madness, considering China's situation from an international standpoint, to embark on a serious civil war. The ugliest part of it was that Canton was flirting with Japan.

Still, when on August fifth the Kwangsi troops actually began marching upon Nanking, there was nothing for it but to get ready to fight. It is difficult to suppose what might have been the outcome, since the strengths of the opponents were fairly equal, if Japan had not chosen that moment to move into Manchuria. The "Mukden Incident" on September eighteenth, 1931, was the first development.

That night the railway near Mukden was blown up, and the Japanese, alleging that it was done by Chinese and that it was their duty to maintain order in Manchuria, as they had stated before, hurried to send troops in. It was a most obviously trumped-up excuse; many students of the matter have since shown with plenty of proof that the original explosion was arranged to give Japan this opportunity while Chiang was busy in the South. As such things go, however, it may be even more illuminating to see what a Japanese has to say about it; Mr S. Akimoto, in his *Manchuria Scene,* writes:

Chang Tso-lin was a picturesque figure who was a mounted bandit, and he became overlord of Manchuria clearly through the sufferance, if not the actual co-operation, of Japan. As years passed, he began to forget his ties and obligations, and to act in a way inimical to Japanese interests. This was natural in a man who, when he had risen to a height, and imagined himself secure, would kick the ladder from under him. This was exactly what Chang did or was going to do. He thought he was not only the nominal but the actual ruler of all Manchuria, and could do very well without Japan, and he began to pursue a policy founded upon this illusion. He made himself Marshal, and then Great Marshal, built an enormous arsenal within a stone's throw of Japan's economic center in Mukden, and laid other plans which could only be interpreted as acts of warlike preparation against Japan, till at last his megalomania ambition was stopped by his own tragic death. That this was the work of Japanese agents was perhaps a natural enough suspicion under the circumstances.

[*169*]

Chang Hsueh-liang, instead of taking a hint from his father's death, made himself Marshal Chang the Second, and continued to pursue the same anti-Japanese policy. Some observers allege that there were foreign wire pullers behind his back, just as there were Soviet wire pullers behind the anti-British Nationalist forces in 1927. Be that as it may, Marshal Chang Hsueh-liang refused to take Japan seriously; he went on thwarting, negatizing, and persecuting Japan at every turn, till at last, it is said, there were accumulated more than 300 "unsolved problems," insults and grievances, such as debts repudiated, treaty rights broken, individual liberties violated, confiscatory levies imposed, commonest justice denied, strikes and boycotts stirred up against the Japanese, and finally, harmless citizens, including women and children, subjected to nameless acts of barbarity. In short, Chang Hsueh-liang's policy of persecution reached such a pitch that even impartial observers feared that a single spark might inflame the pent-up rage of Japan and create a fearful conflagration.

So broke out the Manchurian incident on September 18, 1931, with the comparatively puerile attack of a handful of Chinese soldiers upon the Japanese railway at a point not far from Mukden station. Once started, however, no power of diplomacy, at home or abroad, could extinguish the fire. This military action in Manchuria was approved by all the Japanese in Manchuria, and later by public opinion at home. A section of the Foreign Office looked askance at the incident at first, but so determined was the action of the military, that in less than two months the whole of Manchuria from Tsitsihar in the north to Dairen and Port Arthur in the south had actually fallen under its domination. Nothing short of military intervention by the United States or the League of Nations could have prevented it. But neither America nor the League made any such intervention, so it went on burning till it burned itself out, and till Manchuria was declared independent of China on March 1, 1932.

In brief, China's northern rulers had been grudging Japan the very modest portion of Manchuria which she had earned at so much sacrifice in money and blood, and they lost the whole of it, and what is more, with it, their "face," too. Yes, Manchuria has been lost to the rulers who exploited it for their selfish purposes, but not to the millions of Chinese inhabitants, for they will be the safer, the happier, and the more free for the change.

It is interesting to observe the Manchuria of today, in the light of this last statement. . . .

The Japanese were in control of Mukden in September and there was every likelihood of their spreading their influence further. It was the first definite move made by another nation to break up the newly "unified" China, and in the face of this threat China's civil wars faded in importance. Even those shortsighted members of the Canton group who had been in close touch with Japan joined in the howl that rose on every side, demanding quick action against the perpetrators of this outrage. They did not, however, give up working for their own interests.

Chiang was not ready to fight Japan, and he made his reluctance evident by handing the problem over to the League of Nations and requesting them to settle it. The young people of China shouted for quick revenge, and in Shanghai a mob of students commandeered a train and rode to Nanking, where they joined with other fire-eaters in a march on the Ministry of Foreign Affairs, beat up two officials, and made nuisances of themselves in other quarters. (The students of China have always been particularly free and noisy in regard to politics; it is more or less traditional that they demand a hearing in national affairs when a crisis occurs. Modern classroom discipline has done a good deal to moderate their behavior in recent years, but there is still a phenomenal number of "strikes" and protests in Chinese universities, compared with similar disturbances in Western institutes of learning.) It had not been long since the Generalissimo warned these youngsters not to meddle in politics, particularly in Communist politics, and the lesson was presumably rankling. They welcomed this chance to assert themselves again, and for an irreproachable cause; what right-minded person would not fight for his country? Cheering, they smashed the offices of the *Central Daily News,* tore down the Ministry of Foreign Affairs, and might have settled down permanently in what was left of Nanking if the Government had not taken action with military troops and had them removed to the places from whence they came.

In the meantime there was much discussion between Nanking and Canton as to the best way to resolve their differences and get together. Canton demanded Chiang's resignation; the General-issimo promptly resigned and went home to Chekiang. The Canton government thereupon, according to the bargain, dissolved. Chiang Hseuh-liang resigned also, and T. V. Soong attempted to do so but was retained.

In the new government, Hu Han-min and Wang Chiang-wei with Chiang were supposed to be on the Central Executive Committee, but none of them would take up their posts. Sun Fo was President of the Executive Yuan, Lin Sen President of the Government, Eugene Chen Foreign Minister. Meanwhile Japan was sending troops throughout Manchuria and taking possession everywhere. The new government immediately got into trouble, and showed no signs of getting out.

In January 1932 the three members of the C.E.C., Wang Ching-wei, Hu-min and Chiang Kai-shek, at last decided to play ball and go to Nanking. There they managed to outtalk Eugene Chen, who wanted to break definitely with Japan, and Chen resigned, saying bitterly that Chiang still had all the real power and it was no use to oppose him. Sun Fo followed him in resigning. The new government had not lasted very long.

Chiang was then appointed chairman of the National Military Council, with his old friends Feng Yu-hsiang, Yen Hsi-shan and Chang Hsueh-liang as other members; Wang Ching-wei was named President of the Executive Yuan, and T. V. Soong was Minister of Finance. The entire group removed itself from Nanking, to get away from Japanese gunboats, and went to Loyang.

☆   ☆   ☆

Mrs Soong was not to see the Japanese trouble at its height. Before the Shanghai incident took place she died of the same disease that had killed her husband—cancer. The loss of a less strong personality might have led the family to a dissolution of their unity; her children had chosen their ways by this time, and

[*172*]

were each set upon his own path. Mrs Soong, however, had welded them together so strongly that they were never to feel totally free of the family ties. They could not even bring themselves to give up their mother's home in Seymour Road. Eling had the idea of presenting it to the Methodists to be remodeled as a church, but her brothers and sisters could not agree to this. For the time being they left it as it was, with Mrs Soong's companion still in residence and all the servants continuing to work in the house as if their mistress had been still alive.

When the Japanese attacked Shanghai, Eling and Chingling were both there. Madame Kung was living in the Route de Seiyes house, and Madame Sun still lived in her house in Rue Molière.

It was during this war that Madame Kung began to take an active part in public affairs. Her children were growing up, and now she had more freedom than she had experienced since her marriage. It was the beginning of a third phase for her, the first two being the ordinary development of a Chinese woman; a purely "social" existence before her marriage and the life of a busy mother afterward. Most women stop developing and remain in the second phase, but Eling was a Soong, and, as eldest, the head of the family, an important role in China. The emergency situation created by the undeclared war called for quick action in Shanghai for the troops who held out so gallantly, the famous Nineteenth Route Army from Canton and Chiang's Eighty-seventh and Eighty-eighth Divisions. There was little preparation for the vast number of wounded soldiers who were pouring into the city. One night at twelve o'clock the chairman of the Red Cross telephoned Madame Kung, who had been interesting herself in this matter, and asked her to do something about it.

Madame Kung was angry, because she had been told before this moment that there was plenty of hospital space. When she is angry she becomes very active, and fur began to fly. There was no time for a "drive" or a bazaar or any of the usual methods of raising money, so for quick relief she raised the sum of $80,000 from the large private fortunes of herself and three friends. This money was sufficient for a small hospital, the Pei Teh, which was fitted out with four hundred beds and an efficient, modern staff.

Within a week this hospital was filled. In the meantime, however, Madame Kung had started a general drive among her friends to raise a larger sum, and soon a private hospital of one thousand beds was established in the Continental Emporium. Both these hospitals were run on unusually modern lines, and were rated tops by the Shanghai Municipal Council for efficiency and cleanliness—an innovation in Chinese army service at that time. This group of women also instituted the custom of making clothes and preparing food for the soldiers at the front. It was the very beginning of the new attitude in China toward the army. Chiang Kai-shek had started the reform by teaching his Whampoa cadets to befriend the people they encountered instead of victimizing them; until he taught them manners, soldiers in China were hated and feared regardless of the army to which they belonged, whether they were fighting against or for the province in which they were stationed. Bandits or soldiers, it did not matter to the country people; men in uniform were a scourge. The year 1932, however, marked the end of five years under the new regime, and China was beginning to wake up to the change. The resistance of the Nineteenth Route Army to the Japanese had earned the admiration of the entire world, and the Chinese became aware that there were other heroes in their country than those of antiquity.

Among the richer Chinese there was still of course a tendency to look down on the soldier. The ancient social system that lists people according to their vocations placed the soldier very near the bottom, along with barbers and actors, and the bankers and merchants of Shanghai were inclined to rest upon that assumption, and to think of the men fighting and dying outside the Settlement as part of a machine that had been created for their convenience. The Soong sisters put an end to this conception. Their reactions were characteristic. Madame Chiang, indignantly patriotic, insisted that they be admired; Madame Sun's preoccupation with the greatest good for the greatest number made her demand recognition for these men if only as courageous unfortunates; Madame Kung's mind immediately turned to practical measures. Between them, they mobilized the wives and daughters of China's leading men, and with the help of these women they made the entire country soldier conscious in a manner it had never been before.

Early in 1932 Dr Kung was sent to America in his new capacity of Special Industrial Commissioner. Madame Kung, whose health was not good, accompanied him; she could not resist taking David with her, though the doctor had ordered a complete rest from all responsibility. David was not much of a responsibility anyway; his manners were very good, and he was a quiet boy. He was then fifteen years old.

It was Eling's first visit to the West since her marriage. At the beginning of the American part of the trip it seemed as if her life had not undergone much of a change. No matter where the Kungs went it was the same routine, a round of official parties, particularly in Washington and New York. When she had done her duty for a certain period of time, however, she felt free to visit her old school at Macon. She had written her friends there:

"I long to tread once more the familiar grounds and to see the faces of those I have loved. I shall make a desperate effort to come back."

"I have seen Madame Kung," writes Eunice Thomson, "shed very real tears of feminine vexation and have myself fetched her the spirits of ammonia to calm her nerves. [That was when she came to America in 1932 and the tears were over some extravagant newspaper statements which she considered unbecoming.] . . . She was afraid that even at the last minute she might find it too much to face the possible notoriety. But we promised her that no trumpets would be sounded and were able, with the co-operation of friends who could understand her need for a little peace and privacy, to keep that promise. Her classmates were notified and came from far and wide to join her at Wesleyan. For two whole days she saw none except familiar faces and was able to lay down for a few hours her country's burdens. Those were probably the last carefree hours she has had from that day to this."

They were not quite the last carefree hours. It was decided that Eling should go on for a tour of Europe with David while Dr Kung completed his work in America. T.V. wanted her to visit Italy; David was anxious to see England; she herself looked forward to Paris. They went to Italy first, and Mussolini, who had been advised by T.V. of her arrival, arranged to have her welcomed at Venice in a truly royal manner, by a launch completely covered with flowers.

"It was lovely," she said, "but I was nervous at having such a fuss made over me. I'd been studying books about Italy all the way over in the ship; T.V. brought them down when he saw me off. I was full of statistics and politics, and the flowers were a pleasant surprise. And the rooms at our hotel, and the official buildings! I've never seen so much red and gold in my life."

For three weeks thereafter Madame Kung led a more or less "official" life, dined and wined by the Governor of Rome and various Roman princesses. After that, however, she broke away and with David traveled quietly at her own pace through Europe, using no more letters of introduction. They visited France and England, and saw all the places they should see.

Nine months after leaving China they returned, to a reconstructed Nanking.

CHAPTER XVIII

The New Life Movement

IT HAD BEEN a troublesome and confused year for Chiang and the Government. The Communists began making trouble again, drawing near Hankow, and the Generalissimo decided to go after them seriously, though the younger and more hotheaded Chinese protested that he should concentrate on Japan. Chiang maintained that China was not yet ready to resist, especially since the country was always being torn and weakened by these interior struggles, and he continued to campaign against the Reds until they withdrew to the Northwest.

In December the Government came back to Nanking, to meet a storm of protest against Chiang's non-resistance to Japan. Though the Generalissimo at a meeting of the Central Executive Committee described his warfare against the Reds in detail, some of the leaders, including T. V. Soong, were not satisfied. They ignored the subject of the Reds and suggested a campaign to take Manchuria back from the Japanese.

[*177*]

Chiang insisted that China was not yet ready for such action. He had his way, though many people protested his policy and there was an immense demonstration by the ever-present students, in which the Nanking scenes of the year before came near to being repeated. In spite of the newly inaugurated censorship there was much journalistic grumbling, and the universities were hotbeds of discontent, not only because of the students but also owing to patriotic professors who went so far as to accuse Chiang of pro-Japanese sentiments. The *actively* militant professor was as yet unknown to China; these mentors saw themselves as scholars directing the troops from some safely distant mountaintop. Chiang, as a soldier by training and nature, could not appreciate this point of view. To him the Japanese menace was a practical problem, and the answer to it was not immediate resistance, but steady preparation.

In 1933 the Japanese went after Jehol. It was during this campaign that they initiated the practice of bombing open towns and thus victimizing the civilian population in a manner much more horrible than the ordinary looting and pillaging of conquered cities. The discontented leaders of Canton took early opportunity to demand action from Nanking, and they did not hesitate to allege that Chiang's hesitation in making war on Japan was due to a secret agreement with the island empire.

Jehol was lost to China on March third, when the Japanese occupied the capital, Chengteh. Feeling rose even higher, and the Cantonese felt themselves justified in having attacked Nanking, especially as the Generalissimo was too much distracted to attend to them in his usual direct way. They shouted louder and louder, and threatened to set up another government on the old grounds that the Nanking body was unconstitutional. Chiang, however, continued with his policy of remaining on friendly terms with the Japanese as long as possible while he prepared for ultimate resistance, even when Feng Yu-hsiang started to make a noise about Japan. The Christian General organized an "Anti-Japanese Army," and tried for a while to combine with Canton against Nanking, but the scheme was defeated for the time being. The Tangku truce was signed May thirty-first, 1933, and according to this agreement a demilitarized zone was created near the Great Wall, from which both sides removed their soldiers.

The signing of this truce, with its implications that China was again being bullied, crystallized the Fukien Rebellion, which was engineered by some of the dissatisfied leaders in Canton. In Foochow, on November twentieth, a new government was announced, with Tsai Ting-kai, hero of Shanghai in 1932, as chairman of the Military Affairs Commission and Eugene Chen as Minister of Foreign Affairs. Notable for their absence from the setup were Hu Han-min, Chen Chi-tang, Madame Sun (who publicly disclaimed any interest in the scheme) and Wang Ching-wei, though this last named seized the opportunity to point out that the rebellion was all Chiang's fault for being a dictator.

Though there was, as usual, an outcry demanding that the Generalissimo resign, he took a short cut to the inevitable conclusion by sending out the troops with the Nanking air force against Foochow. In a short time the rebellion was crushed.

☆   ☆   ☆

It was at this time that William Henry Donald came into the lives of the Soongs. His was not a first appearance, for he had been a friend of Charles Soong in the early days when the present Mesdames Kung, Sun and Chiang were small children, years before the Revolution was more than one young doctor's hope. Donald is an Australian who came to China thirty-seven years ago as a newspaperman and who, through close relationship with all the high officials during that period, developed a strong affection for the country, an affection that mingles the watchful censoriousness of a schoolmaster with the proprietory pride of an old family doctor. He had begun to feel anxious and protective about China before his connection with the Soongs, and had already done his bit by becoming adviser to the Young Marshal.

"Adviser" is a word Donald dislikes and refuses to use. In truth it has come to mean so many things that in China it is almost meaningless. In regard to his position with Chang Hsueh-liang, however, no other word will do. He took charge of the young man in a big way, insisting that he be broken of the various dope habits he had contracted, and taking him to Shanghai to be disintoxicated. All through this long and painful process Donald stayed by Chang, laughing at him, cracking jokes, keeping the patient keyed up to the necessary pitch of will power, until the worst was over. Donald has what is probably the only non-irritating bedside manner in the world. He has vigorous health, vigorous principles and vigorous plans. He does not drink, smoke or tell lies. Perhaps it is his particular brand of honesty, a simple yes-or-no attitude toward truth as he sees it, that accounts for his unusual position in Chinese official circles. It is not the ordinary thing to be trusted in China; events, whispers, intrigues and crises have jockeyed most advisers out of position sooner or later. Donald pays no attention to these things, secure in his ignorance of the Chinese language and serenely indifferent to petty quarrels outside of his province; he avoids the temptation to be subtle. It is the ambition of most advisers to outdo Machiavelli; Donald has no personal ambition whatever, even that one. He would abandon his quasi-dictatorship in a moment if he should consider that principle called for such a step.

When Chang Hsueh-liang was pushed out of Manchuria the Generalissimo gave him a consolation trip to Europe, and Donald accompanied him. There was a *contretemps* in Italy when the Young Marshal got into what Donald considered bad company and started dissipating; Donald walked out on him and stayed out until Chang repented and begged him to come back. They returned to China early in 1934, at the end of the Fukien Rebellion and the beginning of Chiang's strongest campaign against the Communists.

The Generalissimo had a series of conversations with the Young Marshal on this matter in Hangchow, and Donald came along. It was just at the time that the New Life Movement was originally inaugurated to stimulate the people in formerly occupied Red districts. The New Life Movement for one or two years was not very well understood among the masses, and in treaty ports such as Shanghai, where critics have always been bolder than in the interior, the press made fun of it. The most publicized of its tenets were the least important: the rule that all collars on Chinese gowns must be buttoned, for example. Government officials and policemen took their duties very seriously, and public places such as the squares outside railway stations were kept scrupulously clean. Spitters and people who threw their cigarette butts about were punished.

There was more to the Movement than this, however. Madame Chiang always stresses the point that the details—modesty and economy in dress, cleanliness, improvement in table manners, moderation in cigarette smoking—are merely outward signs of a more important spiritual reform that the Generalissimo is trying to achieve for the people. He formulated the philosophy of the Movement on the basis of four words familiar to the sages: Propriety, Justice, Integrity and Conscientiousness.

Peoples of the outer world [writes the Generalissimo] may not at first be able to understand the necessity for such a movement, but they will do so if they realize that they have grown up with national consciousness fully developed around and about them, whereas the Chinese people have been deliberately forcibly bereft of it, and, therefore, know nothing of those sentiments and impulses that so quickly move the Occidental peoples when matters concerning their country come forward for consideration or action. It is to correct the evil consequences arising from this serious state of affairs that action is now being taken along a psychological and educational line . . . we have to learn that to correct personal and national failings we must fall back upon the influence of the old teachings. Rudeness and vulgar manners can be corrected by cultural and artistic training, and degeneration can be overcome by developing good personal character. It is difficult, however, to succeed merely through the ordinary processes of education and governance. If we are determined to reform we must start with the most fundamental question—we must reform our habits first. . . . These virtues [the four already mentioned] must be ap-

plied to ordinary matter, such as food, clothing, shelter, and action.
. . . The means of maintaining our livelihood may be divided into
three phases; first, the obtaining of materials; second, the selection of
quality; and third, the manner in which these materials are used. . . .

1. The obtaining of materials should be governed by the principle of
"lien" [integrity]. Clear discrimination should be exercised between
what is ours and what is not. If they do not belong to us, we should
not take them. In other words, the materials for our daily life should
be acquired through our own labor or through other proper means.
Strife should not be encouraged. A parasite is not a good example.
Even giving and taking improperly should be avoided. "What really
matters is the degradation of personality, but not dying in hunger." . . .

2. The selection of quality should be governed by the principle of
"i" [justice]. Do the proper thing in a particular situation. For
instance, it is proper for an old man to use silk and to take meat and
to have lots of leisure; but a young man should be trained to endure
hardship. What is proper in winter is not necessarily proper in summer. What is proper in the North is not necessarily proper in the
South. Similarly, different positions may influence a situation differ-
ently. A ruler, or any army commander, must have some authority;
while those of a lower rank should not enjoy the same thing, but
should respect discipline. Thus, what is proper is influenced by age,
season, location, and rank; the selection of quality varies in different
situations.

3. The manner in which materials are used should be governed by
the principle of "li" [propriety], which includes natural law, social
rules, and national discipline. . . .

As a substitute for the promises of the Communists, we of the
West would consider this code of ethics far too abstract and lack-
ing in action to be useful. After all, the Reds' teachers spoke sharply
and to the point on taxation, distribution of land, and the disposition of the overlords, whereas Chiang's program, though ambitious enough, was almost too large and moral to take these practical matters into account. We must remember, however, that the
Chinese are used to being scolded and exhorted in the name of
Virtue. Verbal uplift in China is a mannerism and does not call

forth the response that we would manifest if we were told to be honest and clean and straightforward, etc. Our reaction, after two or three of these lectures, would be merely to retort, "Oh, yeah?" But in China every schoolboy, as soon as he can write, inscribes pious and dictatorial maxims in his notebook, and not only in his own notebook but in the autograph albums of his friends.

The New Life Movement, then, was not too abstract for the public it was intended for. For the moment of emergency its chief virtue was that it offered a program, the People's Reconstruction, and that it was something that lent itself to publicity. The art of publicity was new to China, but the leaders were not long in catching on to its methods and possibilities. For the American-trained Madame Chiang, at least, there was nothing startling in the concept of going out deliberately to advertise the Movement on a large scale, and she was to find an adept aide in the person of Donald.

His advice and labors were transferred from the service of the Young Marshal by almost imperceptible stages. After Chang had visited the Chiangs in Hangchow he saw a good deal of them, and one day when Donald was there Madame Chiang came in with her arms full of papers—correspondence, reports, suggestions to be followed or rejected, and a host of other things.

"Look at this!" she said in despair. "I'll never be able to finish it —Don, can you help me?"

Donald could. He could make quick decisions as to which matter needed attention and which could wait; his judgment was sound. Most important, he could write shorthand, and he himself says that it was this accomplishment that changed his entire life. After a few days of intensive activity at the Generalissimo's Headquarters, he happened to see the Young Marshal, who came into the room where he was working.

"I never see you any more," said the Young Marshal.

"Well, you know where to find me," retorted Donald pleasantly. "Come in any time."

Chang was not going to give up his adviser without a struggle. He suggested a compromise by which Donald should spend six months with the Chiangs and then, Proserpine-like, return to his Young Marshal, but this was too difficult and in the end the Chiangs won out. Donald is still very much a friend of Chang, however, and is quick to defend him against criticism on the Sian affair.

It was soon after the Young Marshal lost him, or perhaps even during the change-over period, that the entire group, with Dr Kung, started out on a trip that was to have far-reaching consequences in China's history and a very important effect upon the Generalissimo and his wife.

CHAPTER XIX

The Chiangs See China's Northwest

I T WAS AT THE END of 1933 that T. V. Soong left the Government, following a disagreement with the Generalissimo on the matter of finances. He was unwilling to allow as much of the budget as Chiang needed for the army, particularly since he questioned the wisdom of subsidies for the generals of the provinces. Chiang maintained that the nation's safety outweighed all other necessities. He wanted to raise more money; Soong wanted to decrease the national debt. They could not agree, and T.V. resigned his post, later going abroad. To take his place, the Generalissimo appointed Dr Kung Minister of Finance. Kung was experienced in banking, that being the work his family had done for generations, and he had been Acting Minister of Finance before, during the Northern Expedition.

By this time Chiang was the real leader of China both politically and militarily. However, he refused a request from the Kuomintang to become president of the Party and said that he did not approve of dictatorships. Nevertheless he insisted that Nanking was the center of government, and at the psychological moment, when the Japanese placed Henry Pu-yi upon the throne of "Manchukuo" and named him Emperor, Chiang proposed to the turbulent south-ern provinces, Kwangtung and Kwangsi, that they settle their dif-ferences amicably. Terms were found which satisfied everyone, and the Southwest Political Council resolved to support and obey the Central Government.

On October fourth, 1934, the Generalissimo, accompanied by his wife, Chang Hsueh-liang, Donald, and various generals, arrived in Hankow on his way to Loyang. He held several conferences here, chiefly upon the matter of "bandit suppression"; in other words, he was preparing for his big drive against the Reds, and used the few days he spent in Hankow to talk to his generals and to make fresh plans. He departed on October tenth, the most important day in Chinese Republican history.

The trip to Loyang was made in order to open a new branch of the Central Military Academy, and to inspect the administration methods of that city at the same time. The Generalissimo spoke to the cadets, there were celebrations in his honor, and everything went according to schedule. It was all over by the afternoon of the eleventh, and the Chiangs bade fair to keep to their original plan of taking only three days off for the whole affair. They were actu-ally in their private car, waiting for the locomotive that was to take them back to Hankow and quietly drinking tea, when in the course of conversation somebody said that really they were not very far away from Sian. . . .

It was Donald who reflected aloud that with a slight change of plan, i.e., if the locomotive were placed at the other end of the train, they could actually visit Sian.

The idea suddenly took hold of Chiang Kai-shek's fancy. Ma-dame Chiang liked it too. It was not long since those conversations in Hangchow, when the Generalissimo had admitted the truth of an allegation made by Donald that no high official had ever been able to govern China properly because no official ever knew where reforms were needed. The chiefs of local regions were always afraid to report truthfully, and no ruler ever had taken the time or opportunity to investigate for himself. This statement had made the Generalissimo think, and he resolved to go on to Sian at least. The whole party thereupon started out on what was to be an important tour.

The private airplane of the Chiangs took some of them; others went by train. It was an exciting time for Sianfu; nobody could have guessed under what circumstances the Chiangs were to visit that city again. For two days the party saw the sights and were entertained in the usual fashion, but on the fourteenth the Generalissimo and his wife did something that was to have far-reaching consequences, something that had never before happened in China.

From the *North-China Daily News:*

It is generally supposed that the visit is not unconnected with the Communist menace in Szechwan, for in any movement of or against the Reds this province would be one of the main fronts. But General and Madame Chiang are laying stress on the New Life Movement and today a great meeting in support of it has been held in the Min Lo Yuen, the largest hall in the city. One gracious act was the invitation of all the foreign missionaries in the city to coffee and conversation yesterday afternoon. Both General and Madame Chiang made informal speeches, the one in Chinese and the other in perfect and beautiful English, thanking the missionaries for their service to China and urging that they should co-operate with the New Life Movement to the utmost of their power, as had already been done in Kiangsi with excellent results. Those present were, of course, entirely sympathetic with every movement towards manners, cleanliness and the uplift of the people, and a committee representing all the missions in the city was elected then and there to move in the matter. All were much impressed by the dignity and charm of manner of the Generalissimo and his wife and came away thankful that there are people of such gifts, energy and devotion in the highest places of the land.

The missionaries were more than impressed; they were flabbergasted. In their most optimistic moments they had never expected the leaders of China to come to them and to ask to know the truth, which is what the Chiangs had done at that meeting. Madame had explained in English; they, the Generalissimo and herself, were anxious to see that a real reform was carried out. They realized that the missionaries, who lived with the people and understood their problems, would be able to tell them just what was needed in the way of change and uplift. The missionaries were also in a peculiar position of independence; unlike the officials, they could tell the truth without fear or ambition standing in their way. Madame Chiang asked them to be quite frank, and promised on behalf of the Government to co-operate.

It was something that had never happened before, and for a while it is no wonder that the missionaries were incredulous and even suspicious. For many years the more sociologically minded among them had written, begged, intrigued and pleaded for a chance to talk to even the smaller officials. Very few of them had succeeded. Now the Generalissimo himself, with his wife, had come to them and asked them to speak out about what was wrong with their particular areas of China, and their ideas as to correcting these wrongs.

At last one of them took a deep breath and began to speak. When he was through there were half a dozen waiting their turn. It was a long session that afternoon, and an instructive one for everybody.

Madame Chiang also held a meeting of the leading women of Sian, i.e., the wives of the high officials, and urged them to take more of an interest in the public. These women promised to start a clinic for the treatment of opium addicts. Together with Madame Chiang they visited the Provincial Orphanage and the Business School for poor girls. When they left Sian it was believed by the public that they would return to Hankow, but a good deal was to happen before that.

They next visited Lanchow, the beautiful old Tang city. Lanchow on the map is up at the edge of the thickly settled parts of China, in the thin neck of Kansu, next to Kokonor. Until then, Presidents and Generalissimos simply never went to such places. It was considered a very dangerous step for the Generalissimo to have taken, and both the Young Marshal and Donald were severely scolded afterwards by many officials for having allowed the Chiangs to take such risks. Most of the Nanking officials believed with all their hearts that anyone in Chiang Kai-shek's position was always in danger of assassination, especially in those wild far-off regions of the Northwest.

"To have allowed the General to go into a place like that without preparation or warning, without even a strong bodyguard—how could you have dared?" demanded one prominent member of the Government, and he was all the more shocked to hear that Chiang had walked about freely at his sightseeing with only two or three soldiers following him at a considerable distance. Even in 1934 and indeed until well after this tour, most people in eastern China thought of the less-known provinces as we think of Borneo. The fact that the Reds had retired in this direction added to their conviction that the Generalissimo walked in danger of his life every minute he was away.

The Chiangs, after inspecting the ancient architecture and the modern industries of Lanchow, flew north to have a look at Ninghsia, which is even more remote, a genuine border town. There are some wonderful remnants of ancient culture there, but what impressed the Government people most of all was the distance over which they had to travel. It never seems the same on a map as it does when one traverses the actual region.

In Kaifeng, where the party next repaired, the Chiangs followed their policy of inviting the local missionaries to discussion. The Young Marshal dropped out of the tour at this time and returned to Hankow, but Donald remained with them. Newspaper reports of the Kaifeng visit stress the missionary meeting:

Madame Chiang expressed a desire to meet the missionary body working in this capital city. When assured that this could be arranged, she sent her personal representative around to the different missions

[*189*]

to invite them to a tea party at the Governor's yamen. . . . At the tea table Generalissimo Chiang spoke most appreciatively of the good work done by the missionary body in China. He assured all that not only were the days of opposition and oppression past, but that the time of mere toleration was at an end. He said that, under the present government, it would be the policy to give the utmost freedom to, and active co-operation with, the work of the missionaries. He explained in detail the purpose of the New Life Movement, which he has been promoting throughout the country. It is not a mere regimentation of disciplinary movement to control the people, but aims at the moral, cultural and social uplift of the masses. He called upon Mr Liu to make use of the experience of the missionary body in promoting the objectives of the New Life Movement and asked the hearty co-operation of the missionary body.

Madame Chiang next spoke to the company in English. She read from the report of an impartial witness, testifying what had actually been accomplished in rehabilitating Kiangsi province. . . . She made a special appeal to the lady missionaries to co-operate with Madame Liu in initiating a better homes movement; for she felt that was the most fundamental of all needs. . . .

Canon Simmons of the Canadian Church Mission, senior missionary in Kaifeng, responded most heartily. On behalf of the twenty-odd missionaries present, he assured them and Mr Liu of the eagerness of the missionaries to do everything in their power to co-operate in every genuine effort to uplift the people morally and spiritually as well as economically and educationally. . . .

As the party continued on its way, the Chiangs found it most satisfactory to ask in each place for the oldest and most experienced missionary in the community. After he had been produced, everything went smoothly. On all the Generalissimo's walks abroad he would be accompanied by Madame Chiang, the veteran missionary, and Donald. They talked about more than political reform during these expeditions; the industry of the region was studied, and plans were made for improvement wherever they went. Chiang got into the habit, unusual in Generalissimos, of asking questions on these matters of Chinese people, petty officials, even passers-by. The effect of all this upon the government officials will be discussed later; for the moment let us see what effect the officials had upon the populace. Their trip from Lanchow to Ninghsia was described in the Shanghai *North-China Daily News* as from October twenty-first:

For 100 miles or more there is but one continuous mass of miniature sharp peaked, light-brown loess hills, eroded on all sides into gaping gulches and gullies, so crammed together that to the horizon on every side it looks like nothing else than the high steep waves of a petrified ocean-wide tide-rip. Millions of peaks, slashed and torn, of uniform height, barren, inhospitable and hopeless, jostle in every direction, and from an altitude of nine or ten thousand feet, which we were flying at, the limit of every direction is a long way off on a sparkling day. . . . It is all a gloomy land, and when you see vast blank spaces on the map do not imagine they are unexplored. They are there because the land cannot be lived upon, and has been able effectively to resist the pressure of the persistent march of man from the east and the south. . . . Down in the deep gulches no road or track is possible anywhere, for they constitute a labyrinth; and the camel road from Ninghsia is far to the north . . . the only sign of life from such a height is an occasional raft of inflated bullock or sheep skins rushing down the stream laden with wool or hides, the six great yulohs (oars), three each fore and aft, flashing in the sunlight. . . .

About 100 miles out from Lanchow the gnarled loess gives way to a more open landscape but none the less wilderness. . . . We see our first and only camel caravan, camped for the day in the low hills, having just emerged from the sands of the Little Gobi, which now blaze into view, a creeping stream of rusty red sand waves. . . . "What a sand trap," says the Young Marshal, as we see the red desert stretching into an ever-widening horizon in the distance. . . .

Under the protection of the Ala Shan the earth begins to take on a more friendly and more natural appearance, habitations become more pronounced, farms appear, and in the distance tombs show up and we know that Ninghsia is somewhere near. We could see waterholes splashed about the plain, an unusual but a refreshing sight in this region of waste and arid land. Then came the gaunt and crumbling walls of the old-time Ching garrison, with its lone mud-coloured pagoda, and nearby was the airfield, with lines of soldiers drawn up, and cavalry swung round in an imposing circle. . . . As we banked down and roared lower towards the landing field we expected to see the line of cavalry jump out of its skin and jumble itself on the plain, but to our surprise those ponies stood stock still as if a monster plane was but a droning beetle swooping out of the sky.

Bugles played, people cheered, a band or two started in to welcome the Generalissimo and Madame Chiang and Marshal Chang. General Ma Hung-kwei and his brother, General Ma Hung-ping, who one time was governor of Shantung, clutched the hands of the visitors as they stepped out of the plane, indicated that Ninghsia was theirs, and, after the inspection of the guard, piled them in cars and drove them a long way till the city was reached. At the airdrome they passed long lines of waiting soldiery and cheering citizens, and as they drew near the city another long line was also added to their welcome. The band played "Johnnie Comes Marching Home" with a vengeance, which brings to mind that at Sian the troops goose-stepped at the review to "John Brown's Body," and "Marching Through Georgia." . . . The crowds of people craned their necks to an insufferable extent, apparently to catch a glimpse of Madame Chiang, judging by the way their eyes fastened upon her, and they seemed to regard her as being from another world. . . .

In Shanghai the Chinese press waxed enthusiastic over the Generalissimo's discovery of the Northwest, and the *Sin Wan Pao* said:

Much talk has been in the air about the development of China's Northwest. Actual development has been in process ever since the visit of Mr T. V. Soong to that region. Now Gen. Chiang Kai-shek has visited that region himself and there is every reason to believe that plans will soon be set on foot on a large scale for its development.

At this moment when the whole country is focusing its attention on the Northwest we want to remind the public that the Northwest is the cradle of Chinese civilization and the home of mineral treasures. People who have visited those provinces can readily realize the greatness of Chinese civilization. But there is one thing which many people overlook, that is the unseen power and energy of its people.

Specifically, the Generalissimo in Lanchow and Ninghsia visited woolen factories and spinning mills that had fallen into disuse through the vicissitudes of civil war, particularly because of Feng Yu-hsiang's army and their recent visits. In Ninghsia he saw the Mint and a large factory that had been converted from one of Feng's arsenals. He saw the coal mines; he was fascinated by the sheepskin rafts and investigated their manufacture and use. There was a railway being built to Sianfu, an extension of the Lunghai; the Chiangs examined it. *Sin Wan Pao* continued:

Here [in Lanchow] are more Tang dynasty relics than in any other place in China perhaps. The party walked along the ancient city wall which for centuries has withstood the attack of the waters of "China's Sorrow." Gen. Chiang was amazed at the wonderful old architecture to be seen from this wall top. . . . The Generalissimo inspected the old steel bridge which here spans the Yellow River. It was built in 1907, each part being hauled from the rail head to far distant Lanchow on carts. The bridge is as good today as when it was built.

At Kaifeng, Donald half-jokingly suggested that they lunch with Han Fu-chu, governor of Shantung, in his capital city of Tsinan. It had been a long jump from Sian to Kaifeng, but it was no longer to Tsinan. The Chiangs had tasted the joys of wandering, and they decided to do just that. From Tsinan it was a short way, comparatively, to Peking, and it occurred to Madame Chiang that this would be a good time for the whole party to be overhauled at the Peking Union Medical College Hospital there. The Generalissimo had been suffering for years from a mild indigestion, and spent several days with his wife in the hospital, where he learned that his illness was not serious. While he was still in Peking, the Princes Yun and Teh, of the Mongolian Political Council, telegraphed and asked the party to come on to Mongolia.

They compromised by going to Kalgan in Chahar Province, and sending a good-will envoy to the Mongols. From Kalgan they went to Suiyuan, then to Taiyuan, where they were joined by Dr Kung, who had come to Peking. Here the party split up. The Generalissimo was recalled by urgent affairs that had been waiting for him a long time, and he went to Nanchang, about November ninth, while Madame Chiang, Dr Kung and Donald returned to Nanking by way of Peking, Tientsin, Tsingtao, and Shanghai. The most important tour of their lives had taken only a month, and they had seen places in China to which explorers journey many months and weary miles on foot.

It was a most important trip for three reasons. In the first place, the Generalissimo had seen the country thoroughly, had got into touch with local problems in far-off places, and had learned that he need not be guarded like a priceless piece of brittle jade whenever he stepped outdoors. Many historians have noticed that as he increased his power, Chiang Kai-shek seemed to grow in moral stature, to take on more and more of a feeling of responsibility toward his work and his people instead of increasing in self-importance and vanity. The tour of the Northwest was partly responsible for this development, according to some of those people who are close to him. His particular interest in economic development dates from this time. As a hard-working soldier he had never before given much thought to the industries of peace-time.

In the second place, Madame Chiang began to emerge in her own right into the public eye during her wanderings. The necessity of making speeches day after day cured her of shyness and toughened her against the fatigues of what might be called electioneering. In each city she took upon herself the job of marshaling the women and urging them to help in a nationwide reform. She talked against the old ways of China, the incarceration of upper-class women, the menace of opium and of dirt and poverty; she begged them to develop a sense of social responsibility. As leaders of this movement she appointed the wives of the leading officials in each community, a pattern to which she returned at the beginning of the Sino-Japanese war. All of this energetic effort had its effect upon her, and she returned to Nanking with a sense of what she could do by her husband's side. Incidentally, the long trips by plane were tests of her heroism. Madame Chiang gets planesick very easily, and takes some of her longest hops lying on the floor of the plane with smelling salts held to her nose. This weakness has never caused her to avoid a journey, however.

Thirdly, the populace of China's frontiers had had a glimpse of their ruler, and any amateur psychologist knows what a difference that can make. People who would have been passively indifferent to Chiang and his political position in Nanking now felt friendly toward him because of that moment or those few moments of personal contact. Leaders who had been disgruntled by habit with the proceedings at Nanking had had a chance to talk things out with the Generalissimo himself, and many were won over to his cause because of this. For the first time in history, men in the North, men in the West, men in the South and the East were all thinking of one person as their leader. It was not the long, weary years of civil war that had unified China under Chiang Kai-shek; it was that hastily planned journey through the air and over the mountains of the Northwest.

CHAPTER XX

Chiang Is Kidnaped

THE IMPERIALIZATION of Henry Pu-yi had not satisfied the Japanese as to their position on the mainland, and early in 1935 they attacked Sung Cheh-yuan, the governor of Chahar, after accusing him hastily of having sent Chinese troops into Manchukuo. They sent airplanes over the Great Wall and armored cars with their troops, and after only one day, January twenty-third, they were successful. Sung had to sign an agreement giving Japan a promise not to go into the disputed area of Tatan again. Nanking never admitted the validity of this agreement, but at the moment there was nothing more concrete that the Government could do than to deny it.

Evidently the Japanese had decided to take all North China by degrees, first persuading the five provinces to declare independence from Nanking. Chiang could not yet go to war with any hope of success. He knew that the governing body of Hopei was worrying the Japanese, chiefly because of the Young Marshal's Northeastern

Army, which was as strong as ever and very resentful of their expulsion from Manchuria. The Young Marshal himself was heading bandit suppression activity and was stationed at Hankow, but his army remained in Hopei, and the Japanese feared it. Chiang decided to make certain concessions in order to avoid giving the chance to Japan's secret agent, Doihara, to carry out his plans for a northern autonomy. He moved quickly, sending Chang Hsueh-liang's army out of Hopei, and removing Governor Sung from his post in Chahar. Later Sung was sent back at the request of Japan—Chiang had to take this high-handed behavior and like it; he was playing for time. For the moment, however, he had avoided Doihara's plan and the five northern provinces were still part of China.

Sung Cheh-yuan was made chairman of a Hopei-Chahar Political Council, and the Kuomintang branches in these provinces were done away with at the behest of the Japanese, and though the Council was at best a trouble spot, it was also an exhaust for the whole Sino-Japanese question and saved a crisis.

Now that he had breathing space, the busy Generalissimo turned his attention again to the Communists, some of whom were in Kweichow. He followed them there and drove them out. He set to work to reorganize the provincial government and from there went to Szechwan after more Communists. The Chiangs' visit had an important effect upon both provinces, which because of their position and comparative inaccessability were very badly damaged. Szechwan in particular was a scandal, overrun with war-lords and bandits; conditions there were years behind those of Chekiang or Kiangsu. The peasants were badly oppressed. Here with Madame Chiang the Generalissimo followed the pattern of their days in the Northwest, inquiring of missionaries and honest officials wherever they could be found, and taking a special interest in the old city of Chungking, at the top of the Yangtze, hidden in rocky mountains. The Szechwanese were astonished at this unusual behavior of the great, and reforms began in that year which have continued ever since.

Madame Chiang, writing to the students of the School for Children of Revolutionary Heroes, describes in *Messages in War and Peace* her first impressions of the southwestern provinces which she was later to know well:

You know that Kweiyang is the capital of Kweichow Province, a province that is mostly mountains and is poor and very difficult to reach. Or it used to be difficult. Now there is a motor road from Kwangsi, and soon there will be one from Changsha and another from Chungking, in Szechwan. Soon, too, there will be an air-mail service. Only a short while ago all travel was over stone paths climbing the mountains and descending the valleys. It took seventeen days to get from here to Chungking, and about the same time to get to Canton or Yunnan, and one had to travel by chair or walk. There are mountains everywhere. Not great ranges, but a higgledy-piggledy mass of cone-like hills, some very curious to look at. When we were flying from Chungking here we saw these cones lying in long rows as if some giant had put them there to play with, as children make little hills of sand. . . .

Around about us are bandit bands. It is to try and suppress them that the Generalissimo came here. At present they are but twenty miles away from us, but they will be defeated in the end, and then we will really be able to do something to help all the people and make our country strong and great. And that is what you students always must remember—that you are being educated solely to be of help to your country and your fellow men. . . .

. . . To get here we used steamers, motor cars and aeroplanes. From Kiukiang I went by steamer to Chungking, which is in Szechwan, and is some 1,350 miles from Shanghai, and some 600 feet higher than Nanking. Really the steamer climbs up that height through the rapids of the Upper Yangtze. Up to Ichang the river is just a great body of water running strongly and eating its way into the fields on either side and carrying lots of good earth out to sea, making the ocean yellow for some 60 miles out, so strong is the current of the river, so great is the quantity of silt (that is earth) that it carries. . . .

When we got to Chungking it was raining, the first rain since leaving Nanchang. We had to climb high flights of wide stone steps to get to the roadway. We went to live in a big house which the Generalissimo and I did not like because it was not built from honest money. It belongs to a militarist, like many others here. It is sad to say that Szechwan, which is one of the richest provinces in our country, is made poor by the greed of men who get into power and rob people for their own profit. They are ignorant, and do not know what patriotism means. That is what you students must learn and understand. If you do not, then China will never recover. You must always try to teach others what the country is, what the flag stands for, and what all good citizens should do—that is, work honestly to help the country become strong and great.

In Szechwan, and in Kweichow, as in several other provinces in the West, the people are made poor by opium. The bad officials have poppies, from which opium is made, grown and by shipping opium out, make great profits from it. This evil will kill China if it is not stopped. Therefore, the Generalissimo and I, wherever we go, speak strongly against the evil and we work to educate the people to do their best to have the opium stopped so that our race shall not become slaves.

In Chungking we persuaded the high officials to shut up the opium shops, and I am trying to organize the women to work against the evil. The difficulty is that they do not know how to organize anything, or have meetings, and this is one thing I want the girl students to remember. They must try their best to prepare themselves to grow up competent to form societies to do good, to hold meetings, and get things done. At present the illiterate women think that they have to talk about this and that and everything except the one thing they ought to talk about and do. That is not their fault so much as it is their misfortune. They had no chance to be educated, as you girls have, and therefore, they are more to be pitied than blamed. But you can learn a valuable lesson from it, for as time goes on, our women are going to do their share in saving their country. You must, therefore, try to understand things so that you can teach others what to do and how to do it when you get the chance.

In Szechwan there is a great chance for the people to recover themselves for their province is rich in vegetation, as well as in other products. But there has been no systematic development here, as in some other provinces. Lack of development of natural resources is one reason why China is poor and weak. If you look at the great countries of the world you will see that they are strong because they have developed their mining and other industries to make the things they want, and to give employment to their people. In China most of the work is done on farms, and we have to spend our money buying other things that we need from foreign countries. That is not right. Consequently the Generalissimo and I are working hard to have a new movement started to develop the natural resources of the country, start industries to manufacture the necessities we must have, and improve agriculture so that we can grow all we need to eat. This movement will be the People's Economic Reconstruction Movement, and we want all of you students to understand what it means to China. It means that if China takes lessons from the good foreign countries she in time can be strong and powerful, and can get rich, too. Also no one will dare to take advantage of her and rob her of her territory. But we must all work hard and educate the people to understand the reasons for such a new movement. All of us want our country to be strong and rich, and that is the means by which it can be done. There is no magic about it. Riches are not conjured out of a magician's hat. They have to be worked for. We must be wise and open up our country. If we do not we will surely become the slaves of some other country who wants to take what we have. The Generalissimo is doing his utmost out here to teach the officials and the people what they must do. In that work of teaching everyone must help.

. . . So far, we have been only to Chungking. It is a city built on a high hill at the junction of two rivers—the Yangtzekiang and the Kialing. Long flights of steps lead up from the water; up and down go the travelers, jostling with the carriers of water, and the bearers of freight. Now there is a motor road, and many wide streets at the top. Five years ago there were no wheeled vehicles here. Now there are many motorcars and hundreds of rickshaws. Previously people rode in chairs, carried by coolies. The main road goes to Chengtu, the capital, and people can travel there in two days. Just a little while ago it took weeks to do the journey.

Back in Nanking, Chiang turned once more to the ever-increasing Japanese trouble. His own people were being stirred up again to impatience, and whenever the Japanese could they took exception to statements in Chinese newspapers and magazines, becoming more and more petulant and exacting. When Chiang still took the more discreet way and punished the editors responsible for these "anti-Japanese" expressions, the intellectuals and students reached the boiling point of rage. However, there was a general belief that things could not go on forever as they were; and the modern patriots were happy in their expectations, while the old conservatives were apprehensive. Foreigners watched eagerly and laid bets as to the future; rumors swept the treaty ports that Chiang had declared war; that Chiang had defied Japan at last; that Chiang had sold out. . . .

An American newspaperman who was interviewing Madame Chiang at that time asked her with as much delicacy as he could muster if the Generalissimo was ever going to resist. It was just after one of Chiang's statements that China would go into action when the limits of endurance had been reached; Japan had sent one of the courteous blackmailing notes for which she was becoming famous, and the correspondent was endeavoring to discover just where those limits were to be found. He took a long time to ask the question, and he used roundabout words: "Now, Madame, do you suppose that an eventuality is likely to take place soon, uh, I mean, is the Generalissimo planning—that is, in what spirit do you think the nation would take any more aggressive action on the part of Japan? When the Generalissimo says 'limits of our patience,' does he—that is to say, will he——?"

At that moment Donald came into the room, and Madame Chiang with one speech scattered all her interviewer's ceremony. "Don," she said crisply, "Morris is asking me how much longer we're going to stand for this Japanese flimflam."

The reply, however, was not forthcoming.

Public attention was diverted for a time when in November, at the Nineteenth Plenary Session of the Central Executive Committee, there was a nearly successful attempt to assassinate Wang Ching-wei. He was, in fact, wounded, and rumor ran wild about the occurrence. It was said that he was being punished for his friendly attitude toward Japan; some people alleged that the highest powers in the land had arranged for this attempt, and the Fascist secret society of "Blue Shirts" were supposed to have been responsible for what is often termed in China his "execution." Wang, however, lived and went abroad the following February, to seek a doctor in Germany who would be able to extract the bullet, which was lodged near his spine. His post as President of the Executive Yuan was bestowed upon Chiang Kai-shek.

The Japanese continued to grab territory, piece by piece. In January of 1936 they took Kalgan, the capital of Chahar Province, and though the final arrangement did not give this part of China wholly to Japan, their troops remained.

Then one of the chief events of the decade took place; the South revolted again. It was not officially a revolt against Nanking, but the underlying idea was so near as made no difference. In June, Chen Chi-tang, Li Tsung-jen and Pai Chung-hsi telegraphed Chiang and demanded that he resist Japan formally and definitely. (Kwangsi, incidentally, was overrun with Japanese advisers and Japan-made planes, bought on credit.) When Chiang did not obey they started operations toward the North, the Kwangsi army marching into Hunan and the Kwangtung army preparing to go into Kiangsu. The military leaders expected the customary reaction to similar tactics; a joining-up of all the other leaders, who would, they felt certain, be glad of another excuse to challenge the Generalissimo's power, and they also thought that Chiang himself would make concessions and bargain with them. An interesting thing happened instead. Everybody in China and many people outside united in condemning them for taking such action at a time of emergency.

There was an avalanche of telegrams begging them to desist, and word came from people they had counted upon as they counted upon themselves, condemning the time-honored formula. On top of everything else, the Kwangtung air force, which consisted of forty planes, took off one morning—July first—and flew out of Canton to Nanchang, announcing that they were on the Generalissimo's side. The Southern revolt was crushed, and in a few more weeks the entire matter had been cleared up. Chiang explained his attitude and promised that China should go to war as soon as she was forced to recognize Manchukuo. Chen Chi-tang ran away and the other leaders made friends with Nanking. Feng Yu-hsiang came out in defense of his old enemy Chiang and was appointed vice-chairman of the Commission for Military Affairs. Pai Chung-hsi and Li Tsung-jen were placed in responsible positions in Kwangsi, while Kwangtung came under the direct government of Nanking. United China had been challenged and had met the challenge. In spite of mutterings and impatience, Chiang's leadership was accepted.

This proof of consolidation in their Promised Land probably alarmed the Japanese and certainly brought forth a new show of aggression. As a result, "incidents" took place with increasing frequency; here and there Japanese stationed in China were killed. After the murder of a Japanese marine in Shanghai, the island empire multiplied its claims and pushed them. The Kuomintang must be dissolved, they insisted; it was anti-Japanese. Children in China must not be taught to hate Japan. Newspapers and other periodicals must be censored more strictly, Japanese nationals must be protected, and if the Chinese government could not do it the Japanese marines were ready and willing.

For a while China was obedient. The "incidents" were investigated; now and then an arrest was made. Textbooks were censored here and there, and it was a black and exasperating time for all political writers and publishers; many were put into jail and all were cribbed and confined in their work. In Shanghai, where the officials spent their week ends and one could sometimes get a glimpse of Madame Chiang, there was a heavy, expectant sort of silence. The foreign newspapers were the only ones that dared discuss Japanese incidents freely, but there was no limit to bootleg discussion and tea-house gossip. Always sensation-loving and credulous, the Chinese of the sophisticated centers began to give free play to their imaginations. Chiang Kai-shek was pro-Japanese; he was half-Japanese anyway, and educated in Japan, they said. The

Soongs, too, were partly Japanese. . . . Nobody really believed it
and one was not expected to take it seriously, but the childish
allegations kept pouring out, evidence of the petty explosions that
were their only exhaust.

The year 1936 also marked the growth of the Government's summer resort at Kuling. This is a settlement on the top of Lu-shan,
a mountain some miles from the pottery center of Kiukiang, on the
Yangtze. For years it had been a summer resort for officials, schools
and missions when they fled from the terrible heat of the Yangtze
Valley. Lu-shan rises abruptly from the plain, and within the hour
one leaves the dust, the sounds and smells of the lowlands for
fresh blowing air and the scent of pines. A thousand years ago Po
Chu-yi wrote to a friend:

In the autumn of last year I visited Lu-shan for the first time. Reach-
ing a point between the Eastern Forest and Western Forest Temples,
beneath the Incense-Burner Peak, I was enamored by the unequaled
prospect of cloud-girt waters and spray-clad rocks. Unable to leave
this place, I built a cottage here. Before it stand ten tall pines and a
thousand tapering bamboos. With green creepers I fenced my garden;
with white stones I made bridge and path. Flowing waters encircle
my home; flying spray falls between the eaves. Red pomegranate and
white lotus cluster on the steps of the pond. All is after this pattern,
though I cannot here name each delight. Whenever I come here alone,
I am moved to prolong my stay to ten days; for of the things that
have all my life pleased me, not one is missing. So that not only do I
forget to go back, but would gladly end my days here. . . .

So with the Chiangs, who would gladly have spent all their time
in the house on top of the hill, and the walks and paths through
the garden where the Generalissimo loved to stroll with Madame
Chiang on his arm. They set a new fashion here of simple living,
and the rest of the officials pretended, at least, to follow their example.

Chiang's birthday was celebrated that year in the same district,
which was so soon to see the most sensational development of his

career. He had been called to Sian on October twenty-second in order to confer with the Young Marshal on a spot of trouble that was being stirred up by his old enemies the Communists. Chang Hsueh-liang in his new capacity as Communist-fighter had been stationed there for some time, and was not finding his work particularly easy. It was not that the Reds fought back; they didn't. Nobody was fighting at all; that was the trouble. The long uneventful days had given his troops a chance to think things over for themselves, and they decided that they were tired of this civil war. No doubt there was a good deal of judicious propaganda working on them at the same time, and it was effective. If they were to fight, they said, why could they not fight Japan, China's real enemy? The Young Marshal heard these mutterings and pressed the Generalissimo for a visit. He did not at first make clear to his chief how much he himself was now in favor of this argument; Yang Hucheng, the Shensi commander, had practically converted him. Nevertheless he tried to persuade Chiang to come to terms with the Reds.

Chiang did not realize for months that Yang was on the other side. To anyone familiar with the Commander-in-Chief's character it is not surprising that he refused to listen to Chiang's pleas. He was peremptory with both the Young Marshal and with Yang, scolding them roundly for allowing the campaign to slip into what appeared to be innocuous desuetude. Yang was in reality very friendly with the Communists, and the Generalissimo's attitude did not satisfy him, but Chiang Kai-shek felt he had done as much as was necessary for the moment, and went off to Loyang to meet Madame Chiang, to hold a simple birthday ceremony, and to call a military conference on the situation. Chang Hsueh-liang attended this conference.

The Generalissimo's fiftieth birthday was the occasion for nationwide celebration. Never before had it been so evident that Chiang had become a popular hero, held in the same veneration as was Sun Yat-sen. Everywhere were flags and popping firecrackers and parties. In Loyang the Chiangs themselves merely had a breakfast to which the military conference was invited, but in Nanking there was wild excitement over the fifty-five new planes which had been presented to the Government in his honor by the Chinese people. An unsentimental gift, perhaps, but a practical one.

The country's lighthearted hopefulness was due in part to public ignorance of the situation in the Northwest, which had not been settled by Chiang's strong-handed measures, but on the contrary was aggravated. Every action on the part of Nanking that was calculated to stop the mischief merely roused the soldiers, a combination by this time of Chang Hsueh-liang's troops and the Communists they had been asked to fight. They spoke among themselves and resolved to insist upon a showdown, first with the Generalissimo and then with Japan. The Young Marshal realized the danger of this development and again urged the Generalissimo to resist Japan now, saying that he could not be responsible any longer for his men. They were exiles from their own country and eager for a chance to get their own back.

In all his ensuing behavior during the Sian Incident, the Young Marshal's friends stoutly deny that he had any intention of betraying his chief. Donald is especially emphatic that the Sian kidnaping was in no sense a revolt or a mutiny. Chang Hsueh-liang, though he may not be what is called a "strong character," especially in comparison with the Generalissimo's iron nature, is no fool. He was in a difficult position at Sian and the difficulty lay mostly in the fact that he could understand the claims of both sides, Chiang's and Yang's. Too much sympathy with the other side of a question is usually fatal to a soldier's fighting capacity, and that was Chang's misfortune. He was spurred on to violent action by his Northwest associates, yet when the test came he found he could not be disloyal to Chiang. Still his wavering in both cases may well have been the salvation of China; certainly the Generalissimo's capture and release united the country as nothing else could have done.

Chiang Kai-shek went to Sian on December seventh, determined to put down this Red foolishness once and for all. One of his special units, which he had left up in Shensi in reply to the complaint of the Young Marshal's men that he would not use his own soldiers, had been defeated in a battle with the Communists. Yang Hu-cheng's soldiers had just voted on their own to fight Japan. The Generalissimo decided to attend to this insubordination in person. He had no idea that it would not be safe to go; had he not visited there only six weeks before? Two years of traveling about freely, after his triumphant tour of the Northwest and the West with Madame Chiang, had given him complete confidence in his personal safety at the hands of his people. It was to be only a short trip, so Madame Chiang went to Shanghai for a visit and a rest, as she was not well.

Nobody expected anything sensational from this little expedition. The Generalissimo often traveled about on such errands, and though his high officials were aware of tension in Shensi, tension in regard to the Communists was nothing new. Among the many impossible rumors that have circulated since the occurrence of the Sian Incident, there is a hardy one to the effect that the kidnaping was a put-up job, that the Generalissimo had arranged it, and that Madame Chiang and a few personal friends expected it. The advantages of such a piece of play acting, according to this story, lie in the fact that in the crisis the Government people showed their true colors; those who were loyal to Chiang proved it, whereas his enemies came out into the open. Therefore the Generalissimo was never really in danger.

Strange things happen in China, and the Sian Incident was strange enough in truth without these elaborations of fancy. It is most unlikely that the Generalissimo's group found it necessary to go to such lengths in order to discover their enemies. Like other governments, the Chinese leaders are pretty well aware of the sentiments of their colleagues; it needs no melodramatic trick to discover their sympathies. Chiang's astonishment at the revolt was genuine; he attempted to escape, and thus hurt himself badly. Donald in defense of his first protégé still maintains that Chiang would have been better off had he submitted quietly and treated the matter like an impromptu conference and nothing more.

Others point out that this would have been true had the matter been in the hands of the Young Marshal alone, but Yang Hucheng's intentions were not so pacific; Chiang was certainly in danger of his life for a while.

It seems best for the time being to take what we have been told as a framework, and to fill it in with speculation that is not completely idle. The *Diary* extracts that have been published, with Madame Chiang's account of the matter, *Sian, a Coup d'Etat,* supply us with an outline of event.

Active trouble began on December ninth, when a procession of students tried to march out to Lintung, the hot-springs resort near the city where the Generalissimo was staying. When they refused to obey the orders of the police at the city gate to stop and return home, the police fired and wounded two youngsters. This incident, as might be expected, did more harm than many political meetings, however quarrelsome, could have done.

Chiang's uncompromising attitude is best expressed in his own words. In the introduction to his *Diary* the Generalissimo says:

I inquired about the conditions at the front and gave them (the Commanders of the bandit suppression troops) my orders. I told them that the bandit suppression campaign had been prosecuted to such a stage that it would require only the efforts of "the last five minutes" to achieve the final success. I urged them to perform their duty with courage and determination. I also called them to conferences at which we discussed questions of strategy, and I explained to them my views. Judging them with an unprejudiced mind, I found that the Commanders of the Northeastern troops were loyal to the country and fully understood the principle of righteousness. I had not the slightest suspicion of their treachery. Unexpectedly a mutiny broke out, almost under the tip of my nose, and threatened my personal safety. As I had full confidence in them, I neglected to take precautions. For this I should blame myself and not others.

The Generalissimo is a man to whom discipline is one of the first laws of the universe. "I explained to them my views. . . ." No doubt the Commanders felt exasperated at the stoniness of that wall. The first extract from Chiang's *Diary* shows the same frame of mind:

December 11. This morning, while I was walking in the compound, I noticed two men on the Lishan Mountain, standing looking at me for about ten minutes. The incident struck me as singular. . . . Li Tien-tsai (head of intelligence work under Chang Hsueh-liang) suddenly called and requested an interview. As he had made no appointment, I was rather surprised at his unexpected call. During the interview Li expressed his doubt as to the wisdom of the bandit suppression policy. His views were the same as those of Han-ching (Chang Hsueh-liang) which were expressed to me the day before. Finding that his mind had been very much poisoned, I reprimanded him severely.

That evening the Generalissimo invited the Young Marshal with Yu Hu-cheng and Yu Hsueh-chung to dinner and discussion. Chang Hsueh-liang came alone, making excuses for the other two, and Chiang noticed that his single guest seemed uneasy and distracted. However, since the Generalissimo had spent several days scolding the Young Marshal and his friends, he put this behavior down to a natural sulkiness, and was not surprised.

Chiang Kai-shek went to bed that night in a quiet mood, thinking of what he had done, perhaps, in preparation for his morning's entry in the diary. He got up at his usual time—five o'clock. It was five-thirty when he heard gunfire, first thinking that the troops had, after all, revolted. He sent to find out what it all was, and the chief of his personal bodyguard and the twenty soldiers he had brought with him reported that there seemed to be a mutiny. The guard suggested hastily that Chiang take to the mountain back of the house.

Clad only in his nightshirt and without his false teeth, the Generalissimo with two of his men, a guard officer and an A.D.C., tried to leave by one of the side doors. It was locked, and there was nothing for them to do but to climb the wall, "only about ten feet high and not difficult to get over." Doing this, the General-issimo slipped at the top of the wall and fell into the moat outside, a drop of thirty feet. He wrenched his back badly and for three minutes was unable to walk at all. Helped by his men he managed to climb part of the way up the mountain. As he explains, he thought the mutiny was local, and that when the men had dis-covered his escape they would be quieted down before daylight. The party gathered a few more of his bodyguards who were stationed at a little temple, and together they all reached the top of the hill.

Guns were fired close to the heads of the fugitives as they sat there resting. "I then realized that I was surrounded, that the mutiny was not local and that the whole of the Northeastern troops took part in it. So I decided not to take shelter, but to go back to my headquarters and see what could be done. I walked down the mountain as quickly as I could. Halfway down the mountain I fell into a cave that was overgrown with thorny shrubs and in which there was barely enough space to admit me. I felt exhausted. Twice I struggled to my feet but fell down again. I was compelled to re-main there for a rest and to wait further developments."

As it grew lighter the Generalissimo could see that the mountain was surrounded with troops, and he heard the firing of machine guns and grenades at the house. Then a search party came near to his cave, and he was discovered.

I heard one of the mutinous soldiers above the cave saying: "Here is a man in civilian dress; probably he is the Generalissimo." Another soldier said: "Let us first fire a shot." Still another said: "Don't do that." I then raised my voice and said: "I am the Generalissimo. Don't be disrespectful. If you regard me as your prisoner, kill me, but don't subject me to indignities." The mutineers said: "We don't dare."

Having found him, Chang Hsueh-liang's battalion commander seemed overcome. He knelt before the Generalissimo with tears in his eyes and asked him to come back to headquarters. It was after nine o'clock by this time. At the house the Generalissimo was enraged to hear that he must go to Sian to see the Young Marshal, but he had a lot to say to that young man and so he consented to enter the car. He was still under the impression that it was only Chang Hsueh-liang's troops that had mutinied, and when he was taken to the building that was occupied by Yang Hu-cheng and saw the guards wearing the armlet that marked them as Yang's men he could only suppose that the Shensi commander had been overpowered in his defense, and that the men had been looted even of their arm bands. He did not see Yang. As soon as he had arrived he demanded angrily that Chang Hsueh-liang come to him.

CHAPTER XXI

The Generalissimo Refuses to Discuss Terms

I<small>T WAS A STRANGE MOMENT</small> when the two men confronted each other. Chang, the kidnaper, was pale and exceedingly respectful: he "stood with his hands at his sides." Chiang, the kidnaped, was furious, outraged and as peremptory as if the bodyguards and soldiers who lay dead at Lintung were still at his back. He was completely transported with anger; all his instincts as a soldier, his religion of discipline, were affronted. Already he had twice commanded his captors to kill him rather than treat him disrespectfully, and to the marrow of his bones he meant it.

The interview is set forth in the *Diary*. Chang denied having known beforehand of the revolt and tried soothingly to argue with his chief. "I did not know anything of the actual developments, but I wish to lay my views before Your Excellency, the Generalissimo."

"Do you still call me the Generalissimo?" snapped Chiang. "If you still recognize me as your superior, you should send me to Loyang; otherwise you are a rebel. Since I am in the hands of a rebel you had better shoot me dead. There is nothing else to say. . . . Which are you, my subordinate or my enemy? If you are my subordinate, you should obey my orders. If you are my enemy you should kill me without delay. You should choose either of these two steps, but say nothing more for I will not listen to you."

That statement is the basis of the Generalissimo's attitude throughout the Sian affair. His is a sturdily logical mind and he resented the faulty reasoning that had led the Northwest commanders to attempt a forced compromise. A leader is a leader, he said, and if he can be intimidated into taking an action opposed to his beliefs he is a leader no longer. Either these men would obey him or they were his enemies and as such should behave as logical enemies and kill him. A deposed leader was no good to anybody anyway. He must lead or he must die—that was discipline. There were no halfway measures for the Generalissimo. His was no suicide complex, as some people have believed; he was merely living up to his idea of himself. It was not even heroic of him to demand death, in his own estimation; it was *right*.

Chang could do nothing with him. He tried to talk about "the common will of the people" and the Generalissimo's duty to them, but his chief went into paroxysms of rage at this and denied that the mutiny was popular. "Since you are a rebel, how can you even expect to command the obedience of your men who surround this house? . . . How can you be sure that your men will not follow your example and do as you are doing to me?"

The captive Generalissimo then grew kinder and urged the Young Marshal, in a purely friendly spirit, to realize his predicament—the Young Marshal's, that is. "I am really afraid for you," he said sincerely, without realizing for a moment the paradox of the statement. He proceeded to elaborate his earlier speeches and to explain his duty as he sees it. "I must preserve the honor of the Chinese race, and must uphold law and order. I am now in the hands of you rebels. If I allow the honor of the 400,000,000 people whom I represent to be degraded by accepting any demands in order to save my own life we should lose our national existence."

Chang Hsueh-liang at last abandoned the argument and suggested that the Generalissimo come to his home to live where it would be safer; Chiang Kai-shek proudly refused his protection. He also refused to eat anything. In the course of the day he interviewed other people, and steadfastly rejected all offers of clothing and food. He fell asleep that night without having eaten.

In the meantime, in Shanghai, the news had reached H. H. Kung first by way of Nanking, whither the kidnapers had telegraphed a message as to the Generalissimo's capture, setting forth their demands for a future program of the government as the conditions of his release. They wanted eight things: reorganization in Nanking, an end to the civil war, release of all political prisoners, release of the members of the National Salvation Association who had been imprisoned in Shanghai (where Madame Sun had been a protest picketer before the prison), free speech, no restrictions on patriotic movements, a National Salvation Congress and, as usual, "execution of the will of Sun Yat-sen." This, in short, was the ransom demanded for the return of China's leader.

Kung went straight to Madame Chiang, who was interviewing various officials in the course of her work as Secretary-General of the Commission of Aeronautical Affairs, and broke the stupendous news. After the first shock, "I was troubled," she writes, "because this was the only time in years that I had not gone with the Generalissimo on his trip, having been prevented from doing so by illness. I had the feeling constantly with me that if I had been in Sian this situation would not have developed." Doubtless her feeling was correct; in all the Generalissimo's dealings with life since his marriage she has been the softening influence. Mayling does not subscribe wholeheartedly to her husband's worship of discipline: she has faith in freedom of thought and rational discussion. Had she been in Sian, Chiang might not have been so abrupt and censorious with his doubting commanders; feeling would not have run so high and so desperate. But it was too late to regret or to speculate on what might have been avoided: "There has been a mutiny," was the way her brother-in-law told her, "and there is no news of the Generalissimo."

It was not long that evening before the world heard of it. Shanghai even more than Nanking is a factory of gossip, and Shanghai ran wild. The Soongs gathered together—with the exception of Madame Sun, who though personally sympathetic was definitely on the side of the Northwesterners and could not be included in this council of war. Madame Chiang, Dr Kung, Donald and others of their immediate group went to Nanking by the midnight train, which arrives early in the morning. There was not much sleeping that night; they had too much to discuss.

Things were graver even than they appeared. It was far from certain that the Generalissimo was still alive; they had only the assurance of the mutineers for that. If he had been killed . . . but Madame Chiang refused to admit that possibility, though she was to have a tussle with many of the leading minds of the Government about it. They arrived early in the morning to find Nanking in a hubbub, and the Government people divided into two camps. One, of slightly larger number, was in favor of quick and stern retaliatory action. They wanted to make war on Sian immediately; to send bombers over the city and then to march against the Northwest. Already the Standing Committee had taken his appointments from the Young Marshal and denounced him. Madame Chiang was strongly against both actions.

I pleaded for calmness of judgment pending the receipt of definite news; for the avoidance of precipitate action, and for confidence in the spiritual resources of our people. I urged that the leaders in Sian, until proved otherwise, should be taken at their word, but every effort should be speedily made to get at the truth.

"Perhaps they have a reasonable grievance," I hazarded.

This attitude met with few sympathizers. It was not the sort of reasoning the Chinese officials were fond of. Those who were loyal to Chiang were in a frenzy of revengeful rage, and it is rumored that those who were against him were eager to oppose his wife once and for all. If bombing Sian were to prove the fate of the Generalissimo, where would they find a better chance of getting rid of him honorably and painlessly? Only Mayling with her little coterie of supporters stood in the way. In France, Wang Ching-wei heard the news and immediately started for China.

It was decided that Donald should go to Sian immediately. He was confident of his influence with the Young Marshal; he knew him through and through, and was certain that he could counteract the effects of the other commanders' arguments. Madame Chiang wired Chang that he was coming and waited for the reply, during which time she had "stormy conferences" with officials. By lunchtime there had been no answer from Sian, and Donald left for Loyang in order that he would be nearer Sian when the time came to go. Colonel J. L. Huang, the General Secretary of the Officers' Moral Endeavor Association, went along as interpreter, for Donald would not be able to talk directly with Chiang Kai-shek. They carried letters from Madame to Chiang and to Chang Hsueh-liang, in the latter of which she pointed out to the Young Marshal "the disastrous effects his action would have upon the unity of the nation, and expressing my belief that he meant no harm to the country or to the Generalissimo by his imprudent and impetuous action; but that he should retrieve himself before it was too late." The party reached Loyang to find that this city was still loyal to Nanking; later a wire arrived from Chang Hsueh-liang inviting Donald to come.

It is interesting to reflect that by the evening of December thirteenth everyone in Nanking knew that the Northwest leaders had all a hand in the mutiny, while the Generalissimo himself, lying cold and hungry and in pain on his bed, was still unaware of the part played by Yang Hu-cheng and the others. He had had a strenuous day, still refusing to eat although the battalion commander, a former Whampoa cadet, by arrangement with the servants had bought him food with their own money in order that he need not eat the bread of his captors.

"On this day," he writes sturdily, "I did not take any food."

The attendants served tea every hour and were very attentive to me. They showed great anxiety when they saw me take no food. Their sincerity moved me, because it was a spontaneous expression of their feelings.

At 11 o'clock Shao (Shao Li-tzu) again called. I felt a pain in my loins and my legs, and I could scarcely sit up.

Shao wanted Chiang to move from the Pacification Commissioner's Headquarters to a more comfortable house; Chiang retorted that the place where he was, being an organization under the Executive Yuan, was the proper place for him as Chief. He added that if he were not sent back to Loyang he would die right there. Then he sent a long admonition to Chang, reminding him of Chen Chiung-ming's rebellion when the young Chiang Kai-shek had stayed with Sun Yat-sen. He also inquired after Yang Hu-cheng, who had not made an appearance: he could not understand.

The day ended with another visit from Sun, one of the generals, who was evidently in a truculent mood, as he brought a pistol with him. He insisted upon the Generalissimo's moving to the other house, and he stayed until two o'clock, when Chiang grew angry and ordered him to go. "I am your superior. When I order you to go, you should go at once."

Sun went, and Chiang noted in his *Diary:*

I know that these rebels are very dangerous people. I am determined to fight them with moral character and spiritual strength and with the principles of righteousness. When I was young, I studied the Classics of our sages. After I attained manhood, I devoted myself to the revolutionary cause. There are many heroic deeds in our history. The martyrs of the former ages always defied death. In the pages of our history we find vivid descriptions of the circumstances under which they met their death. Being a great admirer of these heroes, I prefer to follow in their footsteps instead of disgracing myself. . . . At this moment, examining my own mind I find it clear and calm. My mental comfort is that I shall be able to carry out my life-long conviction.

Madame Chiang in Nanking carried on with her own fight next

day. She continued with the Aeronautical Affairs Commission work and in the meantime went on explaining to and exhorting her opponents at conference after conference. The veil was slipping; criticisms of the Generalissimo were spoken openly in her presence, and wherever it was possible certain officials began to curtail her powers. When they demanded force, saying that the Government's prestige would suffer if they waited for action against Sian, she asked them who was willing to take charge. This was too straightforward for the most pushing of the aspirants, and they held back.

" 'Anyway, the Generalissimo is already dead,' said some.

" 'What is the life of one man compared with that of the State?' asked another.

" 'She is a woman pleading for the life of her husband,' was one taunt repeated to me. . . ."

Madame Chiang kept hammering away at the military and Party officials, trying to convince them that hers was not merely a wife's plea but an argument based on her certainty that Chiang was necessary to the State. "Place the armies in position if you so desire, but do not fire a single shot. . . . Meanwhile let us use every effort to secure his release. If peaceful means fail, then it is not too late to use force." She proposed to fly to Sian herself, and the idea at first terrified everyone. "I was told that my going would be futile; that I would risk my life unnecessarily; that I would be captured, and tortured to make my husband submit to demands; that I would be held as a hostage, and, at the very least, that I would complicate matters."

Later, when Madame Chiang had proved to be far stronger in her opposition to their plans than they had expected, some of those leaders were delighted that she should go. With both Chiangs out of the way, they hoped, things would move faster in their direction. For the time, however, the matter suddenly took a turn in her favor; Donald wired on the evening of Monday, the fourteenth, that the Generalissimo was alive and well. Further, Chang Hsuehliang urged Dr Kung and Madame Chiang to come to Sian and see for themselves.

Though Donald had been cheerful in his wire, Chiang was not really very healthy just then. He had spent the day with the Young Marshal, during which time they had an interesting conversation on the subject of his *Diary*, which the commanders had seized and read. Among other items that caught Chang's eye was a remark pertaining to himself, in which the Generalissimo had said "It is a pity that Han-ching has not more character." The Young Marshal's reaction was typical; he bowed to the impeachment, examined himself, and went straight to Chiang to confess that the accusation was correct: "Your great fault," he allowed himself to retort, however, "is that you have always spoken too little of your mind to your subordinates. If I had known one tenth of what is recorded in your diary, I would certainly not have done this rash act." For Chang and the others had been very much impressed by the Generalissimo's personal record, his "loyalty to the revolutionary cause" and his determination to bear responsibility for the country. Besides, there had been another argument as to Chiang's removal from Headquarters; Chang said he wanted to send his chief secretly back to Nanking and it would be impossible from that place, but Chiang said he wouldn't leave Sian at all unless he could depart openly and "in a dignified manner." Then he was told that Donald had arrived.

He saw the foreigner at five o'clock that afternoon. "I was very much moved by his loyal friendship," he said. Tears came to his eyes at this first proof that he was not indeed lost. Donald gave him Madame Chiang's letter and persuaded him, with the additional urging of the Young Marshal, who promised to send him to Nanking soon, to move into the other house. . . .

Why had there been so much difficulty and insistence upon this moving? The Generalissimo at that time, at least until four o'clock that afternoon—he saw Donald at five—had not realized that Yang Hu-cheng was deep in the conspiracy, and so it had seemed proper that he stay in the Executive Yuan building. Chang Hsueh-liang, however, knew that he himself was a better and a safer friend to Chiang Kai-shek than was Yang. J. L. Huang, who was waiting

THE SOONG SISTERS

outside in hopes of getting a glimpse of his leader, caught a few words spoken by Chang to a subordinate: "If we can't move him today I'm afraid they will change guards tonight." The guards at that moment were Chang's own; had they been changed to Yang's men it is likely that Chiang would never have come out of Sian alive.

Having changed both his quarters and the tone of his relations with the Young Marshal, the Generalissimo as one might suppose felt a little better about things. Chang now dared to tell him of the eight proposals that had been sent to Nanking and at the same time confessed that he was not going to find it as simple as he had pretended it would be to get the Generalissimo out of Sian and safe to Nanking. Chiang repeated that he would not consider any proposals so long as he was a prisoner, and there followed more arguments both from Chang as radical and Chiang as disciplinarian. They ended on the same note: the Generalissimo would not be forced to do anything. The Young Marshal departed at last, probably controlling his temper with difficulty. What was one to do with the man now that one had him?

Left with Donald, Chiang had time for a little rapid discussion as to ways and means. Madame, he said, must not come to Sian until after his death, but if it were possible he should like to see J. L. Huang. . . .

Meantime that jovial and enormous man had not been permitted so much as a glimpse of his chief, and he was growing worried. Madame Chiang's instructions had been to interpret for Donald and her husband, and above all to see him and to make sure of his state of health. The Young Marshal was obdurate; Huang couldn't interview the Generalissimo.

"But how am I to go back to Nanking in that case?" demanded the Colonel. "How do I know he is really alive? What am I to report to Madame? I could never admit that I haven't even seen him."

Obviously the Young Marshal was not his own boss. Somebody else was objecting. However, he admitted the reasonableness of the argument and thought for a while; then at last he had an idea. Huang, he said, could see the Generalissimo, but the Generalissimo couldn't see Huang. A peep-hole was arranged in the door to Chiang's apartment by the simple expedient of rubbing a tiny space in the whitewash that covered the glass. With a gun jabbed into his capacious back and a stern-faced guard on either side, Huang gingerly bent and peered through this hole. He saw his Generalissimo lying in bed, propped up on pillows and evidently in deep conversation with Donald who sat by his side, while the interpreter stood at attention. Huang was allowed to stare at this tableau for a few seconds, and then was drawn back from the door. Anyway, he had seen the Generalissimo and he had seen him alive, though he looked thin and ill. The Colonel allowed himself to be taken back to his quarters near by in a more cheerful frame of mind. Donald was to fly to Loyang next day to telephone Madame Chiang, and Huang might even go with him and return to Nanking with firsthand news.

It was high time for Madame Chiang's peace of mind that something like this be done. Nanking would not be convinced by Donald's telegram that Chiang was really safe. It was a deep-laid plot, some people insisted, cooked up between the Australian and his old ward, the Young Marshal, to get yet more of the Soongs into their murderous clutches. Far better to send troops and planes, they cried, than to endanger any more people.

The morning of the fifteenth the Generalissimo, who knew that Huang had arrived with Donald and had several times asked to see him, grew impatient when they put off his request. "I am very anxious," he wrote in the *Diary,* "to have J. L. Huang come to see me in order that he might carry a letter back for me to my wife. For all I know, that telegram of the other day may never have been despatched." Although Chang was unwilling and had to argue with his conspirators about it, Huang was at last permitted into the guarded room, not knowing what the Generalissimo had in mind. Neither, evidently, did the Young Marshal, for his orders to the Colonel at the threshold were very firm.

"You must not talk to him at all," said Chang.

"But how can I help it? He'll think I am mad if I stand there without a word," expostulated Huang.

"You may just give him greetings then, and polite talk like that," said the Young Marshal. "But you can't talk about any of his affairs, and he can't talk to you either."

"And if he does?"

"Then you won't be permitted to leave Sian," said Chang grimly. With that they both stepped inside the room, into Chiang's presence.

Whatever stipulation Chang Hsueh-liang had made to Huang, he had not dared give many orders to Chiang Kai-shek. The Generalissimo, who had at last been persuaded by Donald to take food, was brisk and chatty. He asked after his wife's health and then demanded paper and pen and began to write, while Huang stood there respectfully and wondered what his fate was to be. The Generalissimo signed the letter.

"This is to be given to Madame," he said, but did not hold it out. "Letters sometimes get lost, and I am going to read this to you so that you can remember what was in it, in case you cannot deliver it." With a clear voice he read:

As I have made up my mind to sacrifice my life, if necessary, for my country, please do not worry about me. I will never allow myself to do anything to make my wife ashamed of me, or become unworthy of being a follower of Dr Sun Yat-sen. Since I was born for the Revolution, I will gladly die for the same cause. I will return my body unspotted to my parents. As to home affairs, I have nothing to say further than that I wish you would, to gladden my spirit, regard my two sons, Ching-kuo and Wei-kuo, as your own children. However, you must never come to Shensi.

He read this letter aloud three times to impress it upon J.L.'s memory, and the Colonel's heart, as he stood respectfully listening, sank into his military boots. He would never get out of Sian now, he knew.

Outside the room, the Young Marshal flew at him in a fury and took the letter away. "How could I help it?" asked Huang reasonably. He went to his own quarters and awaited his fate, which arrived fairly promptly in the persons of two polite officers and some soldiers.

"We have been so much ashamed of putting you into this dreadful room," said the leader. "You understand it was because you arrived unexpectedly that you have been so inconvenienced. We apologize."

"Don't mention it," said Colonel Huang. "The room is very comfortable. I am quite happy here."

"No politeness, please; it is a most unworthy room and you deserve a better one. We have been able to prepare one in a house a little way off from here, so if you don't mind moving——"

"But I see no reason whatever to move," said the Colonel graciously, trying to stave matters off as long as possible. "I cannot imagine a better place than this. I am near my chief; I am quite comfortable——"

"You are too kind," said the officer. "No, you will be much better in the new place. Really, I insist."

Colonel Huang gave in. "Since you insist," he murmured. "But I assure you that if I had the choice, I would remain here. I am used to campaigning; I have slept in far worse beds. I assure you——"

"No politeness, please," said the officer, bowing.

Then they took him to jail.

CHAPTER XXII

Chiang's Release

THAT LETTER'S MESSAGE was to reach Madame anyway, through the agency of Chang Hsueh-liang's old friend James Elder, who flew to Nanking. In the meantime Donald went without Huang to Loyang on that same day, as he had planned, and they had several long talks by telephone between Loyang and Nanking. Dr Kung could not go to Sian, but Madame Chiang suggested T.V. as a substitute escort for herself. Nanking was opposed to the whole plan; Nanking was acting up seriously, and she was fighting desperately to prevent open war on Sian. The Aeronautical Commission had been placed under direct control of the Ministry of War for fear she would prevent the bombing of the Northwest capital. She urged Donald on the telephone to come away, but he was confident he could avert the catastrophe.

"There may be another way, but I cannot say more."

Elder's arrival with the message from Chiang had given her both hope and fear. If the Generalissimo's noble invitation to kill him regardless were to reach the ears of the hotbloods, nothing could prevent the war. Madame Chiang began to arrange for planes in case they could make a getaway from Sian; she had understood from Donald's last words that Chang Hsueh-liang would probably have to quarrel with his friends in order to effect a rescue, and it would be a ticklish business at best.

The days that followed were days of intense agony and activity for me. Military forces had been in action already east of Sian, and although snowstorms at Sian prevented planes from crossing the mountains, I never knew when some plane or other might get through and bomb the city as they were bombing points along the railway line between Loyang and the mountains.

Shanghai reflected the turmoil of excitement and ignorance that prevailed at Nanking. The writer remembers those days vividly, when all the foreigners who had been favorable to the Nanking government groaned at what they thought was the utter failure of those years of reconstruction; it was like watching a well-loved convalescent who had been slowly and surely climbing out of the shadow of death suddenly fall into a relapse. There was one day when a high official of the Ministry of Finance burst into her house, his voice breaking with grief, his eyes filled.

"They want my chief (T.V.) to go!" he cried. "He'll never get out alive!"

As a matter of fact, however, things were looking better for the Generalissimo. General Chiang Ting-wen, one of Chiang's own men and bearer of the same surname, though he was no relation, had been in Sian all this time. Now he was coming down to Nanking, carrying the Generalissimo's orders to the Government to stop bombing and fighting for three days. These commands were convincing, though many of the officials insisted that Chiang had been forced to write them; with this armistice Madame Chiang went to work as quickly as she could. She prepared the Chiangs' private plane, the Boeing, with Julius Barr, and made plans to snatch Chiang out of Sinkiang if Chang Hsueh-liang should fly off with him there.

[225]

T.V. flew up to Sian on the twentieth. Mayling had tried to go with him, but at the last minute she was forced to compromise and to stay in town a little longer, with the promise that nobody would attack Sian as long as her brother was there. Chang advised her, too, to wait until the fighting was stopped.

Donald and T.V. returned together to Nanking on the twenty-first, a week after the kidnaping, and there was a council of war. The result was that Madame Chiang determined to go back with both of them on the following day. The worst corner had been turned; the most sensational newspapermen still shouted that the Generalissimo had been killed and the rest of it was all a big plot, but it seemed fairly obvious that all the Soong faction would not continue to go back and forth freely between Nanking and Shensi if that were the case. Madame Chiang was certain, too, that it was the moment for her to step in and help the embattled parties to arbitrate. There was a good deal, no doubt, to be said for both sides, but without her influence it is questionable if any one would have been in a mood to listen.

"It was interesting to me," she writes, "to hear from Mr Donald that Han-ching had definite plans to fly out with the General-issimo in the event of an attack. I felt then that I understood Han-ching's mentality, and that gave me more confidence, not only in my intuition, but also in my belief that I could reason with him when I had the opportunity to talk with him. The situation at Sian was, I reflected, that Mr Donald had laid the foundations, T.V. had built the walls, and it would be I who would have to put on the roof."

During these days Mayling had undergone terrific strain, which in her waking hours she never admitted. She lived in the Kungs' house with Eling, who had hurried to Nanking as soon as she realized she would be needed, and the older sister was a great comfort because she believed firmly that Chiang was not dead. Mayling was tremendously busy every second; she never even wept. There was no time, and she does not cry easily. As long as there was hope that Chiang lived—and she never lost hope during those days of waiting—she had a heavy responsibility and she could not shirk it. There were many different undercurrents with which she had to battle: the extremists—among them her own husband—who were sincerely sure that it would be best for the country to take firm measures with the rebels; the plotters who hoped to advance themselves by a complete debacle; the many old-style Chinese whose minds could not see beyond a tangle of petty intrigues, whatever their intentions may have been, and who cluttered up the time to an extent that must have been maddening for Mayling's sharp, Western-trained mind. Above all this was the fact that they were all against her as a weak woman who could not help but rationalize her own behavior. Many of them could not conceive of any woman's taking action for other than personal, sentimental reasons, and this idea colored their opinion of Madame Chiang's attitude and went far to nullify her speeches. It was small wonder that those very natural feelings that they felt they must guard against were stifled in Mayling's heart until she herself could not guard against them, during the few hours when she slept. Then and only then, Madame Kung told her later, did she weep. In her sleep she cried out and wet the pillow with tears.

Those first moments of flight must have been sheer bliss to her after the hectic days and hours of worry and self-control. Even at Loyang, where she saw and noted "bombers fully loaded for action," she was buoyed up with excitement and hope, though now she began to reflect upon the danger she was running. "As I boarded the plane I took the precaution to impress upon the officer in command of the Loyang air force that no planes were to approach Sian till ordered to do so by the Generalissimo." But would they obey that command?

They reached the Sian air field. As they circled about to land, she gave her revolver to Donald and told him to shoot her if she should be seized by the troops. Donald promised: "But I wouldn't have done it," he said later, grinning. He for one had no doubt of his Young Marshal.

Chang met them at the plane, "looking very tired, very embarrassed, and somewhat ashamed." In her usual manner, Madame Chiang greeted him and stepped out into Shensi, pausing only to ask superbly that the customs people should not go through her luggage, "as I disliked having my things messed up." She shook hands politely with Yang Hu-cheng. They had a sociable drive to Chang's house, and Mayling asked for tea before she went to see her husband, wondering meanwhile if they intended to let her see him at all. There seemed to be no trouble in that respect, so she begged that Chiang should not be told of her arrival until she could see him for herself and assure him that she was safe.

Chiang tells of her arrival in a paragraph that shows how much in the dark he was as to developments, and how he was waiting for the end.

December 22. All day today I hoped to hear the noise of airplanes and guns, as from the agitated appearance of Chang, when he came to see me last night, the troops of the rebels must have been badly defeated and those of the Central Government must be pushing forward very quickly. All day there was no sound of planes. My wife arrived at 4 P.M.

I was so surprised to see her that I felt as if I were in a dream. I had told T.V. more than once the day before that my wife must not come to Sian, and when she braved all danger to come to the lion's den, I was very much moved and almost wanted to cry.

"Why have you come?" he demanded as she walked in. Madame Chiang had to exert herself to keep from exclaiming in shocked anger at his appearance. She managed to do so, however; she has learned to control the temper that used to be such a problem to her teachers at school.

"I've come to see you," she said, almost lightly.

Her husband talked rapidly. He showed her a verse in the Bible that he had found that very morning when he opened its pages: "Jehovah will now do a new thing, and that is, He will make a woman protect a man." After so many days of stubborn holding out he was still insisting excitedly that he would do nothing in the

[228]

way of compromise, and he implored her not to ask such a thing of him. Mayling calmed him and reported the almost unbelievable reaction on the part of the public to his detention. "Even the smallest school children were crying as though they had lost a father, and when it was reported that he had been assassinated many soldiers had committed suicide. 'Therefore,' I urged, 'you should not talk of sacrificing your life for the good of the country. . . .'"

It was an interesting point, the difference between the old and the new ideals. Chiang was upheld through these trying days by the traditional, personal heroism on which he had always tried to base his actions: Mayling was speaking from the point of view of the democrat. How far can one travel with either conception before making a compromise with the other? At any rate, Chiang was again with his wife, who could always help him to adjust his rigid convictions to the exigencies of reason. . . . "I noticed that his recital of what he had suffered on the morning of December twelfth upset him emotionally and agitated his mind. To calm him I opened the Psalms and read to him until he drifted off to quiet sleep."

Afterwards she had a long talk with Han-ching and reproached him for thinking that he could have got anything out of Chiang with force. The Young Marshal defended himself: "But the Generalissimo would not discuss things with us. He was so angry after we detained him that he would not talk at all. Please, you try to make the Generalissimo less angry and tell him we really do not want anything, not even for him to sign anything. We do not want money, nor do we want territory."

They talked further, and Chang gave her the rather dubious compliment of commending the sentiments she had expressed in two of her letters to her husband, which he had had occasion to read after confiscating the Generalissimo's papers. He agreed, late in the evening, to argue for Chiang's release with his friends; he himself was now quite willing to let him go. It was not until after two o'clock that he came to report that Yang and the others were not in agreement with him. "They say that since T.V. and Madame are friendly towards me, my head would be safe, but what about theirs? They now blame me for getting them into this affair, and say that since none of our conditions are granted they would be in a worse fix than ever if they now released the Generalissimo."

The next two days were full of conferences and suspicion. As Madame says, the arrival of the Soongs had split the camp; Hanching was now considered definitely on their side, whereas the others felt that to give up their captives would put themselves into danger. The Government troops were getting nearer; the Generalissimo's temper was frayed. T.V. was working all the time explaining, arguing, soothing and suggesting. His party was willing, of course, to give complete freedom to the mutineer, and had the rebels been less worried for their safety they would have found pleasure in the way things were going, for the Nanking group was evidently willing to consider resistance against Japan at last.

"We heard nothing of menaces from the Reds during all this time," wrote Madame. "Quite contrary to outside beliefs, we were told, they were not interested in detaining the Generalissimo. Instead, they preferred his quick release. But we never forgot that their armies were out in the distance—silent now, but menacing and dangerous. We were assured that they had given up their old policies and practices. We refused to believe it. It is a ruse, we told ourselves, and we indicated to the Sian leaders that we would not swallow ruses."

On the twenty-fourth the Generalissimo writes, "The leaders in Sian suddenly disagreed over what they had discussed with T.V. yesterday. They indicated that they could not let me go until the Central Government troops had withdrawn to Tungkwan.

"T.V. is very much upset, but I am taking it quite calmly, as I have not been expecting to leave this dangerous place. The question of life and death bothers me no more."

The entire building must have been a whispering gallery. The Chiangs were never left to private conversation; guards watched them all the time. "I must have seemed very demonstrative to the guards watching us through the peep-hole," said Madame later, "for when I wanted to tell my husband something in secret, I bent very near him to whisper in his ear."

☆   ☆   ☆

Colonel Huang all this time was playing chess with his jailers, philosophically waiting for whatever might come. Nobody ever told him anything. Christmas morning dawned and he said to himself, "This isn't the way I expected to spend the holidays."

Suddenly a messenger arrived and said something to the guards at the door, and then he was simply told that he could go. He stepped out at once for the Generalissimo's quarters, wondering what on earth had happened. The first person he met was Donald.

"Merry Christmas, J.L.," said Donald, and he looked as if he meant it.

"What's merry about it?" demanded Huang.

"Why, we're going back to Nanking. Hadn't you heard?"

Huang started to explain that he had heard nothing, that he had been in jail, but Donald was in a hurry and left him. The Colonel continued on his way toward the house, the front gate of which was at the top of a flight of steps. As he approached, the gate swung wide and T.V. came down the stairs. It was the first Huang knew of T.V.'s arrival.

"Oh, Huang," said T.V. busily, "I've been looking for you. We're leaving, you know. Don't forget to bring my secretaries. They're in the office." Then he, too, hurried away, leaving the Colonel gaping after him.

Next, Madame herself appeared at the gate. "Merry Christmas, J.L.," she said cheerfully. "We're leaving, you know. . . . I leave my *amah* in your care. Don't forget to bring her, will you?"

When Colonel Huang had got his bearings, the departure was almost completely organized. He discovered that the impossible had happened during his incarceration; that the mutiny was over and the Generalissimo was free. There was one more conference going on in that grim building and when it was over the party was

[231]

to leave Sian. The Young Marshal too? Well, nobody seemed to be quite sure. What was sure, and what interested the Colonel rather more than anything, was that the Soongs and the General-issimo were awaited at that moment on the air field, whereas he himself and the secretaries and the *amah* and the other members of the party were to wait until next day, as it was growing rather late for the trip to Loyang. . . .

He stood near the flight of steps with the gate at the top, waiting and watching. Two cars drove up and stopped, their engines idling. It was still uncertain; this moment, perhaps, was the most uncertain of all. Many of the commanders were still reluctant; would they back down at the last minute?

The gates opened. Out came the Generalissimo dressed in a plain long gown, leaning on the arm of his wife. He was pale and thin, and walked with difficulty. Followed by T.V., the Young Marshal and another general, they came down the steps, entered the first car and drove off. Chang Hsueh-liang at the door of the car seemed to hesitate, then stepped in. Other generals followed in the next car, and then there was left only J. L. Huang himself, wishing he had had a camera.

A more pressing matter remained to be settled, however. He did not like the sound of that next day's departure for himself and his party. He commandeered a car and hurried to the air field, from which the Chiang plane had just taken off. He demanded to see the pilot of his own plane.

"Can you make Loyang tonight if we hurry?" he asked.

"Maybe," said the pilot. "It's dangerous, trying to land after dark on that field."

"Never mind," said Huang; "I'd rather die outside of Sian than inside, even if we're still in Shensi. I'll be back in a minute."

T.V.'s secretaries were willing to hurry up a bit, though they were hard at work in the deserted building, but Madame's *amah* objected to being interrupted in her leisurely packing. Huang had to pull her out by the hand while he commended her for her devotion to duty; a few dresses more or less wouldn't matter, he explained. They were all at the plane in record time, and nobody seemed to have reconsidered as to their departure. They took off; Huang heaved a sigh of relief as he glanced back at the cradle of China's civilization, which had so nearly been her grave.

There was a happy reunion that night at Loyang.

☆   ☆   ☆

In Shanghai, strollers in the street under the great illuminated Christmas decorations jumped at the sudden din of joyful cries and exploding firecrackers. The town that had been dull with lethargy woke up with a vengeance. For once no policemen tried to enforce the municipal regulations against fireworks. The Generalissimo was free! He was alive! He was on his way home!

In Nanking the same thing happened, only more so. In all the little towns up and down the river and out in the interior the Christian holiday was celebrated with a fresh fervor unknown to Christian countries. Feng Yu-hsiang, a confirmed teetotaler, drank two cups of wine and let the newspapers know about it. For the first time in troubled centuries all China, traitors and patriots and peasants and Communists and capitalists, even Chiang's enemies, were together as they heaved a gigantic sigh of relief. It had been an irresistibly gripping drama.

CHAPTER XXIII

Chinese Unity

WHAT WAS THE inside story of the Sian settlement? Among the foreigners who watched and puzzled and gossiped it seemed fairly clear; the Soongs had paid a lot of money for Chiang. How else could it all be explained? It was an old story to China, they said to one another, for all the trappings of planes and long-distance telephones.

Only the fact that Chang Hsueh-liang had come along with the Chiangs to Nanking was rather difficult to sum up in the accounting. When the Generalissimo made his statement and offered his resignation, when it became known that the Young Marshal was going to stand trial for his rebellious act, and when the Northwest people kept quiet, it did not seem so beautifully simple, after all. At the same time, it might be even simpler than it looked—it may have been a very deep game, said the treaty port foreigners, who always think they know more than anybody else about these inner workings of the government. Perhaps it was all a put-up job to unify China. Yes, that was it—Chiang Kai-shek had been to Sian before, in October, hadn't he? Well then, the thing was obvious; it was arranged at that time that he should be kidnaped, held for a couple of weeks, and released on Christmas Day. Maybe everybody in Sian hadn't been in on the secret; perhaps Chang Hsueh-liang was the only conspirator, and that was why he had come out with the Chiangs, in order to escape assassination at the hands of the hoodwinked commanders of the Northwest. Oh, it was a clever plan, a deep plan; look at the way the Chinese had risen to the bait! The whole nation had been swayed, and now they were one and all behind the Generalissimo except for those incautious ones who had stuck out their necks in Nanking and shown themselves for what they really were. Now the Chiangs knew who was with them and who against. It was a very good trick. Damn clever, these Chinese. . . .

In the meantime a very nervous Young Marshal was being supported in Nanking by the assurance of the Chiangs and of Donald that he had done the right, the honorable, the only thing, and that no harm would come to him because of it. He waited upon Madame Kung as one of the family for whom he had always had the greatest respect—he had also entertained hopes of a marital alliance between their children. He addressed her as "Big Sister," and expressed his anxiety and his regrets. "Please forgive me," he implored. Eling's heart was touched for him; the Young Marshal had always had this effect on people.

"I wanted to—well, to punish him for what he'd done," she said later, "and yet he was so sorry. . . . Really, it was embarrassing."

Of course he had lost all his appointments, and he would have to stand trial. That was to be expected. If only he would behave himself, now, and confine his behavior at the trial to a quiet manifestation of remorse, everything would be all right.

The Young Marshal, however is not a stoic, and he had taken this adventure very much to heart. At the trial he lost patience with his questioners. "I did it once, and I'd do it again if I thought the Government needed it," he shouted. "My mistake was in trying to coerce the Generalissimo. I wouldn't have injured him. He's the only one of you all that's worth a damn, and none of the rest of you would be any loss to China."

In spite of everything his friends could do, Chang Hsueh-liang was promptly placed under Kuomintang "protection" for ten years and there he remains to this day, rusticating in the country. He plays tennis, golf and bridge. A few select among his friends call on him sometimes, and every so often there is a report in the Chinese press that he is coming back as a General to lead his troops to victory. It may happen; it has not happened, however, to date. He has still a year to go before he regains his civil rights, which were declared forfeit for five years.

Chiang Kai-shek in a message full of humility and apology to the nation attempted to resign; his resignation was, of course, rejected. Twice more he offered it, and then, the amenities having been observed, he took a real vacation in order to get well again and to rest his wrenched back. The Generalissimo in the Introduction to his *Diary* gives his reasons for apology:

As I am a responsible member of the Party and the Government, I should not have allowed myself to be trapped in a city full of rebels. I am ashamed of my shortcomings and have no wish to appear to justify myself. Even if I give a plain statement of facts, still I am afraid that something may slip my memory. Moreover, people may suspect that I have exaggerated my own merits and the wickedness of others. Although the rebels did not treat me as their chief, I cannot deny that they are my subordinates, and therefore I accept full responsibility for the outrages committed by them. In telling the story I place the blame squarely on my own shoulders. Since my friends and comrades are eager for detailed information concerning this incident, I hereby, instead of frequently repeating the story, extract from my diary the main facts concerning my personal experience and the thoughts that were in my mind during those troublous days. This, I fear, may reveal my lack of ability as a statesman and as a military commander.

In truth, however, the Generalissimo could scarcely deny that out of evil good has come. He refused, as we know, to sign any agreement with his captors, but the long conversations in Sian and the manner in which he was treated had the result of putting an end to the civil war between Nanking and the Communists, nevertheless. Both sides found that there were many points on which they could agree; notably the Japanese. Other matters, it was tacitly decided, could wait until the Japanese were settled. When one looks back upon the months that followed Sian, one is amazed at the enormous change in Nanking's attitude. Though the Government put on a show of fire-eating and denounced the Reds, they gave in to many of the important demands of the Communists, who by the way agreed to stop calling themselves Communists. Political prisoners were set free. The now famous "United Front" was announced as an accomplished fact. The Reds placed themselves under the central government. Wang Ching-wei said that China's future program would be devoted to the recovery of the land she had lost. A famous Communist leader, Chow En-lai, came to Nanking; a Kuomintang leader went to Sian. Ten years of strife had been wiped out by the abortive mutiny in Shensi, and the Japanese knew it, and watched keenly for further developments.

Tokyo, as the world knew by that time, was emotionally and inalterably opposed to Communism in any form; the Japanese stood still in horror at the idea that China, their neighbor, was drawing nearer and ever nearer to Russia, the fountainhead of those dangerous ideas. With the last of her internal strife abolished, China was getting far too strong; this truth was not announced outright in the Japanese press, but the newspaper outcry against Reds in the Government amounted to the same thing. The struggle could not be held off much longer. Japan was aware of this; so was Chiang; so were the ex-Communists.

Asia waited.

CHAPTER XXIV

At War with Japan

Asia waited, but she did not do it quietly. The "incidents" crowded in upon one another in such number that even with the newspapers of the period it is difficult to tell in what order they took place. The original "incident" of Shanghai was probably the matter of the Japanese marine in Hongkew who was shot—by a Chinese according to the Japanese authorities; by a private Japanese enemy, according to the Chinese. There were many more to follow, however. Some of the incidents were obviously arranged by Nippon in the same way as the Manchurian episode had been staged; others were just what Japan alleged them to be—outbreaks of hatred and anti-Japanese feeling on the part of the Chinese. Two Japanese newspapermen were mobbed in faraway Chengtu and horribly mutilated. A harmless Japanese shopkeeper in the South, who had lived in China seventeen years with his Chinese wife and had almost forgotten the island of his birth, was mobbed and murdered by patriots who until that day had been his friends. A Japanese vice-consul disappeared from his office in Nanking, and was quite inadvertently found alive and well in the mountains suffering from "amnesia" brought on by private domestic troubles instead of going down in history as a martyr to Chinese bandits. A Japanese sailor disappeared from his ship at Shanghai after the war had begun in the North: he had both governments breathing fire and brimstone, while foreigners began to pack their belongings, before he was found fleeing from shame and disgrace in an up-river town, having gone A.W.O.L. in a Yangtzepoo brothel.

The Japanese press talked openly of Nippon's destiny. Japanese schoolchildren learned to recite, "The oranges of Japan are not very good, but when we take control of Fukien we will have very good oranges." A Japanese news agency man in Shanghai became famous for his Jekyll-and-Hyde behavior; sober he was charming and modest, whereas when he was drunk he was apt to bellow to a party of foreigners, "Be careful, now, or I'll have a squad of blue-jackets upriver to make you behave!"

The Chinese press, on the other hand, was mousy-quiet. Not having the Communists to harry, it suffered a little from paucity of printable material. Yet the propaganda that had been working for years throughout the backwoods had at last made itself felt. Coolies and farmers far from the Coast were learning not only to smoke less and to wash more in order to please their idol, the General-issimo, but they knew now that there was an enemy coming from the ocean. Blond foreigners traveling inland were sometimes greeted with cries of anger and the word, "Japanese!" The Chinese knew no better; their enemy was foreign, not like themselves, and that was evidence enough.

North China felt the strain in a special way. Japan had been taking the upper hand for so long in Peking that by a process of attrition the populace had got used to the idea of Japanese domi-nation and could not be stirred, generally speaking, to the frenzy of horror that was felt by the public in other more southerly prov-inces. Generally speaking; but there were, of course, plenty of people ready and willing to fight as soon as they could clear away the hampering influences of unpreparedness and Nanking's advice to wait. The Japanese were rulers in Manchuria in fact, and in Peking they acted as if they were rulers.

The pitcher took its fatal errand to the well on July seventh, 1937, when some Japanese troops decided to hold maneuvers at Lukuochiao, or Marco Polo Bridge, twelve miles from Peking. Though many of the powers were in the habit of drilling near town, the Chinese felt that Lukuochiao was dangerously far inland. Under pretext of looking for one of their number, the Japanese tried to enter Wangpinghsien, where some of the Twenty-ninth Army was stationed. The Chinese resisted; there was a skirmish; the Japanese retired. In Peking and in Japan they hastily put the finishing touches on preparations that had been waiting for weeks. They did not declare war, but the Sino-Japanese war was on.

The Central Government was in residence at Kuling when the news came. Only a few of the highest officials were not guessing cynically that Chiang's reaction would be true to form. He would counsel patience; he would promise resistance when the limits of China's patience had been reached; he would declare that China's territory must not be lost, while all China watched the northern provinces sliced off and added to the gains of the aggressive little Island Empire. . . . Meanwhile the Twenty-ninth Army began to put up a considerable fight in the district about Peking and there were brisk encounters between troops. A Japanese newspaperman who found himself outside the city wall and surrounded by Chinese soldiery spent an exciting two or three days. His first impulse was naturally to hide from any Chinese he might meet, but hunger drove him into a little town where the peasants were very hospitable. They could not understand his speech, but their good nature had not yet been spoiled by experience; he was fed and clothed and sent on his way wondering. He lived to be pulled over the wall by rope and tell his story.

In those early days even the propaganda of Nanking and Kuling was powerless to battle the innocence of many Chinese peasants. A

Japanese aviator who made a forced landing in a field far in the interior found dozens of willing helpers to repair his plane and send him off again. It did not take long, however, for the most ignorant peasant to learn the difference between his own nation's air force and those others. Today even the Szechwanese are, unhappily, experts in distinguishing the noise of a pursuit from that of a bomber.

Sixteen days after the battle of Marco Polo Bridge, Generalissimo Chiang Kai-shek put an end to the speculation and muttering that had filled Nanking and the treaty ports as well as his own office. He had been closeted in conference with generals and officials for days. He looked tired and yet relieved, younger by years, vigorous for the first time since his vacation after the Sian kidnaping, as he gave the address to the educational and technical leaders who had gathered in Kuling to hear him. For sheer simple statement of fact, sober realization of the trials ahead, and Chinese dignity this speech should live forever in proud contrast to the mouthings of most statesmen:

When China was carrying out its cardinal policy of maintaining external peace and internal unity the Lukuochiao incident suddenly broke out, throwing the nation into a state of profound indignation and causing great concern to the whole world. The consequences of this incident threatened the very existence of China and the peace of East Asia. At this juncture, in answer to many inquiries, I wish to state the following:

First: The Chinese race has always been peace loving. The internal policy of the National Government has always been directed toward maintaining internal unity and, in our foreign relations, mutual respect and co-existence with other nations. In February of this year, at the Plenary Session, a manifesto was issued in which these points were clearly emphasized. For the last two years, as actual facts show, the National Government, in its policy toward Japan, has constantly sought to confine all pending problems to proper, recognized channels of diplomacy in order that just settlement could be reached. Our people should understand our national position. As people of a weak nation we should evaluate justly the degree of our own strength. For the past few years we have bent all our efforts towards patient endeavors to insure peace in the face of grave difficulties and grievous pain in order that we may achieve national reconstruction. For this reason in my report of foreign affairs at the Fifth Plenary Session the year before last, I stated that "while there is the slightest hope for peace we will not abandon it; so long as we have not reached the limit of endurance we will not talk lightly of sacrifice"; and the subsequent explanation at the Central Executive Session shows beyond cavil our anxiety to maintain for peace. But, although a weak country, if unfortunately we should have reached that last limit, then there is only one thing to do, that is to throw the last ounce of energy of our nation into the struggle for national existence. And when that is done neither time nor circumstance will permit our stopping midway to seek peace. We should realize that to seek peace after war has once begun means that the terms would be such that the subjugation of our nation and the complete annihilation of our race would be encompassed. Let our people realize to the full the meaning of "the limit of endurance" and the extent of sacrifice thereby involved, for once that stage is reached we have to sacrifice and fight to the bitter end, though always with the expectancy of eventual victory. Should we hesitate, however, and vainly hope for temporary safety, then we shall perish forever.

Second: There may be people who imagine that the Lukuochiao incident was a sudden and unpremeditated step. But already a month ago there were symptoms that an incident would ensue because of statements from the other side, made both through their press and directly and indirectly through diplomatic channels. Besides, before and after the incident we received news from various sources to the effect that the opposite side was aiming to expand the Tangku Agreement; enlarge the bogus "East Hopei Government"; drive out the Twenty-ninth Army; force out General Sung Cheh-yuan; and try to impose other similar demands. From the foregoing it can easily be seen that the Lukuochiao incident is not a sudden and accidental development. From this incident we must realize that the other side has a very definite purpose toward us and that peace is not to be secured easily. According to our reports the only way by which the Lukuochiao incident could have been avoided was to allow foreign armies to come and go freely within our territory without limitation while our own army must abide by imposed restrictions upon its movements, or to allow others to fire upon our soldiers and for us not to return fire. Any country in the world that has the least self-respect could not possibly accept such humiliation. The four Northeastern provinces have already been lost to us for six years; following that there was the Tangku Agreement, and the point of conflict—Lukuochiao—has reached the very gates of Peiping. If we allow Lukuochiao to be occupied by force, then the result will be that our ancient capital of five hundred years, and the political, cultural and strategic center of our entire North would be lost. The Peiping of today would then become a second Mukden; the Hopei and Chahar provinces would share the fate of the four Northeastern provinces. If Peiping could become a second Mukden what is there to prevent Nanking from becoming a second Peiping. The safety of Lukuochiao is therefore a problem involving the existence of the nation as a whole, and whether it can be amicably settled comes within the comprehension of our term "the limit of endurance." If finally we reach the stage where it is impossible to avoid the inevitable, then we cannot do otherwise than resist and be prepared for the supreme sacrifice. This resistance is forced upon us; we are not seeking war, we are meeting attacks upon our existence.

Our people must realize that today the Central Government is in the midst of preparing measures to defend ourselves. Weak nation as we are, we cannot neglect to uphold the integrity of our race and insure the very existence of our nation. It is impossible for us not to safeguard to our utmost. Let us realize, however, that once war has begun, there is no looking backward; we must fight to the bitter end. If we allow one inch more of our territory to be lost, then we would be guilty of committing an unpardonable offence against our race. What would be left to us other than to throw every resource of our nation into a struggle for final victory?

Third: At this solemn moment Japan will have to decide whether the Lukuochiao incident will result in a major war between China and Japan. Whether or not there is left any vestige of hope for peace between China and Japan depends upon the action of the Japanese army. Even at the very last second before we abandon all hope of peace we would still be hoping for peace; we would still be seeking a solution through proper diplomatic channels.

The following four points will show clearly on what we stand on this issue:

[243]

1. Any kind of settlement must not infringe upon the territorial integrity and the sovereign rights of our nation.

2. The status of the Hopei-Chahar Political Council is fixed by the Central Government; we should not allow any illegal alteration.

3. We will not agree to the removal by outside pressure of those local officials appointed by the Central Government, such as the Chairman of the Hopei-Chahar Political Council.

4. We will not allow any restriction being placed upon the positions now held by the Twenty-ninth Army.

These four points constitute the minimum conditions possible as a basis for negotiation for any nation, no matter how weak it may be. And if the opposite side will place herself in our position and have due regard for maintaining peace in the Far East, and if she does not desire to force China and Japan into hostilities and to make them enemies forever, she will realize that these conditions are the minimum that can be considered.

To sum up, during the Lukuochiao crisis the Central Government, in insuring the very existence of our nation, has taken a clear, unequivocal stand. But let us realize we are one nation. We seek for peace, but we do not seek for peace at any cost. We do not want war but we may be forced to defend ourselves. During this grave crisis the Government may be counted upon to guide the nation with calmness and restraint; the people likewise must show sobriety and discipline. In discharging our obligations to our race let there be no distinction between north and south, age or youth, but let all implicitly and with iron discipline follow the guidance of the Government.

I hope you gentlemen will explain what I have said to all those you meet in order that they will understand the situation and appreciate our policy.

I T IS NOT the writer's intention to give a detailed account of the struggle which followed Chiang's statement. The book *China Struggles for Unity,* by Pringle and Rajchman, supplies an admirable outline of the events of the war in the earlier days, and as a background to this record of the Soongs' activities we cannot do better than to quote it.

Negotiations with the Chinese officials in North China continued until July 28, interspersed by more "incidents" and clashes between the troops of both sides, but it never seemed as if the Japanese Government had any intention of accepting a peaceful solution. The delay between the first incident and the start of major operations on July 28 merely gave the Japanese time to bring up sufficient troops and supplies for the invasion. There is, however, still a genuine doubt as to whether the Japanese Government hoped to restrict the war to North China or whether it even then realised that a general war between the two nations was inevitable. Nor is it certain that the Government was in complete agreement with the Army and Navy or they with each other.

On the Chinese side there was at first some hesitation and indecision. In North China especially there was a strong party in favour of compromise led by General Sung Cheh-yuan, chairman of the Autonomous Council of Hopei and Chahar. But the nation as a whole, as represented by the Nanking Government, seemed to realise that the time had at last come when no more concessions were possible. The indecision of the generals in North China had one disastrous result: the Chinese troops in the North, deprived of leadership, not knowing the truth and torn between patriotism and loyalty to their officers, were caught unprepared and swept aside by the Japanese army when the invasion began. As a result the whole defence of North China was unbalanced and two provinces lost almost before the war had properly begun.

If there existed any doubts that the war would spread to other parts of China they were soon dispelled. The tense atmosphere in Shanghai soon produced the requisite "incident" and the Japanese navy, not to be outdone, made the most of it. It is just possible that a serious clash might have been averted for a few weeks at least and quite probable that the Japanese would have preferred such a delay while they were still occupied in North China; but the recklessness of the Japanese naval landing party and the resolution of the Chinese Government left no room for compromise. On August 13 hostilities were in full swing on land and sea and in the air round Shanghai. The Japanese naval force paid dearly for its impulsive action and was nearly annihilated before the army (a little reluctantly it seemed) sent reinforcements to rescue it from its plight. By then the Chinese troops, massed in a narrow area and strongly entrenched, had the upper hand, and it was not until October that the Japanese began to make any real headway. This effort cost the Japanese thousands of pounds and thousands of lives.

Madame Kung remained in Shanghai until the last possible moment. Though she had not yet conquered the shyness which in those days made public speaking almost impossible for her, she started work once more on the hospitals. She asked the Chairman of the Red Cross if they were sure, this time, that they were adequately prepared. In the first days of the war there was still a strong belief among the Chinese that foreign influence would scare the Japanese away from Shanghai, and the Chairman was quite sincere in his reply that everything was ready for the war. Then the incident of the airfield on Hungjao Road took place, war flamed up in Chapei, and in a week the hospitals of Greater Shanghai were in a desperate condition of overcrowding and lack of supplies.

Madame Kung was not taken by surprise this time. For the interim she bought, from her own funds, three ambulances and thirty-seven military trucks to be used as necessity should dictate. She donated twenty more trucks to Madame Chiang's Aviation Corps to transport machinery and pilots and to be distributed to various division commanders who were stationed at the districts around Shanghai. Several were sent to the Yih Garden after Japanese bombing there had destroyed every one of the army trucks and cars garaged in that district, and they arrived just in time to save a store of ammunition and gasoline that the soldiers were vainly attempting to salvage by carrying it away on their shoulders. The Japanese had intended to hijack and confiscate these trucks when they were loaded; Madame Kung foresaw the possibility and carried out the coup well in advance of their attempt. Other trucks she sent to Chenju and to the division commanders of Sungkiang, small cities near Shanghai. When the eight trucks arrived full of gasoline and completely ready for transportation, the commanders thought their appearance nothing short of a miracle—it was one of the first examples of the development of Chinese efficiency in the war. Bedraggled tired soldiers who had been carrying loads all day had reason to bless Eling's inspiration. She had realized the immense significance of gasoline in modern warfare.

She also ordered and personally paid for five hundred leather coats for the aviators. It was her first venture into this sort of personally executive work, but she developed and exhibited a remarkable talent for it.

The Lido Cabaret was a large building in the International Settlement, hitherto very popular with young people, particularly men who went without partners and spent their evenings with the "taxi-dancers" whose pretty faces are familiar to tourists. Madame Kung inspected the two big buildings, the waxed dance floor and the dining room, and then started to work and make plans. In forty-eight hours the cabaret had been converted into a well-equipped, modern hospital of three hundred beds. Madame Kung's private funds were responsible for this. New clothing, equipment, food and money were given to all soldiers discharged from her hospitals. Later, when these institutions were removed to the interior at the Generalissimo's orders, the equipment was saved and taken along.

Connaught Road, a long street running near the limits of the International Settlement that are marked by Soochow Creek, was the scene for the installation of another hospital, a Children's Hospital with a hundred beds. It was carried on for eight months, partially filling one of the most crying needs of war, until the Municipal Council and other organizations found the time and the funds to set up hospitals of their own. For this venture, too, Madame Kung's own money was used.

No private fortune is sufficient to carry the entire burden of a modern war's relief, but at the beginning of those summer days of bombing, Shanghai and the surrounding country was almost entirely unprepared for anything save actual fighting. The beginning of the sale of Liberty Bonds on September first brought an end to this state of affairs. The leading women of the town and of Nanking took "divisions" under their control and a competitive system was arranged. Madame Kung's division set as its quota a million-dollar sale of bonds. In a short period, however, her canvassers had collected half as much again. For the first time this quiet, retiring woman had found scope for her special talents in organization and finance; she had inherited her mother's aptitude for business affairs. She began to take a keen interest in the economic side of the war. Dr Kung had that year gone to England as China's representa-

Generalissimo and Mme Chiang Kai-shek in Hankow, 1938

tive at the Coronation, and during this trip he negotiated a loan from Engand that sent China into frenzies of joy and irritated and increased Japan's anti-British sentiment. Madame Kung was interested in the complexities of loans and currency and she began to study these matters and to learn how much science there is in banking. Her wartime activities, however, she still kept to herself as much as possible, seeing no necessity for publicity. In her opinion as well as that of other people, too many society women were taking tremendous credit for public work that they were not really· doing. They lent their names to committees and organizations, they allowed their photographs to be published in connection with these activities, they appeared at meetings and bazaars, smiling prettily, but when the time came to make an effort and to fulfill all their promises they always managed to hand their duties over to obscure underlings. This behavior scandalized and disgusted the vigorous Eling, who decided that she had been correct in staying out of the public eye all her life. The old-fashioned Chinese virtues of modesty and anonymity for women, she said to herself, were best after all. Nevertheless her American training and the teachings of her father caused her to make a reservation to the effect that women should and must be financially independent. She must somehow reconcile these two ideas. . . .

In the meantime all this activity and mental stimulation brought her out of her shell to such an extent that she consented, though still protesting that it was Mayling's line of country and not hers at all to make a speech to the women of Shanghai at a meeting at the Park Hotel. She was very nervous about it, but it developed that she need not have feared comparison with her sisters in the matter of public speaking. Her voice was clear and far-carrying, her bearing impressive. Later she was persuaded to send a radio broadcast to America.

In Nanking Madame Chiang was working in such a whirl of activity that she seldom found the time to come to Shanghai to see her sisters. The opening of hostilities in North China had been the occasion for an interesting development of the Chiangs' pet project, the New Life Movement. This platform, as has already been mentioned, was on the way to becoming nothing more than a mild if nationwide joke. The missionary influence had brought into being unpopular strictures upon clothing and such dissipations as smoking and wine drinking and particularly dancing, until the public both inside and outside of China had decided that New Life was nothing but a code of petty rules for behavior. Madame Chiang and the Generalissimo in 1935 had begun to prove that this was not true, but it remained for the war to show how useful such a ready-made organization can be when quick action is necessary. On August first, in Nanking, Madame Chiang rallied to her side these leaders' wives and daughters and proposed to them that the women of China make a concerted effort to help win the war.

Women's work, as Madame Chiang pointed out at the conference, lay not only in the field of munitions manufacturing and hospitalization, but also in the education of China's masses. This war was going to be a long, wearing affair. The bulk of their people were still ignorant of the scale of the coming struggle and its significance. While the country's leaders were directing the battle, these women could teach their sisters the principles of patriotism and the importance of hygiene and proper farming. Many peasant women worked in the fields; it was necessary that China's country-people reduce the disease and ignorance that hampered her production of food supply. At the same time that they were learning these fundamentals they could learn other things—to read, to write, to think. Thus the New Life Movement would be carrying on with a constructive program even though the war had turned it for the time being into a machine for defense.

She herself was far too much occupied with her work as Secretary General of the Aeronautical Commission and as general purveyor of information about China to the world outside Asia to give more than a few moments daily to this latest project. She was snowed under with demands from the press of Europe and America for articles and statements. For as long as possible and as often as she felt she had something to say she complied with these requests. In

America and in England the public read over and over again May-ling's indignant words on the subject of the war. China, she warned the world, was only the first of the democracies to be attacked by fascism. Shortsightedness on the part of the powers had allowed matters to become a menace ever since the first breach of faith in Manchuria, and those same powers would endure to see the griev-ous results to themselves of their "mental myopia."

Then there was the matter of relief for the refugees and the wounded. Madame Chiang spoke on the radio, granted interviews to the dozens of war correspondents who flocked to Nanking, and wrote more and more and more in an effort to put her appeals before the public eye. This was not easy for her; she hates asking for anything. It is not so difficult, however, to request aid for some-body else, and she forced herself to do it. For as long as her time and energy held out she did what she could to collect money. She even agreed to write a series of news reports for an English news-paper, but the editor's constant demands for more sensational material disheartened her. She could not manufacture horrors at will, even for propaganda purposes; the horrors she was witness-ing, day by day, were quite sufficient for her imagination. She gave up that commission very willingly.

Her sisters, too, were being besieged by publications. Madame Sun, who had lived in the obscurity she preferred for many years, had always turned off all requests with the ease born of long prac-tice. Only now and then for a paper of whose policy she approved would she break silence; sometimes a Chinese magazine would obtain an article from Chingling. Madame Kung had never made any attempt whatever to write for publication, and her extreme shyness made any press interviews impossible. She was convinced for a while that an article about her for an American "Sunday Supplement" would be practically painless, and so she consented up to the moment of publication, though there was a long and difficult time during which she had to be convinced all over again in the matter of photographs. Just before the article went to press her spirit failed her and the piece was withdrawn. American editors were effectively discouraged for months by this behavior.

Thick and fast the problems of war were pouring in to Shanghai, and none of the Soong sisters had time to think of the lighter aspects of publicity. Several refugee camps in the Settlement were provided by Madame Kung with rice. In Hongkong, refugees from Canton were given rice, a most welcome contribution by Madame Kung to that crowded and suffering island. She was of one mind with Madame Chiang on the subject of education during wartime, and set up two schools in Shanghai and a hundred more in the interior. One of the most fruitful of her activities was the establishment, through the agency of the Y.W.C.A., of two social centers for workers in the interior, for which she donated largely during the first year. Her idea was to help refugees who were looking for work after they had been torn from their own jobs. With the same idea in mind she sent looms to the interior.

Looms as well as rice, working centers as well as refugee camps, reconstruction as well as relief—it was an idea that fascinated her, an idea that was not new to her. Madame Kung had not yet met Rewi Alley nor had the Chinese Industrial Co-operatives been started, but five years before this she had become interested in the working conditions of the Chinese farmers, and after conferring with Shephard, the New Life Movement adviser, had begun a Rural Reconstruction Movement. She was instrumental in sending out a group of university students to go into the interior during their vacations and to teach the farmers scientific ways of crop raising and marketing. The students had helped to organize schools; they had given lectures on food values and sanitation, had done research work in nutrition, and had begun various "health campaigns." She had also begun to think of a new sort of factory adapted to the peculiarities of the Chinese system, an adaptation of the old relationship between owner and worker (a feudal sort of arrangement which in small factories still works fairly well) and a new system of profit-sharing. It was an idea that had in it the germ of co-operative industry. In those days she had a notion, still very vague, of trying out her theories in some small Shansi town.

[252]

Just now, however, routine war work kept her too busy to do more than think about it.

☆　　　　☆　　　　☆

The war continued. The Chinese were putting up much more of a fight at Shanghai than anybody, themselves included, had thought possible. For weeks the Japanese fought and bombed and burned and looted; for weeks the Chinese resisted in spite of lack of equipment and in several cases of gross inefficiency. They had still to learn the secrets of management and discipline against organized attack, but their bravery was unquestionable and it made up for many discrepancies in the struggle.

Nanking still appealed for help from the other democracies; actual help as well as munitions and supplies. Probably nobody was naïve enough to believe that America would actually enter the war —naïveté is not a characteristic of the Chinese statesman—but the Government did hope for an embargo on exports to Japan of iron, oil and war material. Still the days went on, and though America and England expressed lively horror of the Japanese invasion and full sympathy with China, nothing was done that could injure trade relations between the Island Empire and the democracies. Even when the Japanese fired on the British Ambassador and wounded him, even when incident after incident showed that Japan was determined to shove Great Britain, if not America, out of the Far East, trading continued and war material poured into Japanese ports and then into China. The foreign settlement of Shanghai was swayed by small panics. Women and children were evacuated, spent uncomfortable days in Hongkong or Manila, and then came back or gave up the struggle and retired to their own countries. People observed the fluctuations of the food supply and wailed about rising prices, and continued politely to cheer for the brave Chinese.

"You foreigners are watching this war as if it were a football game," said an official with delicate bitterness. "You clap very kindly."

[253]

However, it may have been some comfort to the Chinese army that the foreigners did more than clap; they worried; they took their own volunteer corps duties very seriously, and in many cases had to close down their firms and retire. Old-timers who had been wont to mutter, "Be a damn good thing for this country if the Japs *would* take over," now had occasion to regret their words. A Japanese China, it became more and more obvious, would be exclusively Asiatic, and all the bright go-ahead methods and efficiency of the "Nips" would be devoted to edging themselves and their businesses out of China. They did more than clap kindly for the Chinese soldiers; they cheered loudly, and indulged in dreams whereby their brave defenders would beat off the invader once and for all. Chiang's stock went up with the foreigners; Madame Chiang was compared not only to Eleanor Roosevelt but to Joan of Arc, to Boadicea, to any military heroine of olden days whose name could be remembered.

The creation in the foreign public eye of a new idol, or rather a pair of idols, was nearly interrupted on October twenty-third by a careless chauffeur. On that day Madame Chiang, with Donald and an aide-de-camp started out for Shanghai in order to inspect the wounded soldiers and to attend to various matters in town. Dressed as usual in her working clothes—a pair of blue woolen slacks and a shirt—there was nothing about Madame's appearance to advertise her identity, save that the car in which she rode was a powerful and swift one, and another one came close behind with a second A.D.C.

They entered the "danger zone" in the afternoon, and began to keep their eyes on the sky, watching for Japanese bombing planes.

It happened at about four-thirty. The car was rolling over a highly banked part of the road when some bombers flew overhead. The chauffeur speeded up: the front wheel hit a bump that sent the car off at a tangent. In the ordinary way the vehicle would have recovered its direction, but it so happened that another bump was lying in wait for that same front wheel, and as a result the car slid off the road entirely, with a great jolt that threw the passengers completely out of the tonneau. Donald felt himself going and even had time to see Madame Chiang's body go hurtling through the air before he, like the A.D.C., landed unharmed, if shaken, near the overturned car.

He stood up and hurried to her where she lay in a mud puddle, unconscious. Her face was streaked with mud and her limbs were limp, but nothing seemed to be broken, though she was as white as paper. Donald dragged her out of the mud and bent to listen to her breathing. She was still alive, at any rate, though she still lay motionless. . . .

"Madame!" said Donald. "Madame?"

A crowd of countrypeople had gathered. The A.D.C. in the second car had hurried to the scene. Donald gave the limp form a little shake.

"Come on, wake up," he said gruffly. "You'd better wake up and take a look around." Then he started to sing, "She flew through the air with the greatest of ease, The dashing young girl on a flying trapeze. . . . Come on, Madame, wake up! I wish you could see yourself now; you're sure a beauty!"

There was no reply; Madame remained unconscious. A horrid doubt assailed him. . . . "You're covered with MUD!" roared Donald. "Your face and your pants and. . . . Oh Lord, she's a goner," he said to himself.

Just then she stirred and moaned. Quickly Donald stood up and, with his hands under her armpits, pulled her to her feet. "There you are," he said, as loudly as if he had never had a misgiving. "*You're* all right. *You* can walk. Come on, let's go and find a house."

Mayling stood swaying, looking bewildered. "I don't think I can walk," she protested. But Donald gave her no time to think; he made her go to the nearest farmhouse, and when they had arrived, still telling her what a muddy beauty she looked, he gave her her handbag with extra clothing and advised her to change her slacks. Alone, she might have fainted again except that he pounded on the door and told her to hurry.

She was still pale when she sat again in the car and tried to make

[255]

plans. "We're right here," said Donald, brandishing a map. "Now, if you want to go back to Nanking, I'm game. But if you want to go on we can still inspect the wounded soldiers before we go into town; there's time enough. What do you say?"

Madame Chiang considered for a moment. "We'll go on to Shanghai," she decided. The car started forward, slowly this time. She sat quietly, listening to her own body, trying now that she had leisure to see what had happened to her. "I can't breathe," she said suddenly, in alarmed tones. "It hurts me to breathe."

"Then don't breathe," said Donald callously. "(Broken rib)," he thought.

"But I can't *live* if I don't breathe. . . ."

Madame lived, however agonizedly. She inspected the wounded soldiers at ten that night, and was safe in her own house by morning. The doctor discovered that the rib was indeed broken, and forced her to lie in bed quietly. Once she was comfortable, Donald was her most sympathetic caller.

"But why were you so cruel out at the wreck?" she demanded.

"Because," said Donald grandly, "once you let a woman lie down and think she's hurt, she never gets up."

Mayling got up, however, and was back in Nanking within six days, hard at work as ever.

CHAPTER XXVI

Attitudes toward War

THE WAR, spread as it was over at least four fronts, became increasingly difficult for the Japanese to prosecute, but their chief efforts were naturally concentrated upon Government centers. Until November twelfth their main attack against Nanking was held up at Shanghai, and though many air raids were made on the capital, it was not until then that the Government began to move inland, to Hankow, Changsha and Chungking. Chiang had not the common Chinese failing of overoptimism. From the beginning he had visualized the necessity of ultimate resistance in the rocky Szechwan city.

During this period various leaders took the opportunity again and again to emphasize to foreign interviewers their determination to resist. Kwangtung and Kwangsi promised to support Chiang to the end, if need be, but most of all did Wang Ching-wei express his horror and indignation at the actions of the Japanese, and on November twelfth he explained that "China's foreign policy should

be to ally with all those states opposed to aggression." All of this
protestation was to be expected; the unexpected and most significant development was that among the ex-Communist guerillas of
the North. Though Japan went into Shansi without much apprehension of resistance from these peaceful and wealthy people, the
Chinese both as soldiers and guerillas put up a good fight. It is
amusing to compare two articles which appeared in American
periodicals about this time; one in the *Forum* (August 1937) by
Madame Sun, and the other in *Liberty* (August 7, 1937), an interview with Madame Chiang.

The latter, "China's Strong Woman Talks," was obviously written before many of the recent events had taken place between
China and Japan. The author, Fulton Oursler, had visited Madame
Chiang at her Shanghai home in Route Francis Garnier and describes her thus:

. . . . she was a slight princess in a native frock of black silk and
embroidered flowers, the skirt slit on either side halfway to the knee.
Her walk was graceful and quick, the positive stride of one who ever
thrived on opposition. My first look into her winning black eyes told
of the great and contradictory passions of peace and action. Her gaze
spoke of some kind of personal access to peace within her own spirit—
and yet I thought I read frustration, too, as if all her life she had
wanted to play and knew just how to do it, too, but never quite found
the time. She was short and her hair was dark satin and plentiful and
arranged so that it fell softly over one side of her lovely and intelligent
face. The skin was of an exquisitely fine texture. . . .

Madame spoke of the missionaries of China:

Back in the United States it is the fashion to condemn them. China
knows better. . . . As the Generalissimo and I have traveled from
one end of the country to the other, we have been astonished again
and again at the devotion of these missionaries and the hardships they
endure. . . . I frankly do not believe we can save China without religion. Political force is not enough.

She went on to say that the regeneration of China was to be accomplished by economic reconstruction, by education, "and especially by the ideals embodied in the New Life Movement."

"I could see," says the writer, "from the sudden excited look on Madame's face that in this movement . . . were all her mind and heart and soul." They discussed the rules of the Movement, particularly the petty ones that had called forth so much criticism abroad. Madame Chiang said:

"Some politicians tried to seize the movement. They used the ideas of the puritan, not because they believed in them but on the theory that any discipline would mold the people to their will. My husband stopped that as soon as he heard about it."

"Then there is nothing of Fascism in the movement?"

"No. China would never take Fascism or any form of the totalitarian state. We can't ever be really regimented. Every Chinese is a personality. He will always think for himself. He has an ancient and magnificent culture, a sense of justice, a love of freedom. The New Life Movement has definitely rejected all forms of regimentation as being opposed to the principles of Dr Sun Yat-sen and so betraying the people."

In that same month of August the American public saw what Madame Sun had to say in her article in the *Forum*, "China Unconquerable."

The unfortunate policy of the Nanking government, which followed the course of internal pacification before resistance of external aggression, has even more played into the hands of the Japanese militarists. But during the past year the situation has changed. The anti-Japanese movement of the people reached a high level, and it became no longer possible for the Japanese to obtain their aims by threats and bluffs. The Chinese people have realized that it is possible for them to resist. They are no longer afraid of their "friendly neighbor."

Mass opinion has made itself felt in China. In the growing demand of the people for resistance to the Japanese, all political differences have become of secondary importance. Military satrapy has given way to the rise of an intense patriotism, which gives hope for a genuine unification of the country.

From my viewpoint, the most important task before China is the realization of Dr Sun Yat-sen's principle of democracy. . . . The democratic nations have witnessed how neglect of the first principle during the past ten years has brought great calamity to China. There have been endless civil warfares; the country has been devastated; millions of our people have perished and millions more been rendered destitute and desperate. The best minds of China have always demanded the cessation of civil warfare and conciliation between the Kuomintang and the Communist Party. Long ago public opinion condemned the insidious belief that before resisting Japan we must first crush the communists. Naturally, this policy was provoked by Japan. . . . far from being defeated, the communists have become the advance guard of the anti-Japanese resistance. . . .

It is a matter of congratulation that General Chiang Kai-shek has stopped further civil warfare and that the Kuomintang at last, in a recent plenary session, discussed the question of reconciliation with the Communist Party. But it is very regrettable that, in the manifesto of this plenary session, conditions for conciliation with the Communist Party have been laid down which will make a ready compromise difficult of achievement. There are such unreasonable demands as that the Communists cease propagandizing and abandon their political program of class struggle. How can the Communist Party renounce propaganda and the class struggle when those are the basic reasons for its existence? In France and elsewhere the communists have not renounced propaganda and the class struggle, and bourgeois parties are successfully cooperating with them. Chinese communists have repeatedly declared that they would not attack the government if the latter would really resist Japan. To work hand in hand to save the country is their only condition.

Therefore for reconciliation with the Communist Party it is necessary only to put into action Dr Sun's principle of democracy, convoke the National Congress, change the electoral system so that the people could really participate and have a voice in the government, release the political prisoners, grant freedom of press, organization, and assembly, mobilize the masses for reconstruction of the country and resistance of Japanese militarists.

The sincerity of the communists in wishing to cooperate with the government was proved clearly through the Sian coup. They exerted every effort to maintain peace between the central government and the northeastern army. It was the communists who sponsored the release of General Chiang Kai-shek and the peaceful settlement of the Sian affair. They have done their utmost to preserve unity in China. Therefore if the Kuomintang desires to follow Dr Sun's policy of alliance with workers and peasants, it must not reject the assistance of the communists in saving the country. Cooperation between the Kuomintang and the Communist Party is absolutely essential. All forces must be united.

Aways remembering that both the interview and the article must have been written before the "United Front" developments took place in the Nanking-Communist relationship, that comparison is a good one from which to trace the subsequent evolution of Madame Sun's and Madame Chiang's attitudes. Madame Sun's activities at this time were still unpublicized. She took a house in Hongkong but spent much of her time in Canton, the scene of her husband's most significant triumphs, and her home was the Mecca of worshiping young radicals. As Nanking and her friends drew closer together she signified her willingness to come more and more into the open, and the year marked a progressive number of personal appearances and publications of her writings. Anything that she thought might help win the war, she did. Even so, she tried desperately to maintain the obscurity which the Russians have taught their Chinese disciples is the proper status of the individual, and her position was difficult, for she had been incorporated into the Sun Yat-sen legend; she was a heroine, a myth almost. To know Madame Sun was the highest ambition of many idealistic youngsters. Hero-worship and the submergence of the individual do not mingle. She was jealously guarded by her intimates, like royalty, and yet like royalty she preserved the paradoxical right to be simple, democratic, and to all appearances extremely easy to get on with. Politically, *not* personally, her relations with her family were still strained. Chiang Kai-shek was on sufferance with the Reds; they were watching him with a sort of grudging, cautious approval. The same attitude was maintained by Nanking in regard

[261]

to Madame Sun and her friends. The net result of the situation was that Sun Chingling throughout almost three ensuing years remained in the region of Hongkong; she could not visit Canton after that city's fall, so she was self-exiled from China. Madame Chiang and the Government traveled inland, working tirelessly for the war. Madame Kung went to Hankow; Madame Sun, the wife of Sun Yat-sen, Father of his Country, stayed in Hongkong in the strange position of refugee, a guest of the British government. She did what she could as a capable writer, an adviser, an example, head of the China Defense League, an inspiration to her group, but the fact remained that she was tied to the British island and forbidden by her own principles to go into China.

Madame Chiang's attitude during the progress of the war swung toward the central point of the United Front at very much the same rate as did her sister's. Certain writers have lately accused her of undying enmity toward the Communists, and it is generally believed among foreign Leftists that this unreasoning prejudice is connected in some way with her missionary friendships. Those who hold this opinion are, in the main, people who do not know China at all or who have been here on hasty trips, journalizing and listening to other journalists who make up a theory and stick to it forever after.

Whatever the former state of Mayling's prejudices may have been, whatever the former state of the Communists' prejudices, both have changed. The "ex-Communists" are represented in Madame's group of workers to the same extent as are the other groups, and for this fairness she is always being accused by the conservative elements in the Government of Communist sympathies. One of her "warphanages" is established in Yenan, the Communist stronghold, and of course receives the same treatment and consideration as the others. The Leftists like working with her because she listens patiently to them and keeps an open mind in regard to all questions. She feels this to be her special duty in a world of extremists. She has managed so far to keep out of anyone's camp.

She has no missionary advisers nor advisers of any sort; though

[262]

there is no particular reason why she should not have, since she is not so malleable that advisers sway her in one direction or another, depending upon the latest interview. It is a difficult road she has taken. However, as long as the Communists call her Fascist, the Fascists call her Communist, the unregenerates call her missionary and the missionaries complain bitterly, as they do, that she will not listen to advice, she feels that she is probably being as fair to all sides as a human creature can possibly be.

(The Protestant missionary of today, in China at least, cannot be called an enemy of Communism by anyone save a characteristically touchy member of that movement. Whatever reprehensible economic processes originally produced this phenomenon and made him a part of the Chinese landscape, he is no longer a forerunner of Western trade. He takes his place in Chinese life. He keeps a watchful eye on the well-being of the poorest people, and in most cases his attempts to reform his world and to procure justice for the downtrodden, officious as they may be, are motivated by principles remarkably like those of Communism, and he knows it.)

During the siege of Nanking, Mayling's chief work was still with aviation. The Chinese air force acquitted themselves well, and there is no doubt that one reason for this was that Madame Chiang took her duties so much to heart. She knew every plane and every pilot. Whenever they took off she was down at the field to watch; she climbed the hills to see the battles and was back on the field to tell them about it later when they returned—if they did return. At that time there was still an international group of aviators, chiefly Americans, flying for China, and they were loyal to Madame Chiang as they would never have been to the ordinary commander. One of them perpetrated a breach of the regulations one day when he wrote her directly stating a grievance; he was rebuked for this by his next in command and retorted, "I wrote to her direct because she's the only man in the outfit who'll show any action." After that Madame made it possible for all of them to address their complaints and suggestions to her, and many difficulties were smoothed out in this manner, and the Air Force was better managed. The toll on her time and energy, however, was terrific. Many emergencies cropped up which she was untrained to meet: unexpected problems arose every day. She knew planes; in spite of her sensitivity to airsickness she has done more flying than anyone else in China who is not himself a pilot, but there is much more to air warfare than flying. There was one time when it was necessary to construct a new road near Purple Mountain in order to bring road-metal nearer the airfield; through the night Madame Chiang conferred with civil engineers making plans, and within a few days, according to her advice, the thing was done and done properly. Several months at this pace, however, tired her out. She could not attend to her other duties. Physically she has never been strong, though like so many small and wiry people her energy is amazing, and her health began to show the strain. One danger signal was a recurrence of the urticaria and sleeplessness that sometimes make life a burden to her. Then too she felt that she should concentrate on her work of organizing Chinese women. It became evident that she could no longer carry on, and she gave up the secretaryship.

For some weeks the exodus had been arranged, but not until November twentieth did the National government make an official announcement that they were removing to Chungking. For the time being, however, the chief officials were to remain at Hankow, nearer the scenes of fighting. Managers of factories, organizations of the Government and private enterprises went on ahead and began the gigantic task of making over the Szechwan capital into a city capable of holding the influx of people that was sure to be the result of this move. That same day Soochow was occupied by the Japanese, who were also advancing through Wusih and Hangchow. In Shanghai the native suburb of Nantao, which had already been partially destroyed by fire, flared up anew with twenty more fires. The next day the Japanese Embassy announced that Japan meant to take over the Customs in Shanghai, the Post Office, the Telegraph Office and the Courts. As the foreign Embassies departed from

Nanking on the way to Hankow, Shanghai fell again into panic. The next ten days brought many tense moments to the international city.

Madame Kung was still occupying the house in Route de Sieyes. It was near the limits of the French Concession, and sometimes during the fighting shells fell near by, into the Chinese garden that had been the scene of so many official parties. Eling had decided not to accompany her sister to Hongkong, and though she has always been timid about small dangers she disclosed a new strength in the face of real peril. The woman who could not face a stray dog knelt quietly in her room during air raids, praying. One day a petty civil official brought word to her that a certain general then in charge of the Japanese forces that occupied Shanghai was requesting an interview with her. He had heard from a certain element in Chinese banking circles—and perhaps foreign circles too— that the Kungs as a family representing the banking interests of China would probably be willing to talk over peace terms with the enemy in return for a price. The Japanese general of course knew of the close relationship between the Kungs and the Chiangs, and he actually thought that he could thus bring the war to a speedy conclusion. He proposed to call upon Madame Kung in her own house.

Eling heard this remarkable suggestion calmly, and then reflected while the go-between waited for her reply. Her friends urged her not to consider it: she might be held as hostage: it was exceedingly dangerous. Finally, "Well," she sighed, "I see all kinds of people; why shouldn't I see this Japanese general? Perhaps, though, you should warn him that I have a very frank nature. Tell him he may come. If he doesn't mind being insulted, he may come."

The General did not pursue the matter further. Eling would never confirm or deny the story.

The day the Government started work officially in Chungking, December first, Mussolini made an official suggestion that China approach Japan for peace terms. Nobody took this hint, but it was not a surprise to anyone that on the following day the German

Ambassador to China, Dr Oskar Trautmann, returned to Nanking from Hankow to see the Generalissimo and Madame Chiang, who were still in the capital overseeing the removal of the Government. The scene that took place, though it has never been officially confirmed, is now famous. Dr Trautmann was shown into Madame's working-room where she sat at her desk. She greeted him cordially, having known him for many years. Somewhat ill at ease, he chatted with her for a while, and then placed the paper of German suggestions on her desk.

"This is not my personal message, you understand, Madame," he said.

Madame Chiang quietly put the paper aside. "I should think not," she said. "Tell me, how are your children?"

Three days later Dr Trautmann returned to Hankow with the Generalissimo's uncompromising reply: no peace negotiations were possible so long as Japan continued to exert armed force against China. There were air raids on Nanking every day. On December seventh, just five months after the beginning of the war of resistance, the Chiangs left Nanking by plane. Whatever could be saved of the air force was removed; the ammunition, gasoline and hangars which could not be taken with the departing army were burned. Even iron gratings from the roads were taken up and carried along to Hankow. The fire raged long after the planes had winged their way upriver, but a week later, when the Japanese forces at last entered the city, nothing remained but charred ruins.

Ten years had elapsed since Chiang Kai-shek began his task of unifying China as the representative of a new, independent government in Nanking.

CHAPTER XXVII

Mayling Aroused

A GOVERNMENT IN TRANSIT" was the self-imposed title of the Chinese organization during its stay in Hankow. Although the official capital for the duration of the war was now Chungking and most of the Ministers traveled back and forth between Hupeh and Szechwan, arranging and preparing and settling into the rocky city, the Chiangs and most of their supporters were to remain in Hankow for eleven months. Madame Chiang and the Generalissimo lived in a small house in Wuchang, across the river from the main city itself. Dr Kung and Madame Kung lived in a flat in the building of the Central Bank of China. T. V. Soong, now President of the Bank, was also in Hankow. The city was thoroughly modern and as comfortable as Shanghai itself; the life was urban and urbane until the last period, save for Japanese air raids and a shortage of certain materials, type among others.

It was in 1938 that the Government publishing office collected and produced Madame Chiang's *Messages in War and Peace*.

Hastily gathered together, printed without adequate proofreading, almost completely unedited, it is today the despair of Madame, who shares with other writers a nervous dislike of most of her work when it has appeared inalterably in print. It is just this formlessness, however, which gives the book a particular fascination for the student of history and biography. A jumble of broadcasts, excerpts from letters, newspaper articles and short stories, it is better than the most formalized guide to Soong Mayling's character and its development under stress.

The early days of the war are here represented by a series of speeches and broadcasts that are full of indignation with the democracies for their failure to come to China's aid. She could not believe her eyes. They had pledged their word and they were breaking that pledge; she could not accept it at first, and when at last she was convinced she rebelled, in scathing words. Until the moment of crisis arrived she had been working too hard for her ideals and had been hoping too ardently for the reform of China to give much thought to the shortcomings of other places than China. For years she had remembered America as the yardstick by which she measured her own country. She had pointed to the Western democracies while she exhorted Chinese students to build themselves up for their country's sake. And now! . . .

She did not give up her dream all at once. For a long time she explained to these strangely obtuse people, feeling certain that they needed only a little knowledge of the true state of affairs to awaken to their obligations and to the danger which lay in wait for themselves as well as for China. "You can see," she said:

You can see by what Japan is now doing in China that she is sinister, ruthless, well armed, well organized and acting on a preconceived plan. For years she has been preparing for this very attempt to conquer China even if she has to annihilate the Chinese to do so. Curiously no other nation seems to care to stop it. Is it because the flood of calculated falsehoods that Japan broadcasts daily is believed? Or is it that she has been able to hypnotize the statesmen of the world? She seems to have secured their spellbound silence by uttering the simple magical formula: "This is not a war but merely an incident." Even the declaration by the Japanese Premier, Prince Konoye, on August 28 that Japan intends to "beat China to her knees so that she may no longer have the spirit to fight" does not seem to have had any effect in awakening the world to a realization of the catastrophe which is now being developed.

It was to avert such a catastrophe that the great Powers signed the Nine-Power Treaty, which was specially created to safeguard China from invasion by Japan. They signed the Kellogg Peace Pact to prevent war, and they organized the League of Nations to make doubly certain that aggressive nations would be quickly prevented from inflicting unjustified harm upon their weaker fellows. But strange to say all these treaties appear to have crumbled to dust in a way that has not hitherto been equaled in history. Worse than that, all complex structure under International Law which was gradually built up to regulate the conduct of war and protect noncombatants seems to have crashed with the treaties. So we have a reversion to the day of the savages when the stronger tried to exterminate the weaker, not only to kill their warriors but their very families, their women and their children. That is what Japan is now trying to do in China. But it is the civilized nations who have really permitted this collapse of treaties and this twentieth century revival of the wholesale brutal murder of innocent civilians. They allowed it to begin in China, in 1931, when Japan seized Manchuria. They permitted it to be continued in 1932 at Shanghai when Japan bombed the sleeping population at Chapei and they now acquiesce in its resumption all over China on a gigantic scale. . . .

And we wonder, does this indicate the fall of civilization? Look at the mass murders of Chinese in various places by bombs, by the naval guns mounted on miles of men-of-war anchored in the sheltered harbor of Shanghai, by machine guns and by rifles. Look at the homes and businesses that have been swept up in savage flames or been blasted into dust. Look at the square miles of bloodstained debris heaped with dead. Look at the fleeing thousands of Chinese and foreigners, screaming, panic-stricken, running for their lives—indeed hundreds of thousands of Chinese mothers and children, homeless, foodless, bereft of everything, leaving their homes shattered and burning behind them when they tried to flee from the horrors of Shanghai.

Look what terrible tragedy overtook them. Thousands of them a few days ago were crowded on the South Station to get into a train when Japanese bombers came overhead, dropped bombs upon them and blew three hundreds of them to ghastly fragments, while over four hundred were wounded. No soldier was anywhere near the station so there was no justification for the terrible massacre. The editor of the *North-China Daily News,* the leading British paper in the Far East, described the barbarous act "as wanton a crime against humanity as can well be conceived." Only a few days later when hundreds of refugees who had managed to escape Shanghai were sitting in their train at Sungkiang Station, some miles out, they were similarly attacked, and another three hundred were blown into eternity by being reduced to torn fragments of flesh while hundreds more were seriously wounded. Not a soldier was on the train. . . .

Tell me, is the silence of Western nations in the face of such massacres, such demolition of homes and dislocation of businesses, a sign of the triumph of civilization with its humanitarianism, its codes of conduct, its chivalry, and its claims of Christian influence? Or is the spectacle of the first-class Powers, all standing silently in a row as if so stupefied by Japan that they do not utter a reproach, the forerunner of the collapse of international ethics, of Christian guidance and conduct, and the death knell of the supposed moral superiority of the Occidental? . . .

Perhaps you can hear over the radio the noise of the cannonade, but hidden from your hearing (though I hope ringing in your hearts) are the cries of the dying, the pain of the masses of wounded, and the tumult of the crashing buildings. And from your sight is hidden the suffering and starvation of the great army of wandering, terrified, innocent homeless ones; the falling tears of the mothers and smoke and the flames of their burning houses.

Good-bye everybody.

In her "Message to the Women of America," printed in the New York *Herald Tribune* March twenty-first, 1940:

If the millions of women in China, who are already victims of the horrors of undeclared warfare, could make their voice heard through their grief, their tears, and the smoke of their burnt homes, it is certain that American womanhood would be shocked into acute realization of the far-reaching consequences of the calamities now threatening civilization. . . . If ever there was menace in the throbbing of distant drums, it is now. . . . Only by collective action, economic, if nothing else, will it be possible to arrest the collapse of democratic ideas of liberty and justice, and prevent America, and particularly smaller, weaker, and less fortunate democratic countries, from being laid open to what are described as "unpredictable hazards," but which are really definitely predictable if eyes are not deliberately closed to the infamies that are now being perpetrated in China. . . . After all, respect for the territorial and administrative integrity of our country was solemnly agreed upon by a congeries of nations. If that agreement were not to be upheld in case of violation what good was served by having the treaty in the first place? . . . It seems to our simple minds, if I may be pardoned for saying so, that if a nation is a signatory to those principles, then surely that nation is both morally and legally obligated to act with other signatories in restraining, by some means or other, not necessarily force, any nation that dares to violate those principles. Or, again, it is puzzling to the Chinese mind why anyone should bother subscribing to something that seems to mean a lot, but, in reality, when the test comes, resolves itself into meaning nothing. . . . We, in China, are thankful that the policy of America has been clarified in general terms. Something specific, however, must be done immediately to compel Japan to understand that her violation of treaties, and her revolting inhumanities and destruction in China, can neither be condoned nor be excused. Above all Japan must be given unequivocally to understand that no so-called peace will be connived at or be tolerated which will in any way sacrifice, or infringe upon, the sovereignty or territorial integrity of China. . . . Japanese propaganda has probably led American people to believe that Japanese troops have conquered great areas of our country. They have not. We are fighting them everywhere. Where flesh and blood, backed only by inferior arms, could not endure against great expenditure of explosives by the enemy, we have withdrawn, but we have not been defeated. Nor shall we be defeated if we are able to procure the means with which to equip ourselves. We are fighting and dying in defence of our soil, and for the principles that other nations profess to espouse; we only ask that those nations demonstrate clearly that there can be no fruits for the aggressor from this barbarous invasion and its monstrous inhumanities, and that the Powers friendly to China and the Chinese people will take collective economic action to compel Japan to abandon her atrocious attempt to conquer our country.

Messages to missionaries, assuring them of the Chiangs' appreciation, letters of thanks for contributions, newspaper articles, speeches—in nervous, incredibly energetic words she poured out her indignation and astonishment and impatience. The following years were to dull the edge of that astonishment; she was to learn the complexities that lurk within the simple declarations of statesmen. "After all, each for himself," she said one later day, with scarcely the suspicion of bitterness, in a Chungking dugout. Those hours of siege in the intermediate stage of Hankow government, however, did not contribute the necessary quiet and repose that were to give Madame Chiang her present-day philosophy. "Japan's Smoke-screen of Falsehoods," "War Progress: News From the Fronts," "America's Disappointing Attitude," "Japan's Campaign of Frightfulness," "Demolition Threat to Nanking," "Hasegawa's Insolent Order," "The Possibilities of Undeclared Warfare"—these titles are merely taken as they come in the collection, and though there has been no attempt to arrange them in chronological order and very small attempt to catalogue them according to subject matter, the very manner of presentation is eloquent of Madame's clear, cold fury and the feelings that set her to making declaration after declaration. She has never been good at appealing; in the name of what she considers right she demands. Often she has decided, after long wrestling with recalcitrant words, to say nothing rather than sound too much like a whining propagandizer.

I am writing this, [she says in an article first published in the *Forum* in December 1937] while I sit waiting for the Japanese air raiders to come. The alarm sounded fifteen minutes ago. I came outside as I always do, to watch the raid and more particularly to observe how our defense is conducted. When the planes arrive, I will write down in order what I see.

[272]

MAYLING AROUSED

It is now two months since Japan started pounding us at Shanghai. During all this time the sufferings of our people have been indescribable. . . .

In the World War the air bases were hundreds of miles from the front. Bombers could manage perhaps two trips a day, if not intercepted by a strong force of defense planes. But at Shanghai we now have no planes to oppose the Japanese, and they have to travel only, at the most, five miles back to their base to reload. . . . Perhaps you wonder why we now have no air force to oppose the 400-odd planes which the Japanese have based at Shanghai alone (altogether they have over 3,000). You must remember that China's air force is less than five years old, and several of those years were wasted through lack of experience in handling the new type of weapon.

This caused us to be without adequate air defenses when the invasion came and compelled us to place large orders in America and elsewhere and hope to have them filled as quickly as possible. We know what to expect from Japan but we never, in our most pessimistic moods, imagined that America. . . .

Now I see the Japanese bombers coming—"three-six-nine," cries little Jimmie, who is taken with me because he has eyes like gimlets.

It is now 2:42 P.M. It is a bright afternoon. Above there are cumulus clouds. High above them, orderly mackerel. Three heavy Japanese bombers come through a blue cleft between the piles of cumulus, heading from the north due south. Three more follow. Anti-aircraft guns put clusters of black smoke puffs around the first three. Now they are bobbing about the second three. Here comes three more—so there are nine altogether. High above the clouds I hear pursuit planes. The detonations of anti-aircraft guns are away in front of me, near the military airfield, which the bombers are heading for. Some of our pursuit planes appear. They have flown behind clouds. The sound of machine-gun fire is now high above me. Above the clouds the pilots are fighting. The nine bombers proceed in steady progress across the city. They have to keep their line if they wish to hit their objectives. The first three are now over the south city wall.

2:46 P.M. Great spouts of flame; columns of smoke and dust ascend. They have dropped several bombs. Then they scatter. Some of our pursuit planes are attacking. North of me a vicious dogfight is going on. It started at 2:34 P.M. All the bombers now are out of sight, in the clouds, but some Japanese pursuits are still being harassed by our fighters.

2:50 P.M. There is a dogfight in the northwest. Any enemy plane, with a Hawk pursuit close on his tail, dives fast. He is out of sight behind Purple Mountain. The combatants are sweeping in and out of the clouds. . . .

2:51 P.M. Suddenly to the southwest of the city smoke and flame and dust in great columns appear. Some more bombers have completed their mission. . . .

Surely, surely, if everyone understood what she was telling them there would be a great movement on the part of the world, particularly America, to save China! She was positive of it. She knew that the great democracies move slowly; nobody knew that better than herself, practiced now in waiting for weary months before the simplest, smallest reform went into the country's program. But America, even from the most selfish viewpoint, would certainly see that all her duty and her common sense put her on China's side; an economic embargo, refusal to sell war materials to Japan—what else could one possibly expect? What else, above all, could an American-trained student expect? Mayling had spent her childhood and adolescent years in the United States, studying American history from the glowing pages of partisan textbooks, and she had first gone to America because of the high ideals her father entertained for that land of promise and glory. Her best foreign friends until now had been American missionaries. The chilly good manners of the colonial British had kept her, perhaps, from appreciating to the full their grim but superior sense of reality in regard to international politics. In other words, those of a British diplomat in the Far East who has naturally developed a defensive attitude: "The United States can still afford idealism: we can't." Now, suddenly the United States discovered that idealism can cost too much, and in Washington if not in the press that expensive item was given up. . . . Madame Chiang, after the first shock of disillusionment, pointed out that it was more than idealism that was at stake, but still nobody listened.

MAYLING AROUSED

In the *China Weekly Review* of August thirteenth, 1938, a year after the "trouble" hit the cozy little world of Shanghai, she began an article with these words:

"Many friends in America have asked me for my views about China's future. Generally speaking, my views are unpalatable—sometimes unprintable."

Edgar Snow, in an article entitled "The Dragon Licks His Wounds" (the *Saturday Evening Post,* April 13, 1940), gives an admirable summary of the work of the Chinese Industrial Co-operatives, but he fails to recount the beginnings of the idea, of which the writer has a vivid memory. It was at a small dinner party in Shanghai at the house of John Alexander, then Secretary to the new British Ambassador, Sir Archibald Clark Kerr. Edgar Snow and his wife, Nym Wales, were present, and Alexander asked Snow what he knew of the co-operative movement in England. Snow said he knew very little, and the Alexanders began to tell him, in the face of vigorous adverse comment from Nym Wales. "I don't even like the words you're using," she said to Alexander. "Commonwealth! Why must you always speak of 'wealth'? That sort of thing is no good here!"

A compromise was effected and for the rest of the evening Alexander spoke of "the common*weal*." That was the beginning. Snow himself tells of the continuation:

Right after the Shanghai war a New Zealander named Rewi Alley and two Americans [the Snows themselves] worked out a plan which they called the Chinese Industrial Co-operatives. They argued that it was pointless to attempt to feed nonproducing refugees for a few months, after which they would starve or be used as slave labor or rice soldiers by the Japanese. They advocated "productive relief" by mobilizing China's refugees and unemployed to start thousands of small "semimobile" co-operative industries, located in the hinterland close to unexploited raw materials, using salvaged tools and machinery to begin with. Financed by relief funds and government loans, and assisted by a staff of organizers and technicians, the refugees could buy over their own plants while learning how to operate them democratically.

Probably the "Indusco plan," as it is now called, would have been interred along with other amateur advice, had it not been ardently sponsored by the dynamic British ambassador, Sir Archibald Clark Kerr. First principle of most career diplomats is actively to avoid action; Clark Kerr succeeds by breaking the tradition at least once a day. He broke it, for example, when he personally presented the Indusco scheme to Generalissimo and Mme Chiang Kai-shek, and Dr H. H. Kung. They agreed to try it out.

Dr Kung pledged five million dollars of Government money to start the Co-operatives, and assumed the Presidency. Madame Chiang became an adviser, and T. V. Soong was on the Committee. Madame Sun in Hongkong entered wholeheartedly into the scheme and did all she could to show her approval and good will. Madame Kung was asked by her youngest sister to be a director, for the project of the Co-operatives reminded her of an old idea of her own, but prospect of such a responsibility with its attendant publicity did not appeal to her, and she would consent only to be an adviser, a position she holds today. Her interest in "Indusco," however, goes very deep.

When Rewi Alley was first requested to join, Sir Archibald Clark Kerr, wishing to make certain that the project would not die from neglect, spoke to Madame Kung and asked her if she would be willing to back it up. Madame Chiang at the same time urged her to lend her special support and interest, since Mayling foresaw that she herself would be too busy with the Women's Advisory Committee and the work attached to it to do the Co-operatives justice. All these people realized the potential importance of the Co-ops, and Eling, talking it over with Kerr and her sister, remembered her reflections in Hankow during the time of the split between Chiang and Borodin. In those days she had first dreamed of some way to reconcile the battle between Capital and Labor. She had been brought up as the daughter of a revolutionary; she had married the heir to generations of capitalists. In her family the struggle was always the biggest bone of contention. She had seen the Chinese rally around Borodin, though to her own mind his promises were vague; they had not a chance, she decided, of ever coming true. Hers is not a political mind: she ignored slogans and war cries, and looked to the economics of the problem. Like many capitalists of other nations she asked herself, why could not Capital and Labor be friends? She did not waste time supposing that the differences between them would ever disappear; she hoped instead for a happy-family relationship in which Capital would be the big brother and Labor the little one. This state of affairs, she said to herself, could never be achieved through legislation. In her experience legislation in such matters has always led to more trouble, even to social upheaval.. Madame Kung quite frankly has a horror of bloody strife between social classes: she has seen plenty of it: she thinks it wasteful and unnecessary—she maintains that such wars are the result of misunderstanding, deliberately cultivated by certain self-seeking factions. She considers any war save one of self-defense a heinous crime.

Some years ago the concept of an experimental factory formed in her mind. Why not try out her ideas in the laboratory? An engineer can make his plans and communicate them to his contemporaries by means of blueprints, but only other engineers will be able to understand what he is showing. The conflict between the "Haves" and the "Have-nots" is universal, and Eling wanted to do something in support of her theories that would be plain to the entire world. A little laboratory-factory in a model village, a cotton plant and mill, schools, training centers for mothers, community enterprises—a community butcher, for example; a modern hospital; good bathrooms—why should it not be done? She resolved to interest some of her friends in this idea and carry it out if it were at all possible. Most of all she cherished the hope of lightening the household work of Chinese women with running water and mechanical appliances. What was the use of all that training in the care of children, what was the use of education if the women were to continue in slavery to their houses?

"Unless Capital voluntarily helps Labor," she argued, "there are always ways and means of getting around the legislative bodies, and that's not only true of China. Our factory might show the men at the top that it's better in the long run to play fair. Why, it might even put a stop to strikes!"

She went further. The cotton mill shares, after the project began to pay, could be retired and used as bonuses for the workers, who would thus become part owners as they grew old. . . . "It may not work," she said, "but it's worth trying, even on a very small scale. We can try to settle other problems too, while we are doing this. Child labor in China—you can't stamp it out just by saying it's wrong to make children work. It may be wrong, but if it's a choice between working and dying most parents will set their children to work. We can make their work lighter and lighter until they are set free."

These thoughts recurred to her when she conversed with Rewi Alley, and in the hopes of putting some of her theories into practice she began to study the "Indusco." She has always interested herself especially in textiles and their manufacture, perhaps because Charlie Soong when she was a child had been fascinated for a time by a venture to make silk out of straw. He had invested some money in the development of this process, which undertaking came to an inglorious end when the chemist died and his son could not make

[279]

the formula work. For thirty years, however, the memory of her father's interest in artificial silk stayed in Madame Kung's mind and led her into a similar venture in 1939.

The Co-operatives suffer somewhat from an excess of advertising; they have been overpuffed by zealous foreign workers, and the public has been led to expect more than it is getting in quick results. In actuality, however, the development is proceeding very satisfactorily and a host of transplanted workers are again occupied, while the Chinese armies are being supplied with necessary material which until now has been imported from foreign factories, often Japanese! Carefully planned to meet the peculiar problems of an agricultural country, the strength of the Co-operatives lies not in size or extent of each center of industry, but in its very limitations. Each co-operative is small and works on an economical basis; the machinery is primitive and light and can easily be moved inland and further inland when necessary.

In Hankow during this period of transit and transition other economic projects were absorbing the time and energy of the Government. While the Ministries were working on moving factories bodily to the interior, Madame Chiang was concentrating on the women workers. The frightful state of affairs that existed in Nanking after the Japanese occupation must not be duplicated in Hankow after the exodus. They knew now what to expect. Factory girls were drilled and taught how to travel when in flight from the Japanese; everything was planned and when the time came the plans worked out admirably.

Madame Chiang called a conference of women in May, at Kuling, for ten days, from the twentieth to the thirtieth of the month. The fifty leading women who fairly represented all groups in China attended, and a standing committee, thereafter called the Women's Advisory Committee, was elected, composed of Mesdames H. H. Kung, Feng Yu-hsiang, Ma Tso-tsi, Cang Hsiao-mu, Chen Cheng, Chang Chih-chang, Chiang Kai-shek and others. There are nine departments: the General Affairs Board, the Training Department, the Publicity Department, the Livelihood Department, Production, War Relief, War Area Service Corps, Refugee Children and Co-ordinating Committee.

The most pressing problem at that time was that of the War Orphans, children lost or left without parents after the Japanese air raids. By the time the Chiangs arrived at Hankow the number of these children had swelled to thousands, and for as long as the Government was in the Hupeh capital Madame Chiang was busy with the work of housing, feeding and clothing them. Homes were made ready for them in Chungking, and the plan of "adoption" was evolved whereby any interested person anywhere in the world could pledge himself to supply at the cost of twenty U.S. dollars a year for each child the living and educational expenses of as many as he wishes to take under his wing—or, at any rate, into his pocket. The adopter receives a photograph of his child and a yearly report of his progress at school and in the orphan community.

The training classes began in Hankow on a far smaller scale than they now exist. Two batches, the first of fifty girls and the second of one hundred and twenty, were sent out from there. These girls, selected in the main from small towns throughout China, traveled as they could to the capital and were trained as teachers, but teachers with a special mission. They were sent into the country in "teams" of thirty, and from their headquarters there they established centers of instruction in schools, temples or any public buildings available, where they held classes in sanitation, rural economics, fundamental principles of reading, writing and arithmetic, and first and foremost, the war and its significance. Some of them have been doing hospital work.

The plan has developed so that now there are new centers of training, but the nucleus of the work is Madame Chiang herself. It is her personality that has worked the miracle of turning these representatives of the middle class, women from what was formerly the most sheltered group of femininity in the world, into young Amazons of civilization. In Hankow she went every day to the classes and talked as only she can talk, nervously, burningly, eagerly, sincerely, until in a burst of young enthusiasm mixed inextricably with hero-worship the girls made themselves over into what they knew she would want them to be. As the classes have grown larger it becomes increasingly difficult for Mayling to give so much time to each individual group, and one of her greatest struggles with her doctor centers about the amount of energy she is allowed to give to public speaking in the classroom every day. This combination of governmental principles and teaching appeals naturally to her: she likes the theory and she likes the work itself. The smallest details of the training school reflect her personality—the fact, for example, that the food is served to the students in individual bowls instead of a communal grab bag; the highly sanitary arrangement for dish-washing (rinsing in three waters, just as Mother teaches us at home); the incredibly neat little barracks where the girls live when they are out in the fields; above all, the *floors,* Chinese floors, yet scrubbed and free of crumbs and fluff and debris—these are super-ficial evidences of Madame Chiang's preoccupation with cleanli-ness and sanitation. Anyone who knows rural China would look at these establishments in amazed disbelief.

What goes deeper is the appearance of the girls themselves and the manner in which the classes are conducted. These teachers are not the delicate, pallid little flowers who walk along the streets of the bigger cities. They are of sturdier stock; taller, ruddy of face, with a freer stride. It is not that they have developed in this way since Madame started her training classes, but that she has released for service this class of women which before lived in a prison of family self-sufficiency. It is impossible to listen to one of them at work without feeling a deep admiration for the manner in which the old methods of teaching are here utilized to impart new ideas. In the mud-floored rooms of a rural middle school or the great three-walled chambers of some old Chinese house anywhere in Free China, a class of small children and worn farmer women who have been working in the fields all day and can spare only the twilight hour chant after the teacher simple truths about hygiene, moral philosophy and nine divided by three.

After Madame Kung went to Hongkong and settled into a small

house on the Bay, while there was still communication between Hankow and Hongkong, Madame Chiang managed to make a visit to her sister. She usually gets away from work once a year for a few weeks, though she does not like to leave the Generalissimo, who has not been to Hongkong since the beginning of hostilities. Madame's departure, though it was kept as secret as possible and was for no more heinous purpose than a short rest and a session with the dentist, gave a chance to the Japanese press to announce that the Soongs were running away from war-torn China in order to live at peace in some neutral country where, of course, they had already salted away their ill-gotten gains in nice safe foreign currency. At this time the Chiangs still had their own plane and pilot; later, in Chungking, when the plane was bombed on the field, it was decided that the expense of a private plane was no longer justified. The area over which the Generalissimo traveled was not so wide that he could not use the army planes when necessary.

The foreign volunteers were still an important element in the Chinese air force at the beginning of 1938. According to the figures supplied by the *Eastern Daily News,* there were one hundred and fifty-two American fliers, one hundred and twenty-four French, one hundred and fifteen Soviet Russian, and fifty-five British. Later, when the American law made it impossible for U.S. citizens to fight for other governments, this part of the force melted away, and the European war took yet more pilots out of action. The Russians continued to give help, however, in trained pilots and teachers and also, which was more important, in equipment.

June brought a fresh blow in the recall not only of the German Ambassador (though Herr Trautmann's departure was not admitted to be of any political significance) but in the departure of the German military advisers who had been at Chiang's elbow since the beginning of the war. It was generally accepted that Germany must retain friendly relations with Japan. However, one or two of the Germans refused to leave: for example, Captain Stennes, whose decision not to return to Hitlerian Germany was dictated as much by prudence as by his friendship for China. Ho Ying-chin, Minister of War, saw the others off at the station, and everything was as friendly as could be. General von Falkenhausen in a press interview later went so far as to say that Japan was wearing herself out.

There was a mass meeting in Hankow on the first anniversary of the Lukuochiao battle. In Shanghai there were many incidents and clashes between Chinese and Japanese. Mass meetings were also held in Canton, Changsha (where some of the Government had rested en route), and Chungking. Japanese planes gave South China a good hearty bombing; in Tokyo too there were mass meetings and speeches.

Madame Sun from Hongkong observed that the past year had been

a significant year, forming as it does another chapter in the glorious history of the Chinese nation. . . . We cannot deny that in China today there are a number of politicians who are cowardly in facing the aggressors but "brave" in dealing with matters internally. These have been defeatists ever since the war began. These politicians have never failed to exert their utmost, scurrying hither and thither like carrion-crows whenever there is the least whisper or hint of "peace." In sharp contrast to their lip-service "support the leader," these hypocrites cherish entirely different aims in their hearts and repudiate what Comrade Chiang Kai-shek has repeatedly declared, that compromise midway would be enslavement. . . . That our political mobilization is far behind military mobilization accounts for the existence of such people and such phenomena as mentioned above, although it is within everyone's knowledge that all comrades-in-arms and all our people prefer to perish as broken jades rather than exist as intact tiles, and that the illusion of achieving a compromise through intrigues is unrealizable. . . . Following the National Congress of the Party, the National Reconstruction Programme for wartime political mobilization was issued. There should no longer be any dispute about its contents and only the practical execution and prompt realization of the various measures proposed by it should claim attention.

Three months have elapsed since the Congress ended. One cannot but feel anxious about the rate at which this programme is being carried out. I wish to mention a few points in the hope that the joint efforts of all responsible political and party comrades and all comrades working at the national salvation front will exert themselves.

The Programme says: "Mobilize the masses of the nation, organize peasants, workers, merchants and students into professional bodies, improve them and consolidate them so that the rich will contribute their money and the able-bodied their man-power to support the war of resistance for national existence." But the work of organizing the masses, particularly the peasant masses in the provinces, is unaccomplished for lack of concrete Organization. The Pao China system, a rural political structure of no positive value, is inadequate to encourage the broad masses of the peasantry to play an active part in the war. Indeed, since the practice involves "assigning and dictation" seen in the imposition of bonds and the conscription of the able-bodied men for training (which are characteristic of their compulsory nature) misgovernment and corruption in all forms predominate. Why not mobilize the peasant masses so that they voluntarily organize themselves democratically into strong bodies like the peasant unions during the Northern Expedition (1925–27)? That would most effectively achieve political mobilization in the villages and enlarge and consolidate the forces supporting our military campaign. . . .

"To improve the political structure, simplify it, rationalize it and increase its administrative efficiency so as to meet the needs of war time," according to the Programme, I think we have to start first of all in the highest administrative offices with the elimination of unnecessary positions and sinecures. Up to the present on the salary list of the Central Government there are still a number of idle officials. All who receive money without doing any real work should be removed. . . . It is more important to do away with the official practice of men hunting after lucrative positions in the same manner as speculators seek after wealth. . . .

The People's Political Council is convening now. Though not all are elected democratically, many members understand well the general suffering of the people and can therefore represent their interests. . . .

It is undeniably Madame Sun's voice that speaks, but that voice has undergone a change. She has softened it, and her admonitions

[285]

are delivered in a spirit that might almost be described as co-operative. Her penultimate paragraph leaves us in no doubt of this new development in her attitude toward the National Government:

Finally I want solemnly to call attention to the "Maintenance of Discipline." The entire nation should support and abide by the order of the Generalissimo. Some even suggest obedience to the leader unconditionally. But in my opinion if discipline is not strictly maintained all voices for support will remain useless. . . .

Who speaks there, Madame Sun alone, or Madame Sun at the behest of her old friends and advisers? The little coterie of foreign journalists who sat in the Y.M.C.A. through the Hankow evenings knew what they thought. There was a large percentage of "Pinks" among the newspapermen in China, just as there was in any similar gathering anywhere in the world. "We looked on Madame Sun as a guiding star, not so much a guide as a star," one of them explained. "She was very remote, of course, but we all felt that we understood her ideas, and we had faith in her activities whatever they were. No, she wasn't considered Orthodox, but still. . . ."

He paused and looked at the foregoing passages of the Anniversary Message. "Decidedly not Orthodox," he repeated. "But this doesn't surprise me. It wasn't a departure exactly—I mean, the Communists during the Hankow period were as quiet as I ever knew them. They meant to play ball until the end of the war and then to collect, if you know what I mean. Madame Sun? Oh, I don't know. You never did know for sure about Madame Sun."

CHAPTER XXIX

Retreat from Hankow

Toward the close of the first year of the war the world had to accustom itself to the practice of bombing open towns, a horror that later became an everyday story to the Chinese. When in June the Japanese began a series of night bombings of the enormous crowded city of Canton there arose a more articulate protest of foreigners to their own governments than there had been in the whole course of the war. This reaction was in part due to the fact that Canton is enormous, full of people and defenseless against attacks from the air, but the chief reason for the telegrams and cables that fled over the ocean was that many foreigners were in a position for the first time to see what bombing—and what being bombed— was like. Then, too, in Canton were represented many foreign property rights, and the city was uncomfortably close to the Crown Colony of Hongkong. . . .

Madame Sun, who had a peculiarly strong feeling for Canton, cradle of her husband's government, took a special interest in this development of the struggle. During the last days of Canton as a

part of Free China she was there almost all the time, leading protest parades and urging her followers to greater efforts of resistance.
Angry and disgusted at the spectacle of refugees pouring into
Hongkong, she wrote to General Wu Teh-chen, formerly Mayor
of Shanghai and now governor of Kwangtung, and called his attention to the number of able-bodied young men whose first interest seemed to be in obtaining safety for themselves. They should
have been ready and eager, said Madame Sun, to fight against the
invaders.

In doing this Chingling was putting her finger on the sorest
spot in the entire history of the war as foreign observers saw it.
The safety of Hongkong and the treaty ports inevitably attracted
all the more prudent types of Chinese manhood into whose psy-
chology the principles of national defense had never penetrated;
from the educated young elegant who said, "Bad iron for nails,
bad men for soldiers, and why should we, the best of the nation,
do purely mechanical work?" to the simple untutored coolie who
did not care as much for his government as for his life. These people crowded the Shanghai streets and made housing conditions in
Hongkong a misery for the poor. The dregs of the country, they
made a bad impression on visitors who could not visualize the
thousands of different quality who remained in the hinterland. A
favorite retort from treaty port foreigners when asked for relief
funds in those days was, "Why aren't all these young men we see
at the swimming pools and the movies doing something for their
own country?"

The answer lay in numbers. China's army was not retreating for
lack of man power, but because of her poverty in armaments. The
fact that this truth was a good excuse for slackers made it none
the less the truth. Whole regiments of reluctant languid young
men, all subscribing to the Chinese maxim that soldiers are on the
lowest social plane, would not have mattered in the progress of
the war; what did matter was the impression they made as they
toiled not and spun not in vaguely governmental posts. But they
are learning; Japan is teaching them. . . .

Chingling, Eling and Mayling with orphans

Canton was bombed; Swatow was bombed; Kiukiang was taken. The famous Eighth Route Army of guerillas continued to trouble the Japanese in the North. Kuling on Lu-shan, where Po Chu-yi and Madame Chiang, in different centuries, had found peace and beauty before the war became the scene of occasional flurries on the part of the missionaries and teachers in foreign schools who continued to live on their beloved mountaintop, stubbornly pretending as only a person who has lived in a besieged city can understand that all was yet right with the world, and that peace and beauty still existed in forgotten corners of the day. They were driven out at last.

Guerillas all over China began to show just how effective they could be. Between Shanghai and Nanking the railroad, which was being operated by the Japanese, seldom ran smoothly. Rails were stolen; stations were blown up; now and then a small outpost of Japanese was isolated and conquered. A new element appeared: the Japanese army man who could be "fixed." There were Chinese guerillas going in and out of Shanghai, relaxing for an evening with the family or at one of the restaurants and then carrying out a consignment of arms next morning, which traveled smoothly enough by waterways and overland to their destination, passed from one well-greased Japanese palm to another. Then the Japanese would go into the country near Shanghai, attack some village, and announce in the press that they had mopped up the district. Thousands of people were driven from their homes once again by floods along the Yangtze, and the Chinese characteristically found comfort in telling one another that these floods, proper homemade catastrophes, good old familiar *Chinese* floods, easily killed far more people every year than those picayune Japs could manage in the course of a whole war.

The Japanese invaded Bias Bay on October twelfth.

Ho Ying-chin and Pai Chung-hsi were sent to take charge of the defense operations in South China, and Li Tsung-jen also made his appearance on the Southern scene. The sudden turn of events bewildered most people, whose attention had been concentrated

[*289*]

on Hankow. It now became evident that the Japanese would take Canton before they conquered the Hupeh capital, and many of those residents who had not been frightened out by the bombings now hastened to evacuate the city. The Chinese had learned a good deal from the air attacks on Canton. In a way they were prepared, though these preparedness measures could not compare with the arrangement of Chungking, later on: there were some dugouts, that is to say, and other people still trusted in the safety of reinforced concrete buildings. The Japanese airmen used more leisurely methods, also, than they applied later to the stubborn Chungking city; flights of from four to twelve planes would circle about and drop their bombs and go away again without much fuss, having done far more damage than the bigger flights were later to accomplish in the interior. It was easy to intimidate the immense sprawling city of Canton.

Just why the Chinese troops put up such a poor show against the Japanese is nevertheless not yet clear. There have been as many rumors as ever, perhaps even more than the usual number, if this were possible. The supreme commander, Yu Han-mou, has been accused in the market place of accepting bribes, and Pai Chung-hsi and Li Tsung-jen, who had formerly been on more or less friendly terms with Japan, were also under suspicion in the public eye. They were all supposedly executed by the Kuomintang officials at one time or other; the Chinese are always ready to believe their officials crooked: this is an aftermath of the corrupt Manchu regime. One truth of the matter is, however, that the Chinese troops were of insufficient strength, both in men and equipment. The main body of the army was fighting in the Hupeh-Kiangsi sector. Time must tell the rest because nobody else can. It is not always easy to be wise even after the event; certainly not in wartime.

From the *China Weekly Review's* record:

Japan's War in China: Oct. 22.—Japanese troops enter downtown sections of Canton at 2 P.M. today. A few hours previously, starting at 2 o'clock in the morning, all Canton was shaken by tremendous explosions, when Chinese High Command ordered systematic blowing up of Government offices, bridges, industrial enterprises and other public buildings. As dawn broke, the city reverberated to the thunder of heavy artillery, tanks and marching feet as the Chinese began to evacuate Canton towards the west. The military withdrawal was signal for last-minute evacuation of civilians. Following the explosions, many buildings were set on fire. and soon large sections of city were ablaze. Canton evacuated by its population first time in history of city. The Japanese, upon entering the city, found streets quiet and completely deserted.

(In March 1940 it was estimated that the population of Canton, including the Japanese who had settled there, was still only one third of its normal figure before the invasion.)

CHINA WITHDRAWS FROM HANKOW

Oct. 25.—Spokesman of Military Affairs Commission announced withdrawal of Chinese forces from Wuhan area; evacuation explained as strategic move and in accordance with policy of prolonged war and resistance on all fronts. . . .

Gen. and Mme Chiang Kai-shek left Hankow for unknown destination. Unconfirmed Chungking report stated that Madame Chiang arrived at Chengtu. Gen. Chiang believed to have gone to Hunan.

. . . Japanese occupation of Wuhan cities completed; 26 Japanese warships arrive at Hankow to control the river. Incoming Japanese soldiers first greeted by Italian sailors. . . .

Night was falling when one aviator, a Chinese who had been trained in America, was sent back to Hankow to take away the last of the coolies and mechanics who had not yet been evacuated. His plan was to spend the night on the field and to take off early in the morning, since he had never done any night flying. He saw what he thought were Chinese planes hovering near the field, made his landing in perfect calm, and was hailed by one of the mechanics.

"Jesus, man," said the mechanic, or the Chinese equivalent for "Jesus, man"; "Hurry up! Those are Jap planes!"

[291]

The refugees tumbled in; in the dark the aviator made his first blind flight, his take-off lit only by the fires of the blazing city.

The Chiangs took one of the last planes out of Hankow that same night. The field was already mined when they flew off. The evacuation of the city was not a hit-or-miss panic, for most of the people had moved out weeks before, by water, by road, by boat. There were, of course, many tragedies. Madame Chiang describes one that occurred when the War Orphans were being moved, in "A Letter From Madame Chiang to Boys and Girls Across the Ocean":

From Hankow and down-river ports we used to use steamers, until one day Japanese planes saw a steamer which was full of them and blew it up with bombs, killing lots of the little ones outright, and pitching the others into the brown waters of the great river, 600 miles from the sea. They, too, were never seen again, having mounted the dragon, which took them far, far away. And we did not use steamers any more.

From *Japan's War in China:*

Nov. 1.—Resolution affirming its faith in Gen. Chiang Kai-shek and China's determination to stand by him in war of resistance adopted at People's Political Council now in session at Chungking. Council's action followed issue of General Chiang's message, in which he re-iterated China's determination to fight to bitter end.

CHAPTER XXX

Digging in at Chungking

T HE LAST MONTH of 1938 was made memorable by Wang Ching-wei's actions, among other things. After a disastrous mention of peace terms earlier in the year following the fall of Canton he retired behind the scandalized excuses of his colleagues and continued to live in Chungking, to all appearances happily enough, until December. During the first week of that month he even made another declaration full of self-determination and united front against Japanese aggression. This was just before he fled.

The other members of the Government were settling in nicely. The militarist's house that Madame Chiang had so disliked in 1935 because it represented war-lordism had been made over into the official residence of the Minister of Finance; Dr Kung lived in what had been "the concubines' house" and the smaller residence was full of A.D.C.'s and secretaries and offices. The Chiangs rented an impersonal sort of house higher up on the hill. All of the Government officials gathered in a district outside the old City, northwest of it. Madame's Advisory Committee and Training School found quarters in a middle school, and the Publicity Bureau was placed in the spacious grounds of another campus, which was soon to fill up with mushroom growths of huts and one-story office buildings. Nearly all of the new buildings were temporary structures of lath and plaster, the exteriors of which were brusque, hasty adaptations of Western style. This fact was very distressing to many of the foreign diplomats, who had learned their Chinese in the old school and were happiest outside their offices, buying curios and dreaming of Li Po. Some of them went to great trouble to acquire genuinely Chinese houses, but it was not easy. War lords had been modernizing Chungking architecture for some years, and the more desirable residences, the really big ones, were liver-colored outrages reminiscent of English suburban villas grown up and surrounded by enormous walls.

A house was built high on a hill further from town and presented to the Chiangs, but they refused it. "We have a house," Madame explained. "We mustn't use money just now for unnecessary things." There was indeed great pressure upon all the living conveniences of the ancient town, and no house went empty for more than a few minutes. Generals, Ministers, Vice-Ministers, Ambassadors, Chargés—they had all to be accommodated. Moreover, the incoming mobs were not greeted with open arms by the Szechwanese. The ruling caste had been severely joggled in 1935 when the Chiangs first visited the West, and a lot of reform had taken place, but the leaders were still the leaders until the Nanking government arrived, and could not be expected to give way graciously. Even so, the newcomers to Szechwan did not meet with the opposition offered to those refugees who went to Yunnan, where the natives accused them openly of ruining their provincial virtue, and mobbed hapless co-educated students who walked arm-in-arm or had curled hair. Nevertheless moving into Chungking called for plenty of settlement and even more tact. Still, by the end of 1938 it had been accomplished.

On the sixteenth of December it was announced that the United

States was extending credits of $25,000,000 to China, and that Great Britain was expected to make a similar gesture. Three days later Wang Ching-wei, Chairman of the Central Political Council, Deputy Chief Executive of the Kuomintang, and one of the Generalissimo's most long-standing contemporaries, aside from being, in the estimation of some people, Sun Yet-sen's spiritual heir, suddenly left Chungking and flew to Yunnan. Most of the public paid no attention to this departure. A few people did.

On the twenty-first of the month Wang Ching-wei continued his trip to Hanoi. The general public began to take more interest in his actions. A few days later, the day after Christmas, it was announced that he had merely flown to Indo-China for medical treatment. A friend of his departed from Szechwan and joined him there.

It was not long before everyone knew, however, that Wang had taken the irrevocable step. He was gone from Chungking, and for good. The bad boy of government circles who had sinned so often and so often had been taken back into the fold was at last out of things forever. The Government itself said so, and indeed after more than a year of waiting, just to be sure he meant it this time, put a price on his head. The Chinese do not like to do this to their officials. There is always the chance, as John Gunther has observed, that the absconders may still be useful, and Wang had had many followers. Moreover, a decade of association with Chiang Kai-shek, interspersed with periods when Wang was playing at treason, had given the two men a sort of companionship. They were practically schoolfellows. It is peculiarly significant of the enormity of Wang's action that Chiang himself crossed him off the list at last.

Wang Ching-wei's behavior is interesting both in view of the workings of his own mind and those of the Chinese public. For years he had been a specimen of the "young man who will amount to something": his amazingly youthful appearance, his energy in spite of his alleged ill-health, his persistence in turning up at what could have been the right moment, were typical of the more attractive sort of successful politician. He has great personal charm.

His adherents are inspired with a sort of unreasoning loyalty that has often carried them into unpopularity and danger. The entire setup of the Wang faction is of the war-lord era; Wang wanted to be head of China because he was bitten by that mysterious insect that infects people with ambition, and his followers wanted him to be head of China because he was Wang, because they, in reflection, were Wang, and because it would pay better: these reasons are arranged in a descending scale of importance. All Wang's actions had been governed by this ambition, from the old days when he aligned himself with the Southerners and Yen Hsi-shan until now when he did the same thing by joining the Japanese. To his mind it was the same thing; Wang may have been the "spiritual heir" of Sun Yat-sen, but he had not inherited the little Doctor's selfless ideal of a united nation, and the later years of China's development were to him only the record of a long duel between himself and Chiang Kai-shek. Joining the Japanese was a natural step in the game. With the Japanese behind him—especially after Canton fell—he had a good chance, he thought, of becoming head man at last.

"Wang feels sincerely that peace should be made, that it will be best for China," said one of his followers. Of course: people always feel these things sincerely. Dictators are very sincere; so are Communists; so are United States Presidents, bandits, and messiahs. Wang also felt sincerely that what China needed was Wang Ching-wei, with a few Japanese to help him at first, and after that no Japanese. The Japanese believed with heartfelt sincerity that China needed Japan, with a little Wang Ching-wei mixed in at first, and afterwards. . . . They were delighted to get a man of Wang's reputation. For many months they had tried to catch a big Chinese to act for them, and without avail. The governments they had set up in the occupied areas were made of small fry. There had been rumors that Wu Pei-fu, the old scholar-general in Peking, would come over to them, but Wu was coquetting and had not committed himself.

Wang failed to take into consideration one fact. He was, perhaps, getting too old and inelastic to realize what he was deserting when he left Chiang Kai-shek's China. That mental picture of a personal duel between two strong men had obscured for him the fact that Chiang's China was not the old scattered heterogeneous mixture of general-governed provinces, but a new entity, an entity that was conscious of being threatened by *an enemy from outside*. This was no civil war, no family squabble, and the Chinese people knew it. Wang's defection, therefore, was definitely shocking. There was all the difference between his departure from Nanking in the old days and his flight from Chungking in the new as there would be between a quarrel in the American government between the President and the Secretary of War and that Secretary's sale of the national defense plans to some foreign agent. He himself could not see the difference because his mentality is as limited as that of a war lord: the Chinese public, with a reasonable number of exceptions, did. Wang Ching-wei, haggling over future power with the Japanese in Hanoi and Shanghai, was out of China, once and for all. His future was linked with that of Japan.

Winter in Chungking is a gloomy time, which is one of the reasons the Government picked it out as a place where they could dig in. A heavy fog lies over the hills by the rivers that segregate it into a wedge-shaped peninsula, and this fog stays there, varying only in density, from October to well into April. In the winter the Chungking sun appears only at long intervals as a watery pale-yellow blob through the fog. Commercial airplanes, manned by pilots who become perforce most skillful at blind flying, make their landings on and take off from a sandspit in the river at the foot of one of the steepest cliffs. Getting into and out of the canyon is only one of their problems. It is not an easy place to fly into, even for a commercial plane with friendly intentions.

Japanese bombers are thus barred from Chungking by weather conditions for about eight months of the year. This fact was the salvation of Free China for two reasons: the temporary freedom from menace to the population, and the opportunity to make more dugouts. The cliffs and rock-cored hills on which the town is built (sooner or later every visitor to Chungking calls it "the city built on rock") offer an ideal material for artificial caves. More and more and more were scooped out by blasting and picking away, and more blasting and more picking away in the endlessly patient, slow, inefficient manner of the Chinese workman, who gets results no efficient laborer could achieve. The city was honeycombed with these caves, public and private, big and little, deep and shallow, and still they wanted more, for Chungking was still filling up to overflowing. As the summer season approached, the military authorities recognized the peril to these crowds and ordered everyone out of town who did not have a good reason for remaining. In vain. There was no possible way to regulate the number of residents. China is no regimented European country: life is incredibly lavish, and the coolie and his children can enjoy at least the freedom of complete anonymity. How were the overworked military and civil authorities to rout out of their huts and corners the thousands of bean curd sellers, itinerant stone workers, storekeepers' cousins' cousins' children?

So they kept making dugouts to accommodate the people, and the people kept flooding into town, depending placidly on the dugouts that they were overcrowding. Downtown the streets, widened since 1935, were still too narrow for the rickety busses, the jogging rickshas, the thick clotting streams of people jammed between rows of framework shops and houses. Opium selling was summarily stamped out by virtue of the government's presence, and the opium smoker's characteristic pallor and vagueness vanished from sight. Native workmen and coolies began to make fortunes. The city hummed, buzzed and rang with chattering and vendors' cries and the endless "clink, clink" of picks detaching crumbs of rock from the mountainside.

It was a cheerful scene, but the army officers and members of the air-raid precaution committee wore worried expressions. The whole gigantic mass of population had been drilled more than one would have thought possible. Everyone knew that a first blast on the siren meant Japanese planes were on their way, and that the second blast would be an urgent warning to get into a cave and stay there until the All Clear. In the meantime, with characteristic calm, the people went about the life-and-death business of daily work.

January 1939 was their first taste of another sort of life-and-death business.

CHAPTER XXXI
Air Raids and Orphans

MAY IN CHUNGKING is still delightful, before the heavy hot blanket of summer descends on the double valley. Most of the population of the town were out in the precipitous streets, sitting on their doorsteps or lounging in the middle of the highway and moving with maddening slowness from the paths of squawking motor cars when the first alarm, the "ching pao," sounded. It is not one siren only, but several in different districts of the city that give tongue, and anyone who has gone through the drill of an air raid will never again hear the upward swoop of a whistle without an involuntary tightening of the heart muscles. After a long steady blast the siren lowers its voice, then heightens it again, then lowers it, then heightens it, in a mad sine-cosine pattern of sound. The nearest one fades away at last, and then from neighboring hills come answering voices as later whistles shriek their messages too. Across the Yangtze and the Chialing rivers the town watchmen beat great gongs in double time—one two; one two; one two.

This is the moment when the people are supposed to start for the dugouts to which they have been assigned. Each person, theoretically, has a place in some cave not too far from his home. In the most crowded districts the public dugouts are far too full, and in those early days the cave space was insufficient for registered people, not to mention the vast numbers who were not supposed to be in town at all. Later the dugout drill became familiar and people calmly collected their most precious belongings and walked to their refuges, but this time, in the beginning, they were simply bewildered and either ignored the warning or ran around in circles, in useless panic. Some of them, but only a few, did go into the caves.

The peculiar situation of Chungking makes possible a lengthy period of warning. Watchers send word as soon as the raiding planes cross a certain point on their way inland. Even then it cannot be told just where they are going, but the Urgent is sounded, in theory, just before they enter an area near Chungking and approach the city itself.

Keyed up as the people were, some of them nevertheless remembered the procedure they had already followed several times. The Urgent would warn them when it was acutely necessary to rush for shelter. They waited anxiously, suspended in action, for that second alarm. It was long in coming. It was so long in coming that the inexperienced people at last decided that the danger had passed, and many were far from their caves when the sirens did blow again and the planes followed promptly on the echoes.

It was a quick, savage raid, but the Japanese fliers too were inexperienced and the damage, compared with what was to follow, was slight. Far too many people were killed; they could have been saved if they had taken precautions. Some buildings were smashed; a few fires were started. Chungking thought it had undergone the worst possible results of a raid, and the next day the authorities prepared more pressing commands and advice. That evening, just at dusk, the Japanese came again.

The first alarm sent some sadder and wiser citizens under cover,

[*301*]

and many more fled to the open country outside the city, where they dawdled and waited. So extremely long was the delay this time that human nature could not remain cautious. People began to drift homeward. A party of foreign and Chinese journalists out on the Chengtu Road decided, watching the streams of humanity, that somehow word had gone around that danger was over. This sudden confidence that takes possession of a mob is just as contagious as panic: the journalists got into their car and started back. A policeman in the street stopped the car and said that the warning still held good: cars cannot run without special permits during the time between the Urgent alarm and the All Clear, and people cannot walk in the open. The crowds were out of hand, but this policeman did his duty. Grumbling but patient, the party went back to the Chengtu Road and safety.

Something went wrong with the alarm system on this evening of May fourth. Instead of the Urgent, the All Clear sounded, and in a few minutes more the planes were over the bustling little city, catching it completely unawares. Lights burned; fires had been started for cooking; the streets were tragically full of life as those hopeful merchants and coolies trudged homeward from their dugouts. . . .

The hell of May fourth has been described elsewhere. There has been nothing like it in Chungking since. In one night thousands of people learned a lesson they will not, cannot forget, and thousands died before they could learn any more. Near one of the ruined sections early in the morning the Generalissimo was seen marching alone up and down, up and down the street, staring at the wreckage. A group of bodyguards followed in a huddled group at a distance of fifty yards.

"What's the matter?" asked an official who knew Chiang. "Why aren't you closer to the Generalissimo?"

"He won't let us come any closer," said an A.D.C. "He says not to come near him. He says it's all his own responsibility that this happened."

One group, perhaps because it had been so well trained, obeyed orders to an unbelievable extent. Throughout that fire-haunted night, while the relief and rescue squads and the police toiled heroically, the War Orphans were being shepherded by the women who were in charge of them and given their orders. Before dawn a little army of over six thousand children had been sent off into the country with directions to march and to keep marching for as long as possible out of the scene of death, until further help could be given them.

Madame Chiang had been on her feet all night, going from fire to fire and making quick decisions as to rescue and relief. It was not until after noon on May fifth that she could think of her orphans. With several members of her staff she followed on their trail in a truck, as her own car with that of the Generalissimo had been sent out to help evacuate bombed victims. (One old couple refused to get into the Generalissimo's car or even to approach it until they were assured over and over that such action would not be a profanation. Even then they insisted upon kowtowing three times to the machine before they would enter it.) They came upon the forlorn, gallant little band well outside of the belt of villages that surrounds the city. The children had marched, stopped by the roadside to rest when they had to, and marched again. The older ones helped the little ones along. Some of them carried others. They were a worn-out army, but not one of them was crying.

Temporary quarters had been prepared for them in a district several miles outside of the city. It was now a matter of getting them to shelter, for it was five o'clock, and of finding food for them. Madame Chiang decided to stop all trucks and private cars that had been pressed into service to evacuate the Chungking populace. Now, having deposited their loads, they were returning empty to the city, and she thought of turning them back once again to transport the children. She stepped out into the road and held up her hand to flag a truck; the driver brought it to a halt. When she told him, however, to load the car with children he shook his head and drove on, unaware that he had cheeked the wife of the Generalissimo. This was no wonder, for her face was streaked with grime and her slacks and shirt were crumpled. The rest of the party was no better, and her aide-de-camp had been sent to scour for food for the hungry children.

Several more trucks were intercepted and lost again, for the chauffeurs could not be convinced of Madame's identity. At last she managed to commandeer the necessary cars, and the orphans were brought to their destination, to food and beds of a sort. It has not gone on record, but Madame admits that a few of the babies, when they realized their behavior had not been too shameful, allowed themselves at last the luxury of a few comfortable howls. . . .

There was not much of vociferous grief in Chungking for several days: the people were stunned and overworked at the same time. Everywhere in the ruins and on the street corners, however, were coffins; some of them were of black lacquer and had candles burning before them, and some were of rough white wood, mere unfinished boxes. Even in this ancient and well-stocked Chinese city there were not enough coffins to go around: not nearly enough coffins.

Wang Ching-wei became a resident of Shanghai, a most unwelcome one. He settled down in Yuyuen Road, at the outer edge of the International Settlement, and his house became an armed camp. Even when there were no fights directly at his headquarters, his presence was a constant stimulation to lawlessness and terrorism, particularly during one somewhat comic period when he was quarreling with his sponsors, the Japanese. Five factions fought among themselves over the dying body of Shanghai; the Ta Tao party, which was made up of opportunist Chinese; the Japanese themselves; the new puppet Mayor of Greater Shanghai, who wanted to become independent; Wang's gang; the Chinese guerillas.

During the summer of 1939 while Chungking learned how to take cover, on into the autumn and the winter that marked a new burst of building and liberated activity in the wartime capital, Wang and his patrons argued about it and about. There was a flurry of excitement in Free China when it was rumored that the enemy had made another important convert in North China, where the spineless puppet government had long awaited a leader—Wu Pei-fu himself. Had he agreed to take on the job he would have found dozens of old acquaintances from pre-Chiang days as his colleagues.

"Peking is fantastic," reported one observer. "Old people who haven't seen daylight in years are coming out and walking in the streets. Tired retired old scoundels, forgotten petty war lords, people who've been smoking opium for the past ten years—they look like something from under a stone. And they're all in the new North-China government."

Now that Wu had evidently promised to deal with the conquerors, however, there was hope for a stronger body of men. The Japanese waited confidently for his acceptance speech.

Wu made the speech. He said he was willing to become the leader of North China again on behalf of the New Order in Asia, IF every Japanese soldier on Chinese soil gave up his post and went back to Japan. China rocked with mirth. Japanese hopes of Wu faded to nothing, and the old scholar-general went back into retirement, dying later under what some people considered suspicious circumstances. He was a national hero before he died, a status he had never before achieved.

Wang Ching-wei, however, reached a compromise at last, and the new "National" government was announced. Several false alarms were given and the inauguration ceremony was announced at various times throughout the winter, only to be postponed. When it did take place at last in Nanking, the contrast beween the city as it is now and as it was during the Chiang inauguration was striking. Japanese soldiers were much in evidence; Japanese "advisers" smiled from behind the shoulders of all the new officials. Under these circumstances it is not surprising that the proceedings lacked spontaneity and merriment. Stubborn Chinese still persisted in talking of the future "when the Government comes back," and a party of foreign correspondents was held up by an accident on the

Shanghai-Nanking railway when some of the track was pulled up by guerillas. Going back they were delayed again by an explosion on the same track. Their Japanese hosts were flustered and disinclined to make explanations.

☆   ☆   ☆

Madame Chiang Kai-shek's health was not in a satisfactory state, though she protested that she was quite all right and was "not one of those people who enjoy ill health." Months of living in the fogginess of Chungking, hours of speech making with her girls in the Training School, sleeplessness and overwork had left her a prey to that most painful of complaints, inflamed sinus. Dr Talbot from Hongkong operated on her in December, and thereafter for a few days was to be seen hovering about and trying to keep her from public speaking. He also urged her to go away to some sunnier spot, but she felt that she could not leave the Generalissimo. An occasional journey to the front was as much of a break as she allowed herself. Another reason for her reluctance was that the Training School was turning out a most important class, a group of girls who were themselves to be teachers in subsidiary training schools throughout the country. She could not leave them to go out into the world without a few more talks from herself.

In February it became evident, however, that the operation had not been entirely successful and that a rest was imperative. Therefore she consented to go to Hongkong, to visit her sister Eling, whom she had not seen for more than a year.

The house in Sassoon Road was very busy for the next six weeks. Madame Sun too moved in, leaving her own establishment for the time being, and for a few happy days the three sisters completely forgot their public roles. It was the first time in many years that they were able to sink political differences with free consciences; the United Front was a fact in that house. They gossiped, they cooked, they made jokes—the old family jokes that outsiders can never understand—they tried on one another's clothes, and Mayling

[307]

was firm about buying a pair of slacks and assuring Madame Kung that she must wear them when they went to Chungking. She was determined to take both sisters back with her.

It was really an excellent idea, coming as the trip would close upon the inauguration of Wang Ching-wei. If the three sisters were to be seen in public, in the capital, no more rumors as to a split in the family and consequently in the Government would be believed. The sisters consented, Chingling stipulating only that Madame Kung promise to return with her to Hongkong after a month or so, and not be tempted by the fear of airplanes and the excitement of the capital to remain indefinitely in Szechwan. She, Chingling, had work to do in the Colony, and she did not want to lose the company of her favorite sister.

There followed a bewildering experience for Eling; a period of photographing and interviews with the press, and meetings held in her own house, and more speech making on her part than she had anticipated in her wildest nightmares. Mayling would not be gainsaid; her big sister was going to do her share in the public eye at last. They had many discussions during which Madame Chiang kept battering at the wall of shyness that Madame Kung had built up in the past years, and Madame Sun earnestly seconded her in urging Eling to come out of her hermitage. Their counsels triumphed when during a meeting of Hongkong's leading women Madame Kung was elected Chairman of the Friends of the Wounded Association. Some of the people there lifted their eyebrows when they realized that it was Chingling, Madame Sun, who proposed this choice—"as there is nobody more eminently fitted for the post." The radical newspapers left the item out of their accounts of the affair.

Before the sisters left and after Madame Chiang had been pronounced cured, they did an amazing thing—they appeared together in the Hongkong Hotel and dined there. The action was amazing for two reasons; first because none of the three ever did appear in such places, and second because they had not been seen all together in ten years. One evening, it is true, Madame Kung had

Mmes Kung, Sun and Chiang. Bombed district, Chungking, 1940

ventured into the great world when her younger brother T.L.
came to see her and insisted upon it.

"It's ridiculous, the way you live," he scolded her. "You may as
well be in a convent. You're living in one of the biggest cities in
the East and you cower at home as if you were a prisoner. Why
shouldn't you come out sometimes and look at people? England's
at war now too, but everyone goes out just the same. Why, look
at the King and Queen!"

Madame Kung explained her reasons—people gossip so; it wasn't
seemly; she was afraid. . . . "Nonsense," said T.L. masterfully;
"Tomorrow night I want you to get dressed up and I'll take you
to the Hongkong Hotel for dinner. Now, don't forget!"

Eling did not forget. As a matter of fact she was very much
thrilled.

She looked forward eagerly if guiltily to the bright lights, the
pretty clothes, the music and the young people. For a long time she
had known nothing of that sort of life except from her children,
and their social activities had been limited to private parties. It
was wrong, Eling felt, to want to hear music and to see nice clothes
at such a time, but she did. She was glad to go, though she still
protested when T.L. called for her.

In a closed limousine they drove solemnly, richly, to the Hongkong Hotel. T.L. hurried her through the lobby to the lift. They
were carried past the "Grips" where everyone was dancing, past
the higher floors, up to the dining hall on the roof, which T.L.
had hired for the evening, and there in solitary grandeur his carefully selected party, all of people Eling saw all the time, dined
solemnly and richly. Not a soul entered that dining room except
the waiters. Afterwards, they went home.

This time it was all changed. The Soong sisters sat in the Grips,
their backs to one of the walls, and watched all the Hongkong
elite, the British taipans and officers, the nice English girls and a
few Chinese millionaires and their wives, eat and drink and dance.
Word went around quickly and in a few moments the dance floor
looked something like the crowd at Wimbledon as couples danced

past the long table, their heads turning as if they had owls' necks, staring as hard as British courtesy allowed. It was undeniable; the Soong sisters were there, all together—Madame Kung quietly splendid, Madame Chiang glowing with new-found health, Madame Sun in black, her hair glossy, her eyes amused.

"I'll believe two of them are there," protested a newspaperman, "but I won't believe that's Madame Sun. She would never, never be with the other two—and in this outpost of Empire!"

"It's Finland," said another man emphatically. "You mark my words, it's Finland. She must be completely disgusted with Russia now, and this is a reaction—it's all Finland."

"No it isn't," said the first suddenly. "I know what it is. It's Wang Chiang-wei."

They turned and stared again at the wall table, at three Chinese ladies who sat quietly eating their dinners just as if they were not Symbols.

It was April first, 1940, when the three sisters slipped out of Hongkong and flew up to Chungking in the famous "D. C. 3," the China National Aviation Company's prize plane. The bustling scene at Kai Tak airport was viewed by very few people, and the machine was hastily loaded. There was oxygen for Madame Kung, and in the luggage of each of the three was a pair of slacks—Madame Chiang had carried the day. Later, although Eling and Chingling were persuaded to wear these garments, they insisted upon huddling themselves in long coats. Only Mayling appears at full length in the photographs without a coat, unashamed of her attire.

Secrecy shrouded their departure, but their arrival was greeted with a blare of publicity. It was the first time in Chungking for either of the elder sisters, and for Chingling it was the first time in years that she had visited any stamping ground of the National government. She went to live in the Kung house, on the top floor of what had been the war lord's concubines' dwelling. (Later a

Japanese bomb sheared off half of this house with miraculous neatness.)

There was such a fever of social activity to welcome the ladies that a rule was made whereby none of them could accept the invitation of any private person. Only Associations and Committees were permitted to entertain them. Madame Chiang introduced her guests at meetings, at parties, at receptions; she was obviously delighted to have her sisters with her, quite aside from the political significance.of their visit. The photographs show her beaming with a simple pride that is touching: for some reason we are always pleased when public figures prove to have private feelings.

The sisters traveled about the beleagured city visiting schools, hospitals, exhibits; they went to Chengtu; movies were made of them inspecting dugouts and orphanages; records were taken of their speeches. They were worked hard. Madame Sun, who does not like public speaking, made many addresses. Madame Kung, who still feared she could not speak to meetings, disclosed an undeniably real talent for this form of expression. The Chungking residents had been keyed up to a pitch of heroic boredom impossible to describe to anyone who has not lived under war conditions, and they were avid observers of the behavior of the Soong Sisters. They stared, and the Soong sisters stared back.

Both newcomers were stirred to their depths by the sight of what had been accomplished. No reports or statistics however impressive can convey the effect of Chungking itself at first sight; the stubborn cheerful busyness of the people and the hundred makeshifts and improvements. Chingling confessed that she had never seen manifestations of better spirit among the countrypeople. Eling was particularly pleased with an exhibit of machinery and arms made from the remnants of Japanese bombs and planes at the Oberlin-Shensi Memorial School, Dr Kung's favorite project and the organization for which she had worked when she was a bride. Transplanted to Chengtu, they were all there, teachers and students.

The sisters were overworked, they were rushed, they were bewildered by quick journeys, welcome celebrations, sightseeing tours of schools, and speeches, speeches, speeches, but the overwhelming impression of hope and vigor carried them through the ordeal. After their departure from Hongkong the papers all carried the story of their presence in Szechwan, and since it was the beginning of the bombing season they came in for special attention from the Japanese. Routed out of their beds on moonlight nights they crept down dugout steps and spent hours discussing the situation by candlelight.

"I don't think I ever appreciated those women properly until I saw them on that Chengtu trip," a foreign correspondent said later. "*We* know what it's like, traveling in China and putting up at local inns and being bitten by bed bugs and chivvied by airplanes, but you wouldn't expect Madame Kung, for example, to take very kindly to it. She looks as if she would be more at home in a nice safe city house. She belongs in a nice safe city house. . . . But she's tough. They're all tough. They turned up smiling in the middle of an air raid in Chengtu after a most trying trip, and they were the best sports imaginable. They spoke as well as if there'd been no trouble. A raid in Chengtu is no fun for the best of us."

Chengtu is probably one of the most easily bombed open towns in the world. Built on a flat plain, there is no possible way to dig caves for the population, and the first alarm is a signal for the whole town to make for the countryside. They go out in rickshas, barrows and chairs; they crowd on trucks or walk, carrying their belongings and their babies. When they have gone several miles they scatter in the fields, among the old graves, and wait until the planes have left their loads, or, as the Chinese language has it, have laid their eggs. Then they troop back again to take stock of the damage.

The Soong party had undergone three alarms during the two-day journey to Chengtu, and another alarm overtook them just as they approached the city. A flood of humanity met the car caravan and they were enveloped in a counterprocession of hurrying people. They sat there, waiting for the flood to diminish, watching China as it streamed past—the peasants, the coolies, the merchants, the babies, plodding patiently and without panic into the fields.

[312]

CHAPTER XXXIII
Appraisal

Cᴏᴍᴘᴀʀɪsᴏɴs may be odious, but they are necessary in writing about the Soong sisters. During their sojourn in the glare of Chungking footlights the ladies were observed and compared constantly, of course. Those among the women working for them who had schoolgirl "crushes" on one or another would quarrel and grow heated as they claimed superior beauty or virtue for each of their idols, and a typical photograph shows the long-suffering sisters sitting on a lawn drinking tea, surrounded by a dense crowd of standing admirers who could only stare and beam down at them, too shy to say a word.

Of the three, Madame Kung has probably the most spontaneous and kindly manner—the sort of manner which is known in America as "human." Madame Chiang is more intense in her moments of communication, and Madame Sun is often overwhelmed by shyness. Like Madame Chiang, Eling's photographs do not do justice to her face, which is most attractive because of its nobility, vividness and coloring. Her eyes express her wit and the keen, sympathetic interest she takes in her surroundings. Though she is short, like most Chinese women, her fine figure and dignified walk always give a first impression of height. One must know her well to see that she has her moments of childlike pleasure in small things—an escape from routine, a victory in some good-natured battle of words.

She has had children; the other two have not. There is, therefore, a hint of authority and added ease in her manner when she visits the war orphanages; she seems to take charge of the entire party, and the children recognize her seniority.

A most characteristic anecdote of her centers about a side street in Hongkong at night, when Madame Kung from the recesses of her limousine watched the crowd walking past, under the blazing lights of shop windows. She said suddenly in a startlingly angry tone, "Look at that man!"

A Chinese dressed in a long gown walked by the car, a baby in his arms. The child lay stretched out, wrapped in too many clothes, its face turned up to the invisible sky.

"Carrying them like that, so that their poor little eyes stare straight into the lights and are weakened," continued Madame. "Men will do it, every time. Men!"

She sighed for all the masculine stupidity in the world that she will never be able to conquer.

☆   ☆   ☆

Madame Sun gives the impression of austerity and a self-control won through years of practice. Her personality is all in low tones— quiet clothes, a house stark in its simplicity, a deep reserve. When she does appear in public and makes a speech one feels that she has had to steel herself for the effort. Yet her voice when it comes out is strong and forceful, and so are her words. She can be downright, even violent, when occasion demands; when she is stirred to indignation, for example.

She is almost a legend with China's young radicals. A few of them know her and have the privilege of calling on her in the cool, underfurnished Kowloon house, where they drink tea and discuss painting, poetry and the principles of Dr Sun. Their faces glow when they speak of her. There is probably as much jealousy and heart burning among Madame Sun's adherents as there is in Madame Chiang's circle, though the Russian philosophy frowns upon this sort of personality idolizing.

In the first days of the sisters' Chungking visit, the Generalissimo and Madame Chiang in honor of Mesdames Kung and Sun gave a lawn party to which all the leading women of Chungking, Chinese and foreign, were invited. It was a strenuous affair for everybody, but particularly for Madame Sun, who was mobbed by a special crowd of eager young students and women with Communist sympathies. Most of them had never seen Chingling and were over-joyed at this unexpected opportunity. They brandished autograph albums and cameras; they pushed so closely about her chair that she could not breathe; they hid her from sight as if they had been a swarm of locusts. Shyness and a sense of duty battled for right of way in her face. Suddenly, as if she could bear it no longer, she broke from her adorers and ran like a young girl into the house.

Madame Chiang's beauty is unusual because of her eyes. They are truly enormous, the long outer corners extending to the edge of her cheekbones. Her famous chic is not the result of effort, but is a natural quality: Mayling looks smart in anything she wears, and is usually indifferent to her clothes.

"This dress?" she will say to an admirer. "I think it belonged to my niece Rosamonde. Yes, this is the one. I said in Hongkong that I liked it and she gave it to me."

She has tremendous vitality, but it is the expression of a grave, almost anxious earnestness, and during her spells of bad health she always fears that she will lose this energy, with the same unhappy foreboding that haunts the writer who thinks he has lost his will to work. She realizes it is her greatest gift, and she has dedicated it

[*315*]

to her job. At forty she has not lost the student's capacity to seek the truth in all matters, and she never doubts the existence of that one truth. The schoolmate who said that Mayling "kept up an awful *thinking* about everything" described her perfectly. Sometimes in her eager concentration she is like a good little girl learning her lessons, but lately she has developed a shrewd, amused cynicism that has matured her and given her a greater understanding of the ways of statesmen.

Oddly enough, considering the work Fate has given her to do, Soong Mayling is of a reflective nature and was cut out to be a scholar rather than an active go-getter. Her real passion is for the art of translation. She spends much of her rare leisure reading ancient Chinese history, and can forget everything in the fascination of putting some of these anecdotes into English. Both languages attract her and she is always trying to reconcile them. She loves to tell these stories, and she does it with great vivacity and charm: her husband would rather listen to her recount an anecdote, though he has read it a thousand times, than read a new one. Her eyes, her gestures, her absorption in what she is saying, her genuine and naïve desire to draw a moral precept from the story no matter how trivial it may seem—the result is bewitching. Charlie Soong must have had the same talent for narrative. There is a teacher's personality just as there is an actor's or a politician's, and it is this quality that Mayling possesses.

It is an amusing truth that in the Generalissimo's recent speeches, in which he follows the time-honored custom of retailing the deeds of heroes, he quotes more and more from the lives of great Westerners, whereas the Americanized Mayling in her anecdotes is falling further and further under the spell of the ancient Chinese.

I remember her most vividly during an air raid, when I shared the shelter of the Chiang dugout with a few of her attendants. We sat at the mouth of the cave, watching the Japanese planes fly over the military airfield and drop their eggs. Madame Chiang was impatient with the necessity of staying under cover—there is nothing more boring, save unremitting fear—but every few minutes the dugout telephone rang and the Generalissimo called up from town to make sure that his wife was staying in the shelter like a good girl. He knew that she would be tempted to desert the damp cave and return to the house, and he wasn't risking it.

While we waited and listened to the drone of the planes Madame Chiang looked over the draft of *Resurgam,* which she was getting ready for the press, and discussed the proper word for this or that idea. The appearance of these articles in the local Chinese press had made a great stir among the officials they criticized, and Madame Chiang was still stirred up by this excitement and perhaps slyly amused.

It was a clear, hot day. In spite of the explosions, the ringing telephone, and the possibility of machine gunning as the planes swept low, there was an atmosphere of quiet in that dugout which emanated from Soong Mayling herself. She has always been brave: recently she has found a new strength that is akin to spiritual peace, and her placid demeanor, even in a country of placid people, made a refreshing little island of that air-raid shelter.

The All Clear sounded and we were released. Pine trees and flower bushes surrounded the stone steps that we climbed to the house. Madame Chiang was thoughtful, and I wondered about her thoughts. Was she busy meditating revenge on the Japanese? Did she have a feeling of personal hatred for those venomous little silver insects that had just winged away toward Hankow?

Suddenly she asked, "Tell me, what is your idea of happiness?"

I didn't know. Hers, she said, was a life of uninterrupted work at reading, studying and writing. . . .

The telephone shrilled as we entered the house, and there was an immense heap of papers waiting on her desk.

☆ ☆ ☆

The noise of girls shouting and applauding at a picnic in honor of the Soong sisters had spread three blocks and reached the door of the Chungking Hostel. We foreigners watched them marching back to their school afterward, several hundred of them in uniform.

The Soongs had just time to keep their next appointment, a visit to a hospital for wounded soldiers. They paused in the prisoners' ward, where four Japanese patients sat in their kimonos in bed and stared at the ladies.

An American man approached Madame Chiang. "I've just arrived overland from Nanking, where I attended the inauguration of Wang Ching-wei," he said. "I've got some photographs here of the ceremony. Would you like to see them?"

"Oh yes," said Mayling; "I haven't seen any pictures of Wang since he—well, since he left us."

The three sisters crowded around and examined the photographs, singling out this face and that as they recognized old acquaintances. They looked absorbed, fascinated; their faces, even in this unguarded moment, carefully schooled against bitterness. From their beds the Japanese prisoners stared solemnly, wondering what it was all about.

☆   ☆   ☆

It is four o'clock in the afternoon. Under a glaringly bright blue sky the walls of Chungking houses—ancient gray and yellow, modern gray and black—stand out so clearly that even from the South Bank one can count the windows. It is a jumble of rocky hill and climbing road and perching buildings. There is a heavy silence over the city that is uncanny. No smoke comes from the chimneys; the lanes and alleys are empty of coolies in their faded blue shirts. There is not a soul in the streets; not even a dog or a cat moves. In the distance, behind a row of hills, a cloud of smoke and dust drifts out, lazily swelling and thinning—the last trace of a bomb that fell fifteen minutes ago.

One cannot see very well from the South Bank; the full effect can be had only from an airplane, but most of these walls enclose charred emptiness. There are places where not a roof remains on a house for whole blocks. There are empty hillsides where a few beams and a little plaster dust is all that remains of a group of houses. Some of those walls have just been rebuilt. The telephone and electric system is made of wire that has just been replaced since yesterday's raid. Still, from the South Bank the impression is of a standing city, unaccountably deserted.

A hum comes from the hills; the drone grows louder and louder. Then from behind a group of fleecy white clouds they come in a formation, approaching at terrific speed. Winging over the airfield in the water, some of them drop bombs that strike the river, blowing up fountains of smoke and water. The roar comes later, horrible in the stillness. More bombs have been dropped in the town; spouts of black debris are shooting up in a line that follows one of the main roads. The roar fills the air with an irregular rhythm. It is not for long: the planes have passed over the town and are away again, with one last bomb plowing up a fountain over the hillside.

Silence for a second. Then the whine of an attacking Chinese pursuit sounds through the air, and there is again silence. The dust spouts grow. From a group of shattered houses there rises a tongue of red flame. The semblance of life it gives to the dead city is not the only activity on that part of the foreshore. Surprisingly there comes a thin note, the call of a bugle. Dozens of small figures appear out of nowhere; they are fighting the fire. All over the rest of the town, however, it is still perfectly quiet.

Twenty minutes pass. The flame has been defeated and the foreshore is quiet again. On several high points, sticking up from street corners and buildings, there are masts that can barely be seen against the glaring sky. At the end of those twenty minutes something happens to the masts; they bear fruit. Two little red lanterns appear on each. There is another quiet space of about ten minutes. Then the red lanterns disappear and a green one takes their place. At the same time a siren starts hooting.

It is the same siren that has given the alarm, but now it carries no hint of horror. The whistle sounds long and clear, and other whistles answer it on the same note. Suddenly the city is transformed. As if they have shot up from the ground, there are people everywhere, climbing out of their caves and starting up the hills toward their homes. The dead city is transformed; there is life and color and noise everywhere, particularly noise. It throbs through the air, it carries over the river, it fills the city—chattering, calling, laughing. It clears away the obscene noise of the bombs. It brings the spirit back from another and more horrible world. Outrageously, without reason, it recreates that hope which is the only reality. God himself takes heart when he hears it—the undefeatable din of China.

Appendix

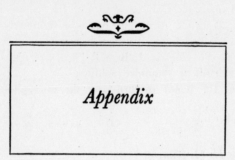

Appendix

THE SOONG SISTERS' BROADCAST TO AMERICA
CHUNGKING, APRIL 18, 1940.

(By Madame Sun Yat-sen)

FRIENDS OF DEMOCRACY:

The struggle of the Chinese people against the aggression of Japanese militarism will soon be almost three years old. The fifth part of mankind that Japan, with her superior military power, boasted she would bring to her knees within three months, has successfully fought and is continuing her fight with determination and full confidence in final victory.

The future history of the peoples of the Pacific and of the whole world will be different and brighter because our 450,000,000 people, instead of becoming the helots of an all-conquering slave empire, have taken up arms for their own freedom as well as yours.

You will listen to the impressions of Madame H. H. Kung from Chungking, our war capital, of how our people and Government are meeting the problems of our armed resistance, wartime reconstruction, rehabilitation and relief. Madame Kung is eminently fitted for this task as she is not only one of the foremost pioneers who blazed the difficult path to enable Chinese women to participate actively in our national life alongside men, but has also rendered most valuable patriotic services and is the distinguished sponsor of such significant movements as the Chinese Industrial Co-operatives, Child Welfare work, and "Friends of Wounded Soldiers."

I now have the honor to turn over the microphone to Madame Kung.

☆   ☆   ☆

(By Madame H. H. Kung)
Good morning, everyone:

When I am speaking to America I feel and know that I am speaking to truly sympathetic friends of China. We have evidence of that sympathy in a much-needed practical flow of contributions to our relief funds.

That help has been received with abiding gratitude. It has been used to good purpose. How great is the extent of the requirements, however, was only borne in upon me by the airplane flight I recently took over several hundred miles of our western country. It was all mountains—an illimitable sea of them. They stretch as far as the eye can see, and thousands of miles further than that.

Into this great remoteness have poured millions of people. They fled from the invading Japanese troops and their far-flying bombers. But the migrating masses came westward with hope; and great numbers have joined the old inhabitants cultivating the mountainsides. I saw terraces of cultivation climbing up steep slopes thousands of feet above sea level.

Away to the east, far beyond sight, were the great plains, the granaries of China, which fed and nourished the bulk of our population.

These are the productive areas which the Japanese invaders have always longed to bring under their control.

These they sought to conquer for exploitation when they began their ill-starred aggression. They can never conquer them. Already the Japanese forces are shrinking under the blows our armies have dealt them. Already they are shortening their lines to go on the defensive.

APPENDIX

Already their military leaders have endeavored to hide their shamed faces behind the flimsy curtain of the pathetic puppet show that they have at last set up at Nanking after so many futile failures.

That so-called government is a mockery; it is an insult to human intelligence. Instead of possessing power to make treaties, it has been formed to break treaties and destroy foreign interests in China at Japan's dictation. It represents nothing in China but the dregs of the political cesspool. The names of the treacherous tools of Japan are anathema in China; as they should be in every respectable part of the world. Those people who may curry their favor will frown at their own folly soon enough. Nemesis rides hot upon the heels of the traitors. It will not be stayed by the barriers of falsehoods which they and their Japanese masters are erecting to frighten old friends of China.

An array of facts stands out as clear as crystal. The chief one is that Japan has already shot her bolt in China. China, without any assistance at all, and with comparatively feeble armament, has fought Japan to a standstill.

The unity among the Chinese defenders is beyond question. The determination to continue resisting is staunch and resolute. There is no thought of peace; there can be no talk of peace while Japanese soldiers are on our soil.

At the end of almost three years of war our fighting strength is greater than ever it was. We are planning with the hope of being able to carry on to the end both financially and economically. We are erecting in West China a reservoir of man-power and products which we hope will always fortify us against want.

We have dragged machinery for hundreds of industries from the eastern provinces. We have created some fourteen hundred industrial co-operatives so far, with units of from less than ten up to as many as three hundred members each, and they are all in places where they cannot be bombed. There are perhaps thirty thousand actual worker-members of the Industrial Co-operatives, and they are supporting families and dependents.

The whole of this western country has been transformed by the influx of technical experts, educators, producers, artisans. An astonishing spirit of vital energy seems to invest everyone and everything.

But the most revealing and impressive manifestation of our inherent power and will to win to victory is embodied in the women. We have never seen anything like it. Women have escaped from their cloistered lives and are working everywhere: at the front with the fighting men and the wounded; behind the lines with the war-shocked country people; far in the rear, in rural work, in hospitals, in war orphanages, in industrial and community services. And so we are digging in to resist to the bitter end.

A remarkable change has come over the attitude of the whole of our people toward the troops. In olden days soldiers were mercenaries, and were ranked low in the scale of life. Now we have a Citizen Army. It works with the people, and the people work with it. The Friends of the Wounded Soldiers, sponsored by the New Life Movement, has become nationwide. It is a Movement of voluntary service by the people for their defenders. The people feel that through it they are all helping to resist the invader; and that spirit of unity will yet defeat the invader.

While unceasing warfare has been disastrous to life and property in China, it has, however, done a thing acutely observable in these western regions, if not in our coastal cities. It has stimulated the people to respond again to the old national spirit of co-operation. That, coupled with our age-old ability to survive the most overwhelming calamities, will, I am confident, ensure that we will save our heritage, and preserve it for ever.

Now my sister, Madame Chiang Kai-shek will speak to you.

(By Madame Chiang Kai-shek)
GOOD MORNING, FRIENDS IN AMERICA:

I have only a few minutes in which to add a few words to those of Madame Kung. They must be confined to a direct appeal to all liberty-loving people to see that China is promptly given the justice that is her right; the justice she has earned by almost three long years of unparalleled bloodshed and suffering.

We in China ask that a stop be put to one of two things: either the Congressmen, who are the law-makers of America, should stop expressing horror at aggression, or they should stop encouraging aggression by permitting gasoline, oil, and other war materials to go to Japan.

APPENDIX

We are fighting the battle of free men under dire handicaps, but we could have surrendered.

I wonder if your Congressmen have ever given one thought to what would have happened if China had surrendered to the believed invincible might of Japan?

The answer is obvious. Japan would have had her naval, military, and air strength intact. She would have been able to use our territory, our man-power, and our resources in support of Totalitarian operations against the Democratic countries.

She would have been able to strike swift and powerful blows in the seizure of Indo-China, Burma, the Malay States, the Dutch East Indies, Australia, and New Zealand.

She would have avoided the Philippines. She has been taught to believe that so long as she does not actually touch the possessions of America, the Congressmen will take no steps against her, no matter what the people of America may think.

But she would have been able to secure complete mastery over the Pacific, and been able to hold it with resources under her own command. She would no longer have required American markets, gasoline, oil, or anything else.

The swift defeat of Democracy was, however, prevented by the resolute resistance and sacrifices which we have been making in China. But if continued American assistance to Japan compels us to succumb there is no telling what still may happen.

If such a fatal thing should occur, this much is certain: Japan's navy, which, it is reported, is being feverishly enlarged by the construction of several great and secret battleships, will be free to take possession of the Dutch East Indies, if the opportunity arises. That opportunity will surely arise if Japan can contrive it. You already have the spectacle of her coldly calculating upon the embroilment of Holland in the war; and you see her unable to hide the plans she is eagerly making to prevent the Democracies from placing a Protectorate over the islands. So far as Japan is concerned her success, if she steals a march, would merely be further fulfillment of the notorious Tanaka Memorial; but it would be a windfall gained by her because of Democratic failure to recognize the importance of fostering China's resistance.

Through our refusal to accept Japan's dominance we have bogged

APPENDIX

down her army in China; and can keep it there. While we can defeat it in time, we will do it all the sooner if justice is done to us. Then it cannot possibly be of any service to the Totalitarians in this present world upheaval. That is help to the Democracies which is beyond price at this juncture.

The question is, will justice be done to us? And that can only be answered by the people of America and by their Congressmen.

The people of China are deafened by bombs, but they are anxiously listening for your reply.

THREE RADIO BROADCASTS

By Madame H. H. Kung

I

GOOD MORNING TO ALL WHO ARE LISTENING:

I am speaking from Shanghai, China. I am glad of this opportunity of speaking to you and greeting you, for I look upon America as my second home. I spent my school days there, and among you are many who remember me, and whom I remember with affection. Apart from my personal friendships in your country, America is China's traditional friend, and realizes that Japan's armed aggression in China—the dangers and horrors of which are revolting to all who have human instincts—threatens not only China's national life but the peace of the world itself.

After the Great War it was believed that future peace in general was hedged in safely by a structure of treaties and facts—while that of China was particularly iron-barred—as a house is protected against burglars—by the Nine-Power Treaty. But just as any burglar would become active if the policeman disarmed himself, or weakened in his watchfulness, so did Japan bestir herself as soon as she felt that the greater nations had become indifferent, and were being swallowed in the whirlpool of world depression. Japan, who suffered least of any nation from the Great War, or its aftermath, spent her substance, her strength, and her time in arming to take advantage of the world weakness which she saw increasing all about her. She intensified her industrial production to steal world markets, but, more than that,

[328]

she accumulated armaments in sinister quantities for the sinister purpose of stealing more territory from China.

Out of the world's troubles Japan calculated she could reap great fortune, and out of China she decided she could carve an expanded empire. She was prepared to take any risks, and chance any consequences, to secure the loot she coveted, because she was convinced that she could, if the worst came to the worst, defeat any nation, or combination of nations, that might try to curb her ruthless aggressiveness and her treachery with regard to treaties. She was encouraged in this belief by the world's failure to resent her contemptuous violation of treaties, or her invasion of China, when she seized Manchuria in 1931.

Her successful tearing from the doors and windows of China those bars provided by the Nine-Power Treaty decided her to go further, and with more ferocity, in the hope of being able to burgle as she wished. So we find her plunging into widespread destruction of life and property in our land, and, so far, she has found herself unimpeded by the metaphorical policeman.

Japan has, however, found something else much more of a surprise to her. Utterly unexpectedly she finds China up and fighting as she never fought before; fighting with courage and skill out of all imagining. China has consequently caused two things to be revealed; first, that we Chinese are not cowards, and second, and of greater significance, that Japan is not invincible. Even though we be overwhelmed we have pricked a bubble, or exposed a bogey, for the wide world to see. And what the combined great powers can now well ask themselves is: "Why be afraid any longer to insist upon proper respect for the sanctity of treaties in order to ensure the preservation of mankind?" Why be afraid, indeed? But if the world is still afraid then the whole outlook is black and forbidding.

I imagine your asking what you can do about it? You can do a lot. To have peace you must have the courage to work for peace. Otherwise, you may wake up one day to find war brought to your very doors when you are still shouting from your house tops for peace, isolation and neutrality.

How then can you help China to check Japan's aggression and defend the peace of the Far East in accordance with the terms of the treaties that should be upheld? It is our conviction that you need not go to war. We do not ask you to fight our war. But short of

going to war, there are many effective ways in which you can help
us and the cause for which we are fighting. We know we have your
sympathy and your moral support, and we appreciate them. But we
need from you more than that. We need within measure your material support. If that is denied us you help Japan to crush us. We
need arms and ammunitions; we need help for the millions of innocent homeless women and children whom treaties have failed to
protect, and for the tens of thousands of wounded. At the same time
we want your co-operation to prevent Japan getting money to continue her aggression. That can be done by buying nothing from,
and selling nothing to, the Japanese. Let no ship leave American
shores with arms, ammunition, or any cargo for Japan which will be
used for killing thousands upon thousands of innocent and peace-
loving Chinese.

We refuse to believe that militarist Japan can defy the overwhelming
force of the world's conscience and pressure. In fact, after the exhibi-
tion that has been going on for the past eleven weeks right here at
Shanghai we know she cannot. Do you realize that we ill-armed and
unready Chinese held up the most modern machine of murder and
massacre all these weeks mostly with our flesh and blood and manual
weapons? We did not move till flesh and blood could endure it no
longer. Can you not realize then how easy it will be, if they wish,
for the Powers to compel the Japanese to abandon their predatory
policies?

As you all know, the nations of the world are soon meeting at Brussels to seek a peaceful settlement of the Sino-Japanese situation on the
basis of the Nine-Power Treaty. It is therefore timely to ask what
will be America's attitude at that conference, and what concrete
steps will she be prepared to take in concert with other Powers to
back up the Nine-Power Treaty? Japan bluffed the world before,
and is trying to do so again. She claimed among other things that
time has revealed as false, that she wanted no territory when she
invaded Manchuria. She claims it again now that she is invading
China Proper. But she controls Manchuria through a puppet regime,
and she is already busy making puppet states in North China and
Inner Mongolia to control those regions. Her armed forces and her
advisers exercise supreme power in the puppet states despite the
pretense that popular "independent" movements created them. Will

APPENDIX

America and the Powers refuse to have their intelligence insulted once again, and tell Japan so in plain and unmistakable terms?

America has so vital a place in determining what the future of the world is going to be that we in China are anxious about her attitude at this conference. Is it going to be an assertive one in support of a determined move to have treaties honored? Or will it be negative for the sake of salving conscience and avoiding trouble? We are anxious because we saw the League of Nations become impotent before the *fait accompli* of a seized Manchuria. Since then much has gone wrong in the world, and we fear lest China will once again be victimized, and betrayal come to the hopes of all weak nations. The eyes of these countries are fixed upon America because they sadly need leadership; because they are waiting to see if the days of treaties and international law are dead. And all law-abiding peoples are watching because they are wondering if peace on earth is passing.

It is difficult to visualize America in any other role than that of the champion of the weak and the oppressed. It will be a stimulating thing to see her, as expected, standing up fearlessly for the sanctity of treaties and justice, and refusing to be bluffed and bullied by a nation that can perpetrate such horrors as those for which Japan is responsible in China today.

Treaties will stand or fall upon what happens at Brussels, and peace in the world will correspondingly be blessed or be damned. The great Powers have great responsibilities. They are the ones who are to determine whether civilization is to be sacrificed, and whether the inhumanities that are spreading bloodshed and ruin broadcast over China today are to become the lot of other countries to-morrow.

We cannot believe that America will do other than resolutely act to mobilize the other responsible Powers in a move to take the simple steps required to stop for all time what otherwise would become the recognition of a violent era of undeclared war and brutality.

We cannot believe that America will do other than stand firm for the restoration of confidence among nations, and the revival of respect for treaties. Concrete, courageous leadership and action are all that are required now to right the ghastly wrongs that have been done in China. This is no time for quibbling, or, as you would put it, "passing the buck." This is a time for stark realism. We must not fool ourselves or others, wittingly or unwittingly. Let us be courageous,

[*331*]

and, above all, be honest. Unless America and all the Powers are ready to take a bold and forthright attitude at the Brussels Conference, that conference will go down in history as one of the most futile and meaningless gatherings of world's statesmen that has yet to be seen, and will seal the eternal doom of the cause of humanity, democracy and world peace.

Good-by.

II

On behalf of the Chinese women of Shanghai I extend to you, our foreign friends, a cordial welcome. I need not tell you how much we appreciate your presence here this afternoon, because, in spite of the advice of your governments to return to your own countries you chose to remain and endure with us the dangers involved in the close proximity of warfare.

Whatever bonds of friendship have united us as women in times of peace have been now further strengthened by a more fundamental tie which has been forged through sharing a vital common experience. I am referring to the Japanese invasion in the very heart of Shanghai. We have all seen with our own eyes the wanton ruthlessness and callous waste of life and property and businesses in this great city and in our peaceful countryside, and you have shared and are sharing with us the deep indignation against this madness on the part of Japanese militarists in defiance of all sense of human decency. You have also worked with us side by side to alleviate the sufferings of our innocent people—helpless victims of this ruthless undeclared war to the accompaniment of the thundering cannonade the echoes of which, at this moment even, have not yet died down, and which with each reverberation is bringing about us more death and destruction and havoc.

From time immemorial women have assumed the role of comforters to mankind. Which one of us, as mothers, do not remember, that when our toddling babies fell, and we kissed the little bruised knee or head, it was ready sympathy as well as anything else which assuaged the hurt and comforted the little ones. Truly sympathy was and is a great factor bringing balm to the human heart. At the present moment, however, we women in order to insure world peace must

[332]

go a step further. We should strive to influence the upholding of justice—international justice as well as social justice. And if we women of the world would unite and work for this ideal, which is not at all Utopian, but really a practical common-sense ideal, then surely we can put an end to the miseries around us which are being augmented as each day goes on.

I thank you again for your loyalty, for devotion to your adopted country, for the many expressions of practical help you have given our people, as well as for your moral support.

III

RADIO AUDIENCE OF AMERICA AND FRIENDS:

I appreciate this opportunity of speaking to America for two reasons. First, America is my second home. I spent the formative years of my life in your land. I received my modern knowledge and training from your fountainhead of learning. I derived my ideals of freedom and democracy from your institutions and traditions, and these have become an essential part of my being. Even as I talk to you now over the radio thousands of miles away, I know many of my friends are listening in. America is China's traditional friend, and before my mental eyes I can see in this audience well-wishers of my country all over your land. To you all I take this delightful opportunity to extend my warm greetings.

I appreciate this opportunity also because I am going to speak to you on a subject which concerns not only the life and death of the Chinese people but also the vital interests and honor of the American people. I refer to Japan's armed aggression in China, the dangers and horrors of which are shocking with revulsion anyone who has human instincts. Day and night, a terrible though undeclared war is raging between two of your nextdoor neighbors. Peace of the Pacific is seriously disturbed. The whole future of democracy, humanity and world peace is at stake. How this war in China affects your own country must be a question burning in the heart of every alert American.

You all remember that, not long ago, your country and others went through immense sacrifices and untold sufferings to fight against

[*333*]

militarism, in order to make the world safe for democracy and to restore the peace and security of the human race. Following the World War, the League of Nations was conceived by your great statesman, President Wilson, as an instrument to insure world peace. Farsighted statesmen of the world, however, early realized the dangers in the Far Eastern situation. They saw how, when they were busy fighting in Europe, Japan had taken advantage of weak China, forced upon her the infamous "Twenty-one Demands," sought to establish domination over her, threatened to close the Open Door in China, and sown the seed for another world conflict. Under the leadership of your Government, therefore, the Washington Conference was convened in 1922 which, among other things, sealed the Nine-Power Treaty. In that treaty, the contracting Powers solemnly and unequivocally pledged to respect China's sovereignty, independence, and territorial and administrative integrity and to uphold the Open Door principle with respect to China. Japan was one of the signatories. Subsequently, as a further effort to insure world peace, the Anti-War Pact, which customarily bears the name of another American statesman, Secretary Kellogg, was signed by a number of Powers. Japan was again one of them. Thanks to these painstaking efforts in the interest of a better world order and achieved under the leadership of America, the human race enjoyed a short respite of comparative peace. The world rejoiced and China was particularly thankful.

Unfortunately, the world was soon disillusioned. For, no sooner had Japan solemnly signed these treaties than she began unscrupulously to scrap them. In an even more reckless and intensive way, she renewed her aggression in China and in 1931 she startled and defied the whole world by marching her troops into Manchuria, the throat of China. Having thus successfully bluffed the world, she proceeded to carry out persistently a series of further encroachments on China, in utter disregard of the sanctity of international law and morality. Her undeclared war in Shanghai in 1932, her invasion into Jehol along the Great Wall in 1933, her armed aggression in Hopei, Charhar and Suiyuan Provinces in 1935–36, her official connivance at the scandalous orgy of wholesale smuggling in North China, her illegal stationing of troops in the same region, her intrigue in creating the so-called "East Hopei Autonomous State," her numerous other acts of murder, bully, intrigue and interference throughout China, and finally her latest aggression which has thrust war upon the whole of China, are well known to the world. All these acts of aggression, I must point to you, friends, have been due to the fact that when Japan grabbed Manchuria from China, the Powers of the world conveniently looked aside and allowed themselves to be bluffed and flouted through their attitude of inaction and impotence. Had the Powers in 1931 firmly and courageously brought home to the Japanese militarists that international treaties could not be violated with impunity, subsequent history in the Far East and even in Europe would have been different and the world crisis today avoided.

Now, my American friends, I need hardly tell you that we Chinese people are pacifists like you. We are by nature peace loving. We are taught by our sages to worship peace and to abhor war. In our moral conviction, we cherish the Christian principle of "world brotherhood." In our political belief, we uphold President Roosevelt's policy of "good neighborhood." Our people have, consequently, been extremely patient with Japan's militarists, while our Government has persistently endeavored to maintain peace and friendship with Japan. In fact, we want to live in peace with all nations so that we may devote ourselves to our spiritual and material reconstruction, for the benefit of the world as well as of ourselves.

But, militarist Japan does not wish to see the development of a united, peaceful and progressive China. At last, the repeated aggressions of her militarists, and especially their absolute lawlessness and horrible brutalism, have left our people absolutely no alternative but to take up arms in self-defence. The national existence and independence of China's 470,000,000 people cannot be sacrificed. The soul of China cries out for salvation. Though regarded as spineless pacifists, we are pitting our brave hearts and flesh and blood against all the odds of Japan's mighty fleet, her mechanized armies, her warplanes, tanks, shells, machine guns, incendiary bombs, and the most powerful weapons of killing and destruction. And, let me assure you, we are determined to resist our aggressor to the last man and the last inch of territory. The daily horrors of brutal killing and wanton destruction visited upon thousands and thousands of innocent and peace-loving Chinese would shock any human being with revulsion. You who have gone through the horrors, agonies and sufferings in the last World War can surely appreciate the feeling that is beating in every Chinese heart at this moment. The soul of China is indeed pained. But, believe me, the soul is stirred, not depressed. And as long as that soul exists, united China will resist her invader to the bitter end, cost what it may.

My friends, you who are thousands of miles away from China, may ask how this Japanese aggression affects your country. Let me tell you, it affects you in a most vital and dangerous way.

First of all, Japan's policy of war and aggression aims not only at the conquest and domination of China; it aims also at the exclusion of all foreign interests from any market where the Japanese sword holds sway, and at the eventual expulsion of America and Europe from their territorial possessions in the Pacific and Asia. The experience of foreign interests in Korea and Formosa has given stern warning in the past; in Manchuria and Jehol they have already been kicked out through the "Open Door"; and a foretaste of what they may expect in other Chinese territory under Japanese domination has been clearly indicated in North China today. Driven by unbounded lust for power and supremacy and by frantic belief in a "divine mission," Japan is ruthlessly seeking the domination of China as a steppingstone to establishing her hegemony in the Pacific and finally world domination. Her former Premier, Tanaka, stated in his well-known memorial to the Emperor that to conquer the world Japan must first conquer China. Read some of the books written by Japan's responsible leaders today, such as *The Pacific Crisis, The Next World War* and *An American-Japanese War Is Inevitable,* and you can readily see for yourselves how they openly advocate war against your own country, preparing for that emergency, and aspiring to grab and smash the Philippines, Hawaii, and your western coast, once they succeed in commanding China's vast natural resources. Already Japan's hand of economic penetration has reached the heart of your land in the form of her colonists, cheap labor and price-cutting goods. It is only one step to striking you with her mighty sword.

But the menace of Japan's aggression is not limited to your material interests. The moral and spiritual aspect of the situation is equally, if not more, significant. If Japan's flagrant violations of international law and treaties are tolerated, what will become of all the past and present efforts in which your country leads towards building a peaceful world order? If Japan's aggression and domination are to extend unchecked, where will be the security of all her neighbors? If Japan's lawlessness and brutalism are to go unchallenged, who can predict the future of humanity and civilization? If Japan's militarism is allowed to defy the world, what will prevent other aggressive countries from copying her dangerous example in other parts of the world?

Now, let me put myself in your position and be absolutely frank with you. You are a peace-loving nation. You wish to avoid involvement in war in any part of the world. You have built up an "isolationist policy." You have enacted the "Neutrality Act." I can fully appreciate your position and aspiration. But have you ever stopped to think that a nation by ignoring the dangers of destructive forces cannot live in peace, any more than an ostrich can bury its head in the sand? As your illustrious President has poignantly pointed out in his epoch-making speech at Chicago, "In the modern conditions of international interdependence, no nation could isolate itself from the upheavals of the rest of the world." It is not only essential to your ideals of freedom and democracy that the sanctity of international treaties and the maintenance of international morality should be restored; it is vital to your peace and security that the forces of destruction and aggression in the Far East should be checked in time. When your nextdoor neighbors are being attacked by robbers, do you, like frightened children, duck yourselves in your bedclothes, or do you like brave and farsighted men seek to rid the community of the public enemy? Friends, no people is more peace loving than we Chinese, but we have war forced upon us no matter how peace loving we may be. Do not deceive yourself by thinking that mere canting of pacifist aspirations or sole reliance on an attitude of aloofness and isolation will give you immunity from the baneful effects of Japan's gangsterism. To have peace you must have the courage to work for peace. Otherwise, you may wake up one day and find war brought to your very doors when you are still shouting on your house-tops for peace, isolation and neutrality.

How then can you help China to check Japan's aggression and defend the peace of the Far East? It is our conviction that you need not go to war. We do not ask you to fight our war. But short of going to war, there are many effective ways in which you can help us. Yes, we have your sympathy and moral support and we appreciate them. But we need from you more than that. We need your full material support in the form of money, relief work, arms and ammunitions. At the same time, let no American buy anything from or sell anything to the Japanese. Let no ship leave American shores with arms, ammunitions or any cargo for Japan, which will be used for killing thousands upon thousands of innocent and peace-loving Chinese every day. We refuse to believe that militarist Japan can defy the overwhelming force of the world's conscience and pressure.

Now, you all know that tomorrow at Brussels, nations of the world are meeting to seek a peaceful settlement of the Sino-Japanese situation on the basis of the Nine-Power Treaty. It is therefore timely to ask, what will be America's attitude at the Conference? and what concrete step is she prepared to take in concert with other Powers to back up the Nine-Power Treaty? America's moral leadership in the world is going to be put to an acid test. The eyes of the world are fixed on her.

Permit me to ask you a few point-blank questions. Does America intend to make the Conference a face-saving affair, just to salve her conscience? Will she be satisfied with another meaningless Japanese reaffirmation of respect for China's territorial and administrative integrity and the Open Door principle and destroy the spirit of the Nine-Power Treaty? Will she go to the Conference with the idea of "Head, China loses, Tail, Japan wins"? Will she allow Japan to confront the Conference with a *fait accompli* and get away with half a loaf if not the whole loaf? Will she sacrifice China's essential rights as a price for the kind of "peaceful settlement" which Japan secretly seeks?

Or, will America let her conscience speak out aloud and bravely call a spade a spade? Will she exercise her right as a judge and see to it that the violator of the Nine-Power Treaty is properly dealt with? Is she determined to do all she can to uphold the letter and spirit of the Nine-Power Treaty? If need be, is she ready to back up her noble principles by concrete, courageous action? Is she prepared to defend and not to forfeit her moral leadership in the world?

My American friends, this is no time for quibbling or passing the buck. We must not fool ourselves or others, wittingly or unwittingly. Let us be courageous and, above all, be honest. Unless America and all the Powers are ready to take an honest and courageous attitude at the Brussels Conference, it will go down in history as one of the most futile and meaningless gatherings of the world's statesmen and will seal the eternal doom of the cause of humanity, democracy and world peace.

The world awaits America's answer.

Index

INDEX

INDEX

government in 1890, 13–15
industrialization (*see also* "Industrial co-operatives"), 24
Japan
   relations with, during Northern Expedition, 149–150
   war with, 238–320
Japanese invasions
   Canton, 290–291
   Chahar, 196
   Hankow, 291–292
   Jehol, 178
   Kalgan, 202
   Manchuria, 169–171
   Nanking, 263–266
   Shanghai, 173, 238, 246, 264–265
   Soochow, 264
Manchu rule, 1, 14, 35–37, 67, 76, 80, 83
missionaries, 1, 7, 15, 35–40, 258, 262–263
   co-operation with Chiang Kai-shek, 187–190
monarchy restored, 104
Nationalist Government, 127–132, 137, 143, 150
politics, 13–15, 82–86, 103, 107–115, 116–118, 121–124, 126–127, 131–132, 172
recognition of Nanking Government by foreign powers, 150
reconciliation between Hankow and Nanking governments, 137
religion, 73–74, 82, 97, 102–103, 139, 162–164, 258
Russian activities, 116–118, 125–133
Southwestern provinces described by Madame Chiang Kai-shek, 198–200
Twenty-one Demands, 98
Western civilization and education
   impact of, 14–16
   views on, 1–3, 14–17, 47, 63–65, 70
war declared on Germany, 104
war with Japan, 238–320
China Struggles for Unity, 245–246
Chinese Educational Mission, 5
Ch'ing Dynasty, abdication of (*see also* "Kuang Hsu" "Manchu rule" "Tzu Hsi"), 83

Ching, Tseven, 22
Chinkiang, 14
Chow En-lai, 237
Christianity (*see also* "Religion") 15, 73, 82, 97
Chungking, capital of China during war with Japan, 257, 264, 267, 293–294, 297–299, 300
Cohen, General Morris, 120
Communism (*see also* "Russia"), 117–123, 130–131, 143, 162, 166, 177, 197, 205–207, 237, 260–262, 286
Communist's reconciliation with Chiang Kai-shek in order to pursue Japanese war, 237, 260–261
Concessions, foreign, 14
Co-operatives, see "Industrial co-operatives"
Craven, Dr Braxton, 7
Craven, Mrs Braxton, 7, 8

Donald, William Henry
   Chang Hsueh-liang
      association with, 179–184
      defense of, in Chiang Kai-shek's kidnaping, 207
   Chiang Kai-shek
   friendship with, 179–184, 216–233, 254–256
   negotiations for release, in Sian kidnaping, 216–233
Durham, N. C., Charlie Soong's life in, 7–8, 10–11

Education
   Chinese children's, 23–24
   Western, of Chinese (*see also* "Western civilization and education"), 1–3, 63–65
Elder, James, 224
England, see "Great Britain"

Fen Yu-hsiang, 167, 172, 233
   anti-Japanese army, 178–179
   Boxer Rebellion, record of, 123
   demands for reward, 151
   Peking, occupation of, 123
   Chiang Kai-shek
      adherence to, 132, 143, 149, 203
      revolt against, 152, 160–162

INDEX

INDEX

Special Industrial Commissioner, sent
    to America as, 175
Sun Yat-sen, aid to, 123–124
Y.M.C.A. work, 89–90
Kung, Jeannette, birth, 118, 155–156
Kung, Louis, 128, 154–155
    birth, 118
Kung, Madame H. H., *see* "Soong,
    Eling"
Kung, Rosamonde, 155
    birth, 102
Kuomintang, 84–86
    Chiang Kai-shek expelled from, 131
    Communists
        break with, 132
        relations with, 237, 260–261
    Japan
        abolished in Hopei and Chahar at
            request of, 197
        demands for dissolution by, 203
    reorganization along Soviet lines, 121
    Sun Yat-sen, strengthened by, 99
    Yuan Shih-kai, ordered dissolved by,
        89
Kwangsi declares independence from
    Yuan Shih-kai, 99
Kwangtung declares independence from
    Yuan Shih-kai, 99
Kweichow declares independence from
    Yuan Shih-kai, 99

Lamb, Dr, 62
Li Chi-sen, 131
Li Chi-wen, 141
Li Hung-chang, 37
Li Tsung-jen, 152, 203
    revolt against Nanking Government,
        202
Li Yuan-hung
    President, 103, 107, 110
    dissolves Parliament, 103
Lin Sen, 172
Lukuochiao Incident, 240, 241–244
Lu-shan, 204

Macao ceded to Portugal, 14
Mainwaring, Elizabeth, 94
Manchukuo, 196, 203
Manchuria invaded by Japan, 169–171
Manchuria Scene, 169
Marco Polo Bridge Incident, 240, 241–
    244

McTyeire School, 31–34, 40–43, 50
Medicine, used by missionaries, 15
Messages in War and Peace, 198, 267–
    270
Missionaries, 7, 258, 262–263
    Boxer Rebellion, 35–40
    Chinese resentment of, 1, 15
    Chiang Kai-shek, co-operation with,
        187–190
    medical, 15
Missions, spread of, 15
Moore, Col. Roger, 6
Moss, Mrs, 59–62
Mott, John R., 90
Murphy, Henry Killam, 156

Nanking, 17, 137, 202
    Nationalist Government capital, 84,
        131
        description, 144
    retreat from, in Japanese war, 263–
        266
Nanking Government, recognition of,
    by foreign powers, 150
Nanking, Treaty of, 15
Nantao, 16, 17
Nationalist Government, 84, 127–132
    Chiang Kai-shek
        rejoins, 143
        resignation, 137
    recognition by foreign powers, 150
New Life Movement, 180–184, 187, 250
    Communism, as a substitute for, 182
New Shan-chow, 5
Newchang, 14
Nine-Power Treaty, 269
Northern Expedition, 127–137, 149–150
Nyi, Miss (Kwei Tseng), *see* "Soong,
    Mrs Charlie"

Oberlin-in-China Junior College, 99
Officers' Moral Endeavor Association
    (O.M.E.A.), 146–147, 163
Oursler, Fulton, interview with Madame
    Chiang Kai-shek, 258–259

Pai Chung-hsi, 152–203
    Nanking Government, revolt against,
        202
Peiping (*see also* Peking), 161–162

[345]

INDEX

INDEX

INDEX

Schools for Children of the Revolution, 145–146
Sian: a Coup d'Etat, 93, 208
Southwestern provinces described by, 198–200
war work, 249–251, 252, 254–256, 262–264, 274, 277–278, 280–282
Wellesley, at, 91–95
Y.W.C.A. work, 105
Soong, Mrs Charlie
  biography, 22–23
  Chiang Kai-shek, antagonism toward, 137–138
  children's education, 23–24
  death, 172
  discipline, 23, 26, 46
  education, views on, 46
Soong sisters (*see also* "Soong, Chingling" "Soong, Eling" "Soong, Mayling")
  America, life in, 59–63
  American education, 59–65
  Americanization, 98
  childhood, 29–34, 44–55
  Chinese opinions of, 72
  dress, styles of, 56–58
  early education, 40–43, 44–46
  home life, 25–30, 44–46
  political views, 133–136
  religion, 42
Soong, T. V. (Tseven), 125, 128, 130
  Chiang Kai-shek
    disagreement with, over government finances, 185
    negotiations for release of, in Sian kidnaping, 226, 230–232
  government work, 118
  Harvard, at, 92
  Japan, feeling against, 177
Soong, Tsean, 22, 68
Soong, Tseliang, 22, 68
Soong, Yao-ju, *see* "Soong, Charlie"
Southgate, Annie, devotion of Charlie Soong for, 9–10
Southgate, James H., 9, 21
Soviet Union, *see* "Russia"
Sun Fo, 108, 172
  Southern rebels, sympathy with, in 1931, 168
Sun, Gen., 217
Sun Wen, *see* "Sun Yat-sen"

Sun Yat-sen
  administration, 82–83
  America, trip to, 78
  Canton
    escape from, 111–115
    headquarters in, 103, 104, 107, 108, 109–115
    relieved of power in, 108
    return to, 109
  Chiang Kai-shek, association with, 77, 96, 99, 114–115, 117–119
  Communism, attitude toward, 117, 120–123
  constitutional government, efforts toward, 103, 107
  death, 124
  Director of Railways, 88
  inauguration, 79
  Japan, flight to, 89
  London, in, 78
  marriage to Chingling Soong, 97–98
  Northern Expedition collapse, 109
  Northern Government, refusal to cooperate with, 110
  Peking, trip to, 1924, 123
  post-Revolution activities, 96–99
  President, 78
    second election to presidency, 109
  Revolution, 23–25, 65–68, 76–79
  Russia, friendship toward, 116–122
  second revolution, 96
  Soong, Charlie, association with, 23, 24–25, 65–68, 98
  Soong, Chingling, marriage to, 87–88, 97–98
  speeches, 122
  tomb, 157
  World War, opposition to China's entry into, 104
Sun Yat-sen, Madame, *see* "Soong, Chingling"
Sung Cheh-yuan
  Chahar, governor of, 196
  Hopei-Chahar Political Council, chairman of, 197

Tau Zeta Epsilon, 92
Thomson, Eunice, 175
Tientsin, 14
Treaty of Nanking, 15
Treaty ports, 14

[*348*]

INDEX

Trinity College, Charlie Soong's education at, 7

Tsai Ting Kai, 179

Tsai Yuan-pei, Dr, 141

Teull, Prof., Annie K., 93

Tufts, Dean Edith Souther, 93

Tuttle, Rev., opinion of Charlie Soong, 9

Twenty-one Demands, 98

Tzu Hsi, Empress Dowager, 67, 76
Boxer Rebellion, 35–37
ruling power, 14
Western civilization and education, views on, 1–3, 14

United States
Charlie Soong's education in, 7–11
China
aid to, in Japanese war, 295–296
sympathies with, in Japanese war, 253

Vanderbilt University, Charlie Soong's education at, 8–10

Wales, Nym, 276

Wan Bing-chung, 5, 49

Wang, Dr C. T., 90, 157

Wang Ching-wei, 72, 167, 172, 216, 237, 257–258
Canton Government, in, 127
desertion to join Japanese, 293, 295–297, 305, 306–307
People's Army rebellion, 161

Wellesley College, Mayling Soong's education at, 91–95

Wesleyan College for Women, Soong sisters at, 47, 49–55, 59

Western civilization and education, Chinese views on, 1–3, 14–17, 47, 63–65, 70

Whampoa Military Academy, 121, 125, 146

Wheeler, Hetty, 94

Winton, Dr George B., opinion of Charlie Soong, 8–9

Women's Advisory Committee, 280–281

World War, 104

Wright, J. B., opinion of Charlie Soong, 9

Wu Pei-fu, 129, 306
failure to maintain peace in North, 123
Northern Government, control of, 110

Wuchang, 77, 78

Wuhan, 77

Yang, Hu-cheng, participation in kidnaping of Chiang Kai-shek, 205–233

Yangchow, 17

Yangtze Valley riots against missions, 15

Yen Hsi-shan, 90, 102, 167
Chiang Kai-shek, support of, 143, 149, 150
reward demanded for, 151
People's Army rebellion, 160–162

Y.M.C.A., 89–90, 147

Y.W.C.A., 105, 252

Yu Hsueh-chung, 209

Yu Hu-cheng, 209

Yuan Shih-kai
activities following Revolution, 79
administration, 84–86, 89
death, 99
declared Emperor, 99
opposition to, 99
political ambition, 82–86
President, 83
reforms under Ch'ing Government, 76
seizure of power, 89
Twenty-one Demands, 98

Yui, Dr David, 139

Yung Wing, Dr, Chinese Educational Mission, 5

Yunnan independence declared from Yuan Shih Kai, 99

[349]